SILVER SURFER

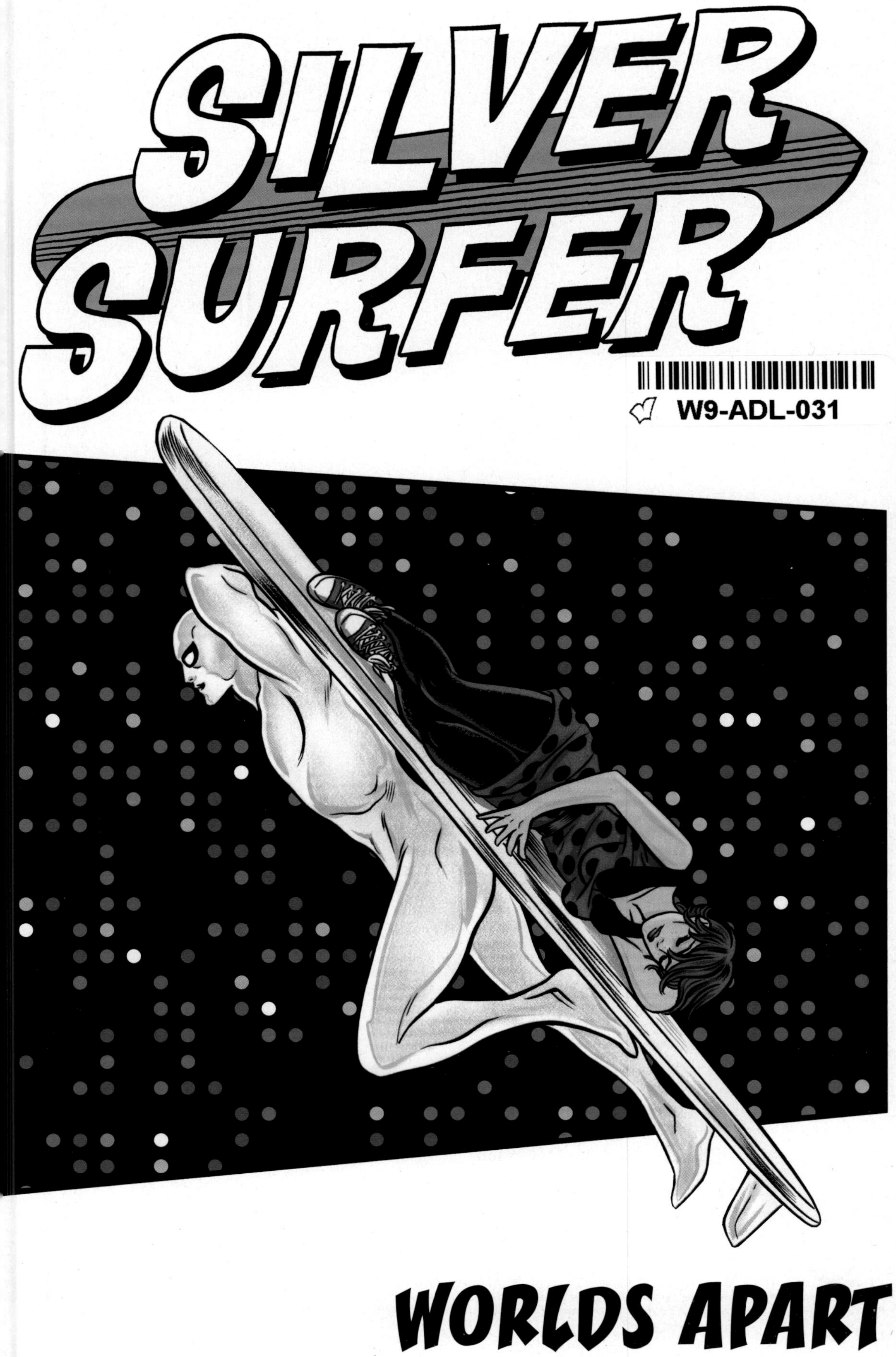

WORLDS APART

Collection Editor: **Jennifer Grünwald**

Assistant Editor: **Sarah Brunstad**

Associate Managing Editor: **Alex Starbuck**

Editor, Special Projects: **Mark D. Beazley**

Senior Editor, Special Projects: **Jeff Youngquist**

SVP Print, Sales & Marketing: **David Gabriel**

Book Designer: **Rodolfo Muraguchi**

Editor in Chief: **Axel Alonso**

Chief Creative Officer: **Joe Quesada**

Publisher: **Dan Buckley**

Executive Producer: **Alan Fine**

SILVER SURFER VOL. 2: WORLDS APART. Contains material originally published in magazine form as SILVER SURFER #6-10. First printing 2015. ISBN# 978-0-7851-8879-7. Published by MARVEL WORLDWIDE, INC., a subsidiary of MARVEL ENTERTAINMENT, LLC. OFFICE OF PUBLICATION: 135 West 50th Street, New York, NY 10020. Copyright © 2015 MARVEL No similarity between any of the names, characters, persons, and/or institutions in this magazine with those of any living or dead person or institution is intended, and any such similarity which may exist is purely coincidental. **Printe** in Canada. ALAN FINE, President, Marvel Entertainment; DAN BUCKLEY, President, TV, Publishing and Brand Management; JOE QUESADA, Chief Creative Officer; TOM BREVOORT, SVP of Publishin DAVID BOGART, SVP of Operations & Procurement, Publishing; C.B. CEBULSKI, VP of International Development & Brand Management; DAVID GABRIEL, SVP Print, Sales & Marketing; JIM O'KEEFE, V of Operations & Logistics; DAN CARR, Executive Director of Publishing Technology; SUSAN CRESPI, Editorial Operations Manager; ALEX MORALES, Publishing Operations Manager; STAN LEE, Chairma Emeritus. For information regarding advertising in Marvel Comics or on Marvel.com, please contact Jonathan Rheingold, VP of Custom Solutions & Ad Sales, at jrheingold@marvel.com. For Marv subscription inquiries, please call 800-217-9158. **Manufactured between 4/17/2015 and 5/25/2015 by SOLISCO PRINTERS, SCOTT, QC, CANADA.**

10 9 8 7 6 5 4 3 2 1

SILVER SURFER
WORLDS APART

STORYTELLERS:
DAN SLOTT & **MICHAEL ALLRED**

COLOR ARTIST:
LAURA ALLRED

LETTERER:
VC'S JOE SABINO

COVER ART:
MICHAEL ALLRED & **LAURA ALLRED**

ASSISTANT EDITOR:
JAKE THOMAS

EDITOR:
TOM BREVOORT

SILVER SURFER CREATED BY STAN LEE & JACK KIRBY

6

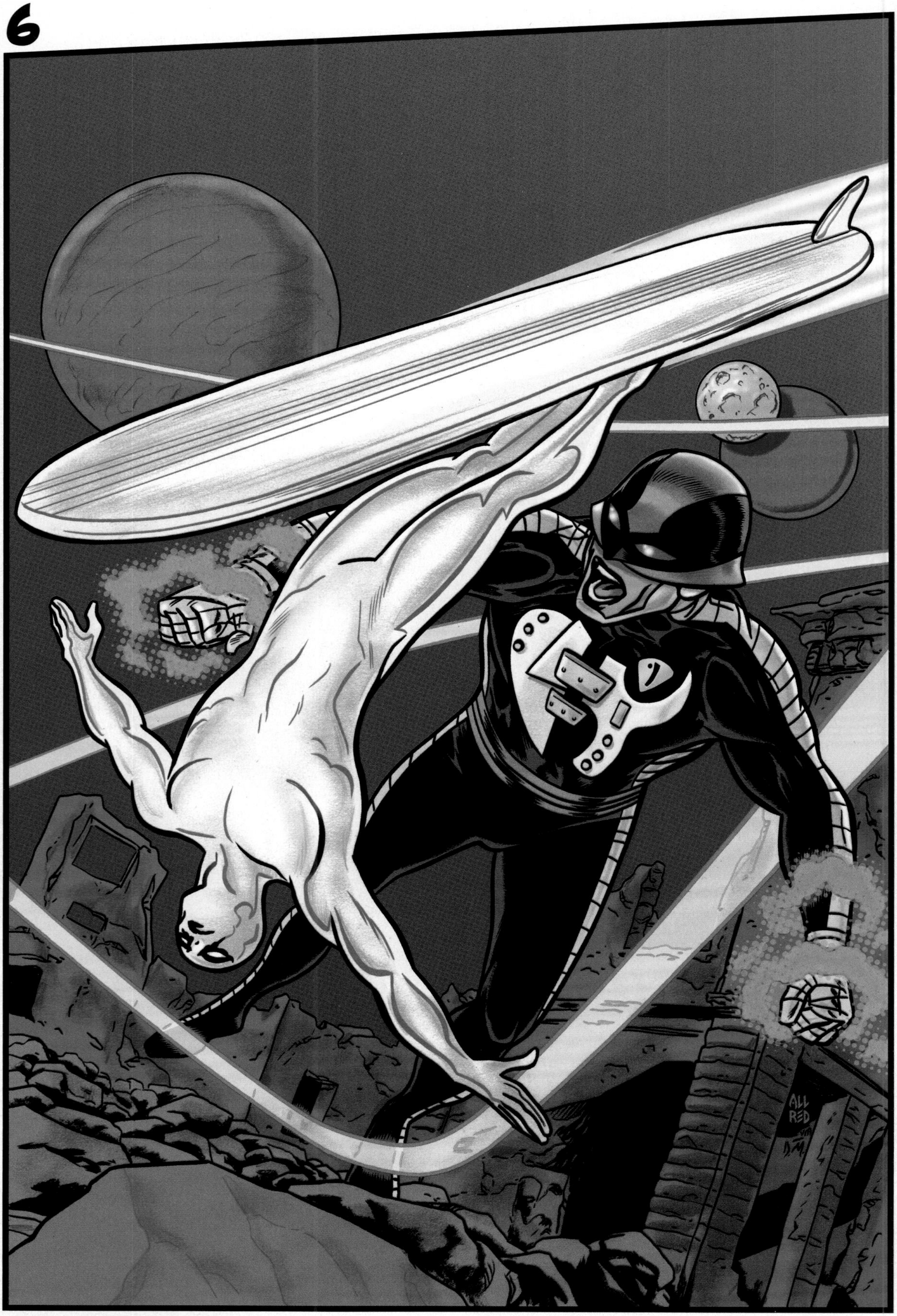

IMPERFECTIONS

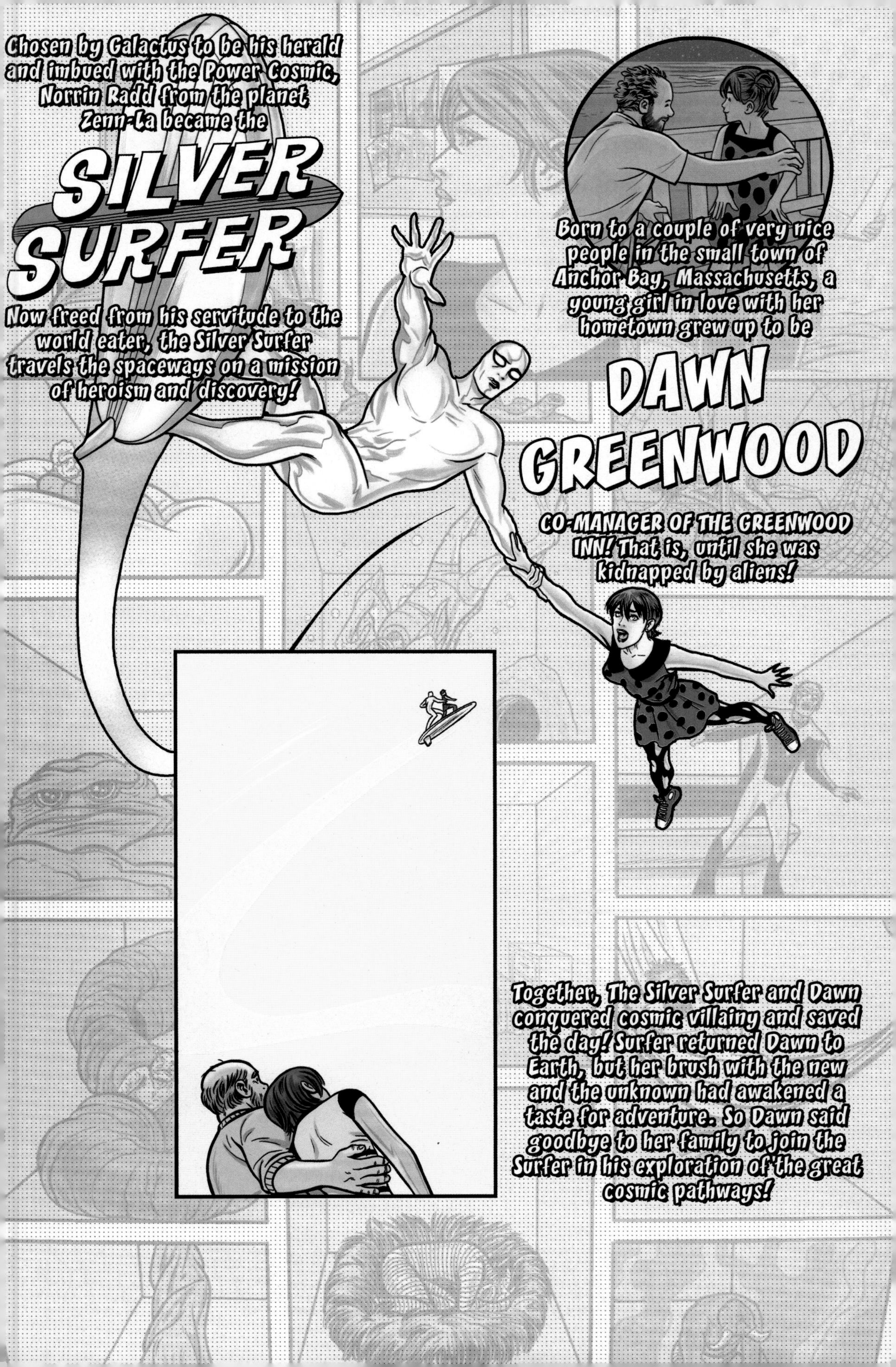

Chosen by Galactus to be his herald and imbued with the Power Cosmic, Norrin Radd from the planet Zenn-La became the

SILVER SURFER

Now freed from his servitude to the world eater, the Silver Surfer travels the spaceways on a mission of heroism and discovery!

Born to a couple of very nice people in the small town of Anchor Bay, Massachusetts, a young girl in love with her hometown grew up to be

DAWN GREENWOOD

CO-MANAGER OF THE GREENWOOD INN! That is, until she was kidnapped by aliens!

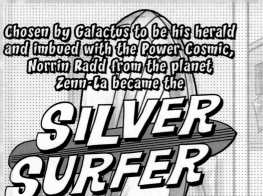

Together, The Silver Surfer and Dawn conquered cosmic villainy and saved the day! Surfer returned Dawn to Earth, but her brush with the new and the unknown had awakened a taste for adventure. So Dawn said goodbye to her family to join the Surfer in his exploration of the great cosmic pathways!

THE MILKY WAY GALAXY.
NOW.
SURFER, I'M HUNGRY. FIND ME A PLANET.
IMPERFECTIONS

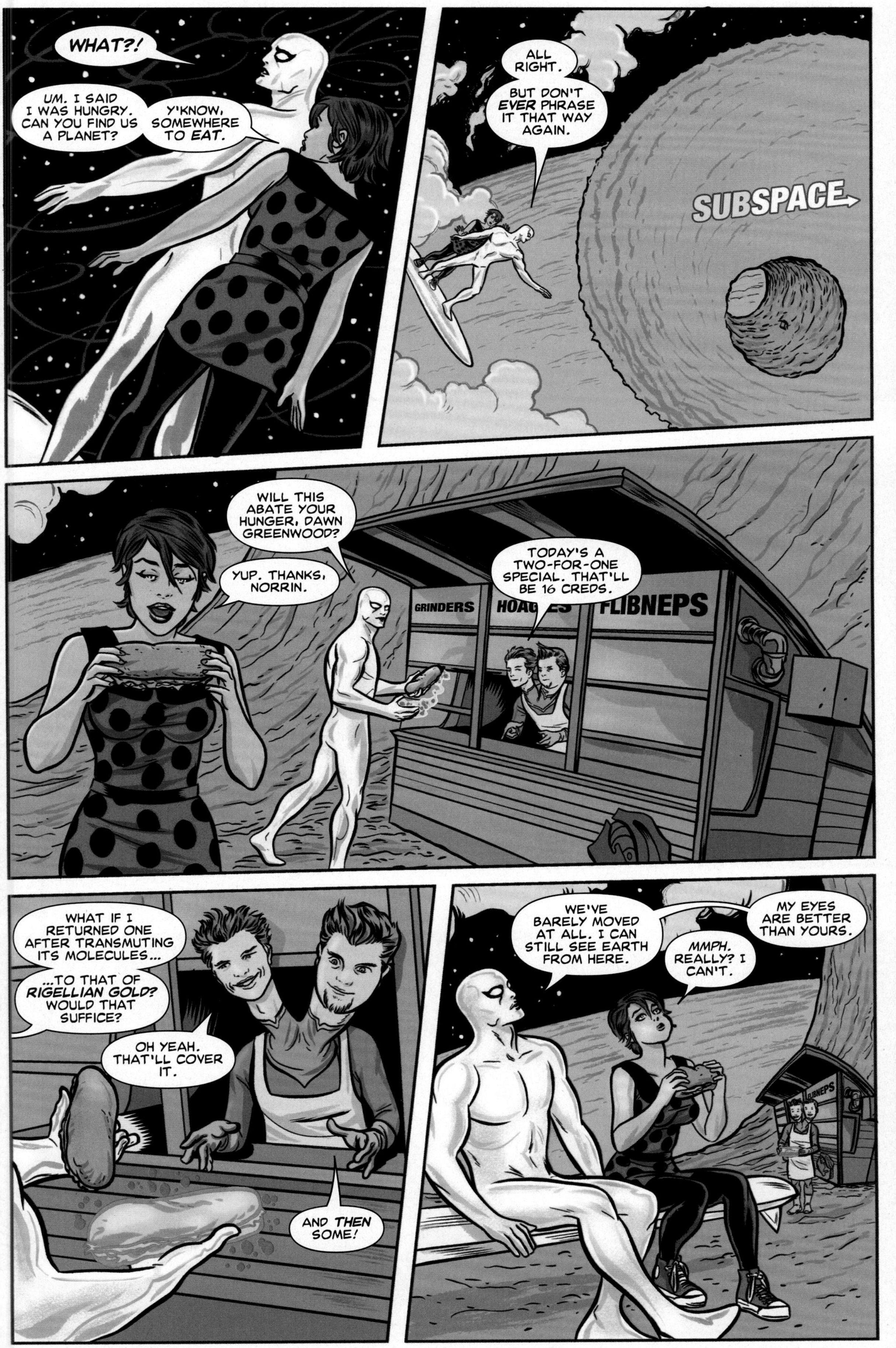
WHAT?!
UM. I SAID I WAS HUNGRY. CAN YOU FIND US A PLANET?
Y'KNOW, SOMEWHERE TO EAT.
ALL RIGHT.
BUT DON'T EVER PHRASE IT THAT WAY AGAIN.
SUBSPACE
WILL THIS ABATE YOUR HUNGER, DAWN GREENWOOD?
YUP. THANKS, NORRIN.
TODAY'S A TWO-FOR-ONE SPECIAL. THAT'LL BE 16 CREDS.
GRINDERS
FLIBNEPS
WHAT IF I RETURNED ONE AFTER TRANSMUTING ITS MOLECULES...
...TO THAT OF RIGELLIAN GOLD? WOULD THAT SUFFICE?
OH YEAH. THAT'LL COVER IT.
AND THEN SOME!
WE'VE BARELY MOVED AT ALL. I CAN STILL SEE EARTH FROM HERE.
MY EYES ARE BETTER THAN YOURS.
MMPH. REALLY? I CAN'T.
FLIBNEPS

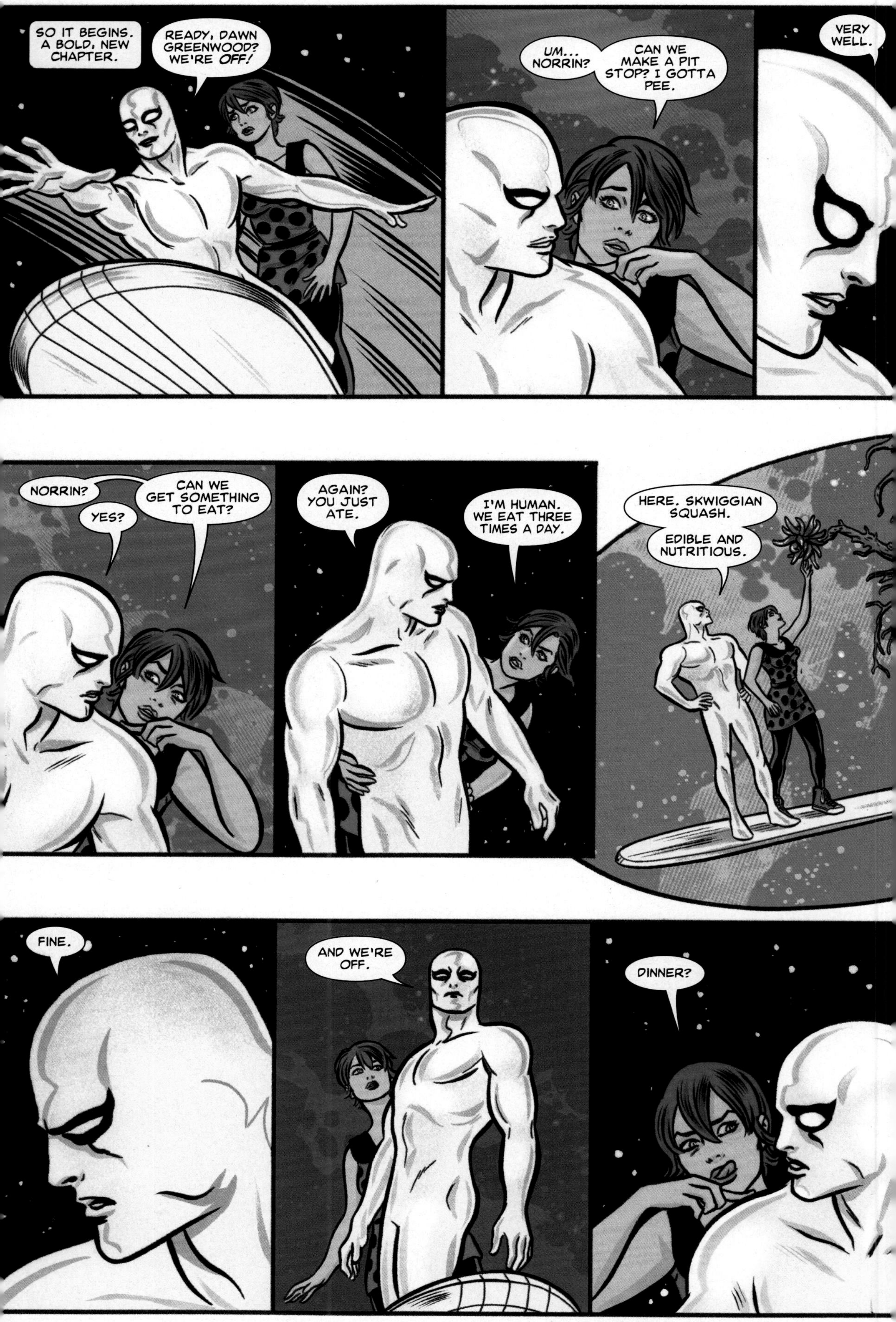
SO IT BEGINS. A BOLD, NEW CHAPTER.
READY, DAWN GREENWOOD? WE'RE *OFF!*
UM... NORRIN?
CAN WE MAKE A PIT STOP? I GOTTA PEE.
VERY WELL.
NORRIN?
YES?
CAN WE GET SOMETHING TO EAT?
AGAIN? YOU JUST ATE.
I'M HUMAN. WE EAT THREE TIMES A DAY.
HERE. SKWIGGIAN SQUASH.
EDIBLE AND NUTRITIOUS.
FINE.
AND WE'RE OFF.
DINNER?

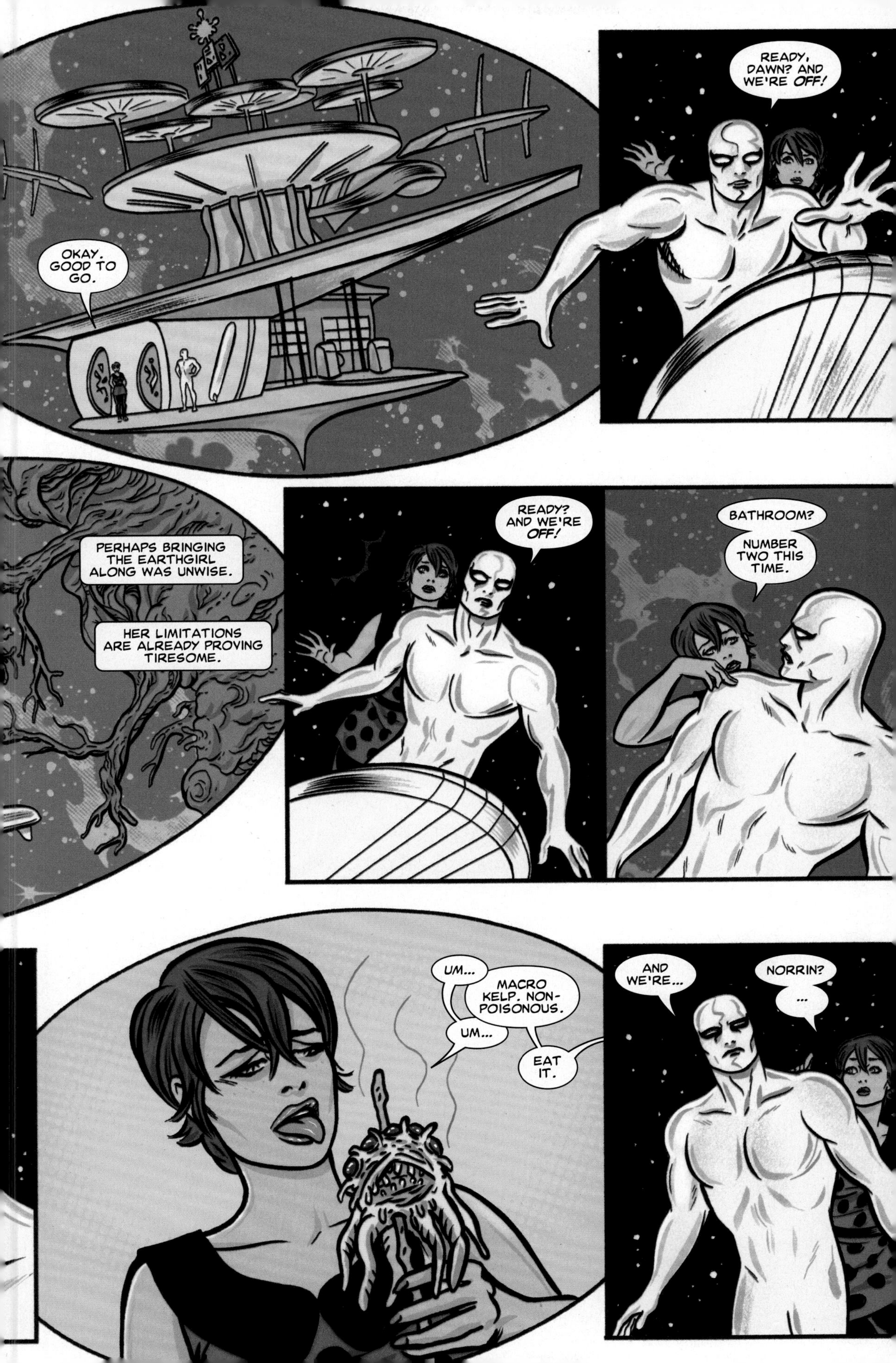
OKAY. GOOD TO GO.
READY, DAWN? AND WE'RE *OFF!*
PERHAPS BRINGING THE EARTHGIRL ALONG WAS UNWISE.
HER LIMITATIONS ARE ALREADY PROVING TIRESOME.
READY? AND WE'RE *OFF!*
BATHROOM?
NUMBER TWO THIS TIME.
UM...
MACRO KELP. NON-POISONOUS.
UM...
EAT IT.
AND WE'RE...
NORRIN?
...

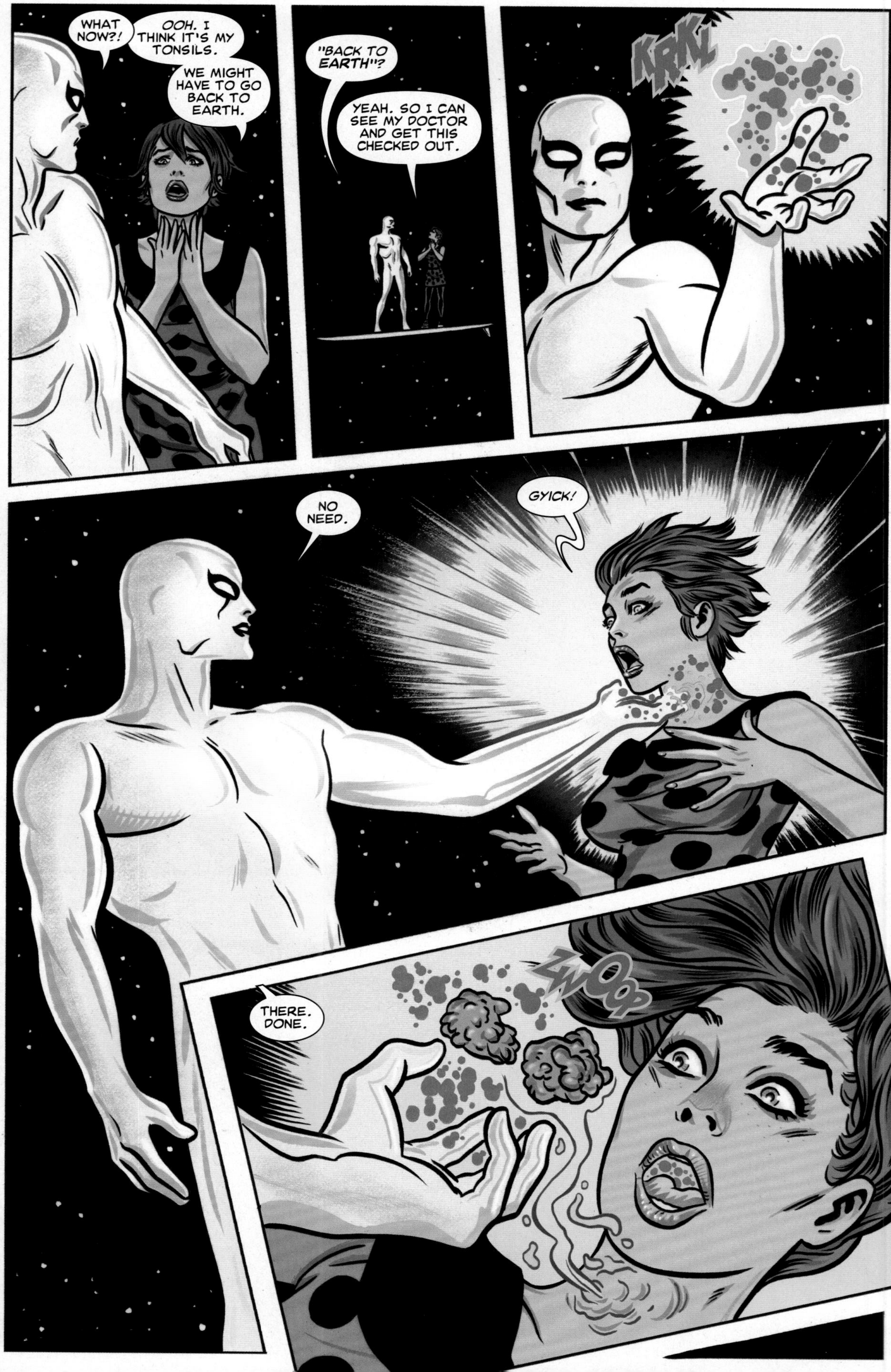
WHAT NOW?!
OOH. I THINK IT'S MY TONSILS.
WE MIGHT HAVE TO GO BACK TO EARTH.
"BACK TO EARTH"?
YEAH. SO I CAN SEE MY DOCTOR AND GET THIS CHECKED OUT.
KRKL
NO NEED.
GYICK!
ZWOOOP
THERE. DONE.

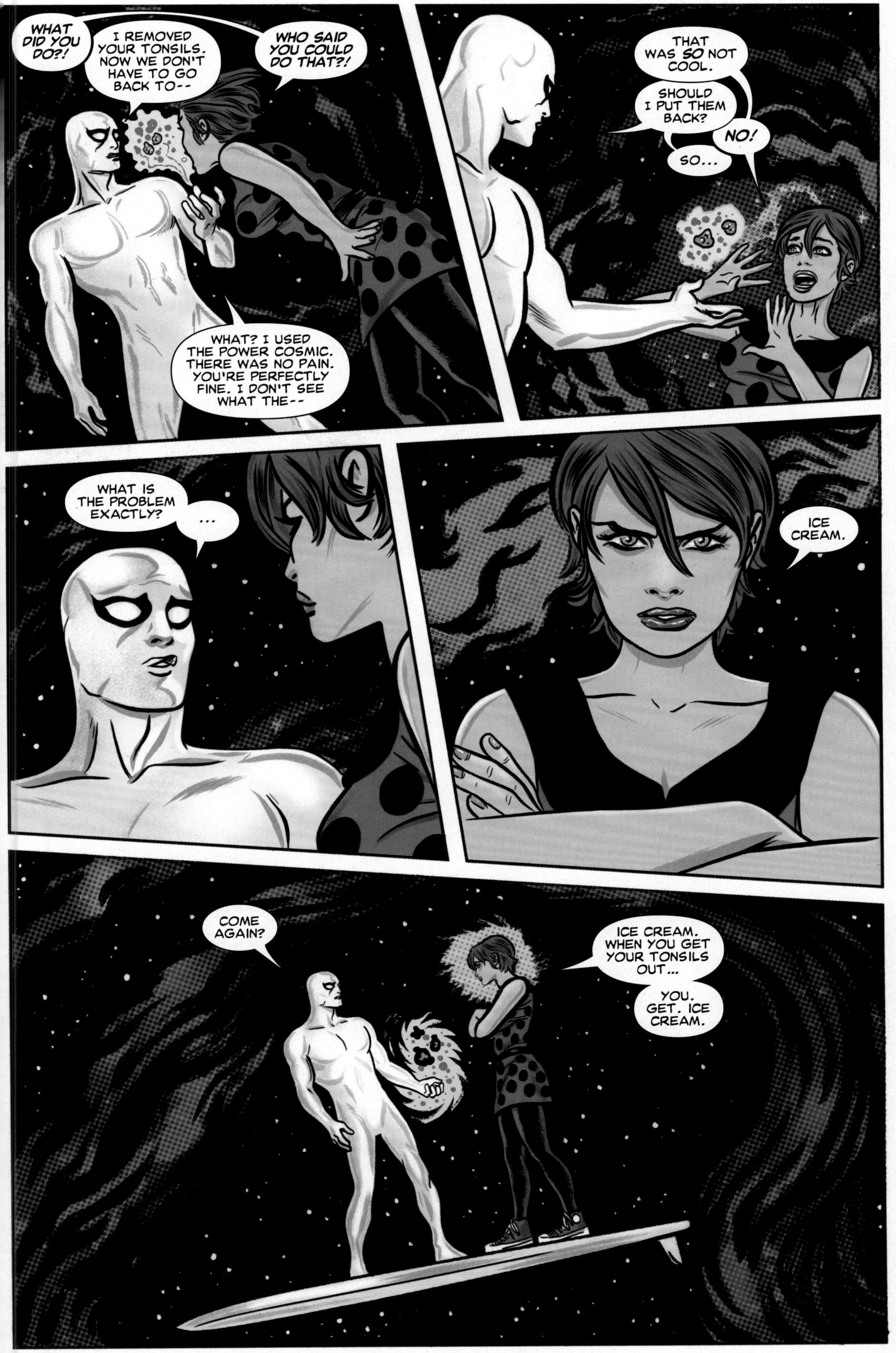
WHAT DID YOU DO?!
I REMOVED YOUR TONSILS. NOW WE DON'T HAVE TO GO BACK TO--
WHO SAID YOU COULD DO THAT?!
WHAT? I USED THE POWER COSMIC. THERE WAS NO PAIN. YOU'RE PERFECTLY FINE. I DON'T SEE WHAT THE--
THAT WAS SO NOT COOL.
SHOULD I PUT THEM BACK?
NO!
SO...
WHAT IS THE PROBLEM EXACTLY?
...
ICE CREAM.
COME AGAIN?
ICE CREAM. WHEN YOU GET YOUR TONSILS OUT...
YOU. GET. ICE CREAM.

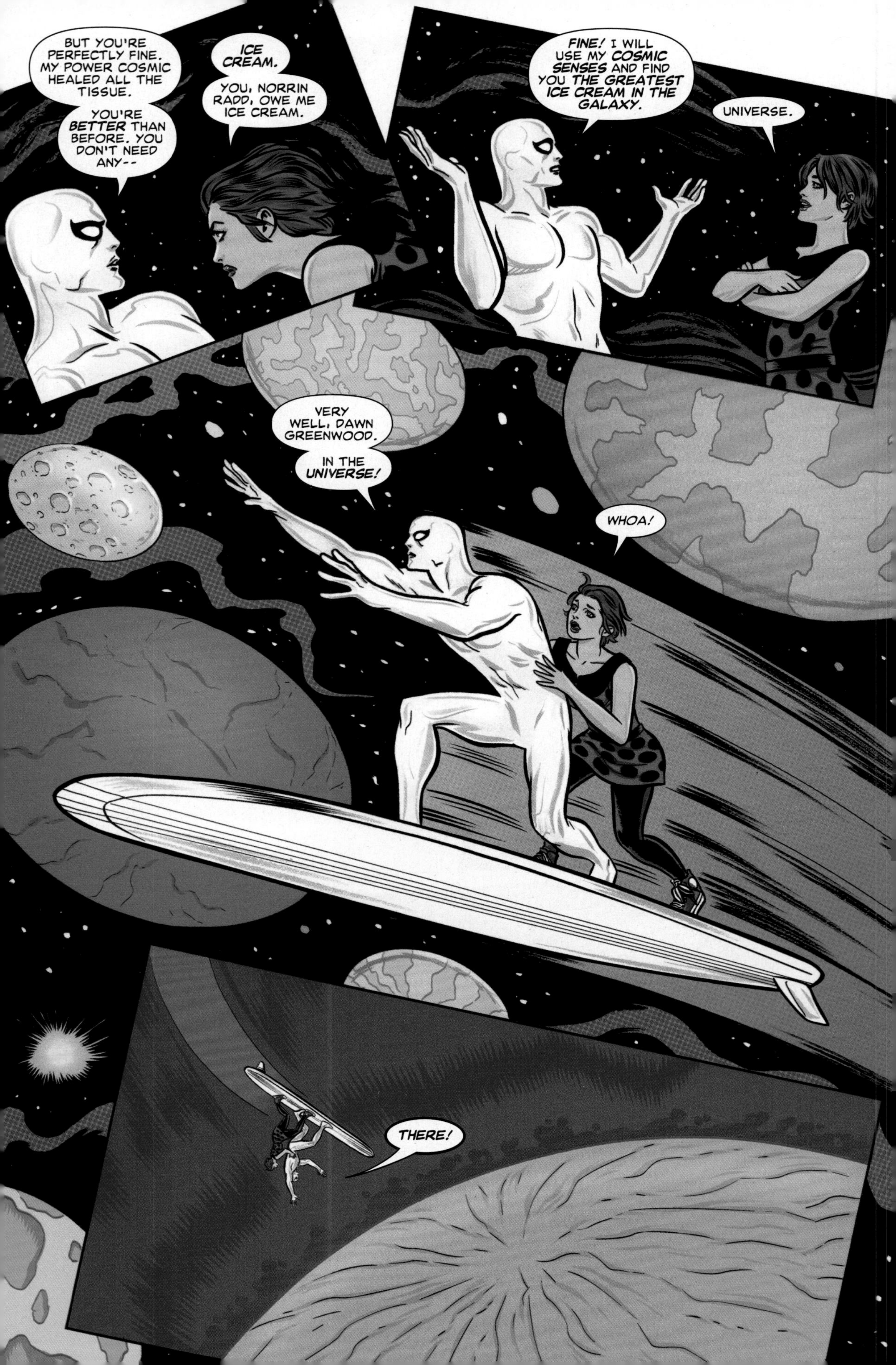
BUT YOU'RE PERFECTLY FINE. MY POWER COSMIC HEALED ALL THE TISSUE.
YOU'RE BETTER THAN BEFORE. YOU DON'T NEED ANY--
ICE CREAM.
YOU, NORRIN RADD, OWE ME ICE CREAM.
FINE! I WILL USE MY COSMIC SENSES AND FIND YOU THE GREATEST ICE CREAM IN THE GALAXY.
UNIVERSE.
VERY WELL, DAWN GREENWOOD.
IN THE UNIVERSE!
WHOA!
THERE!

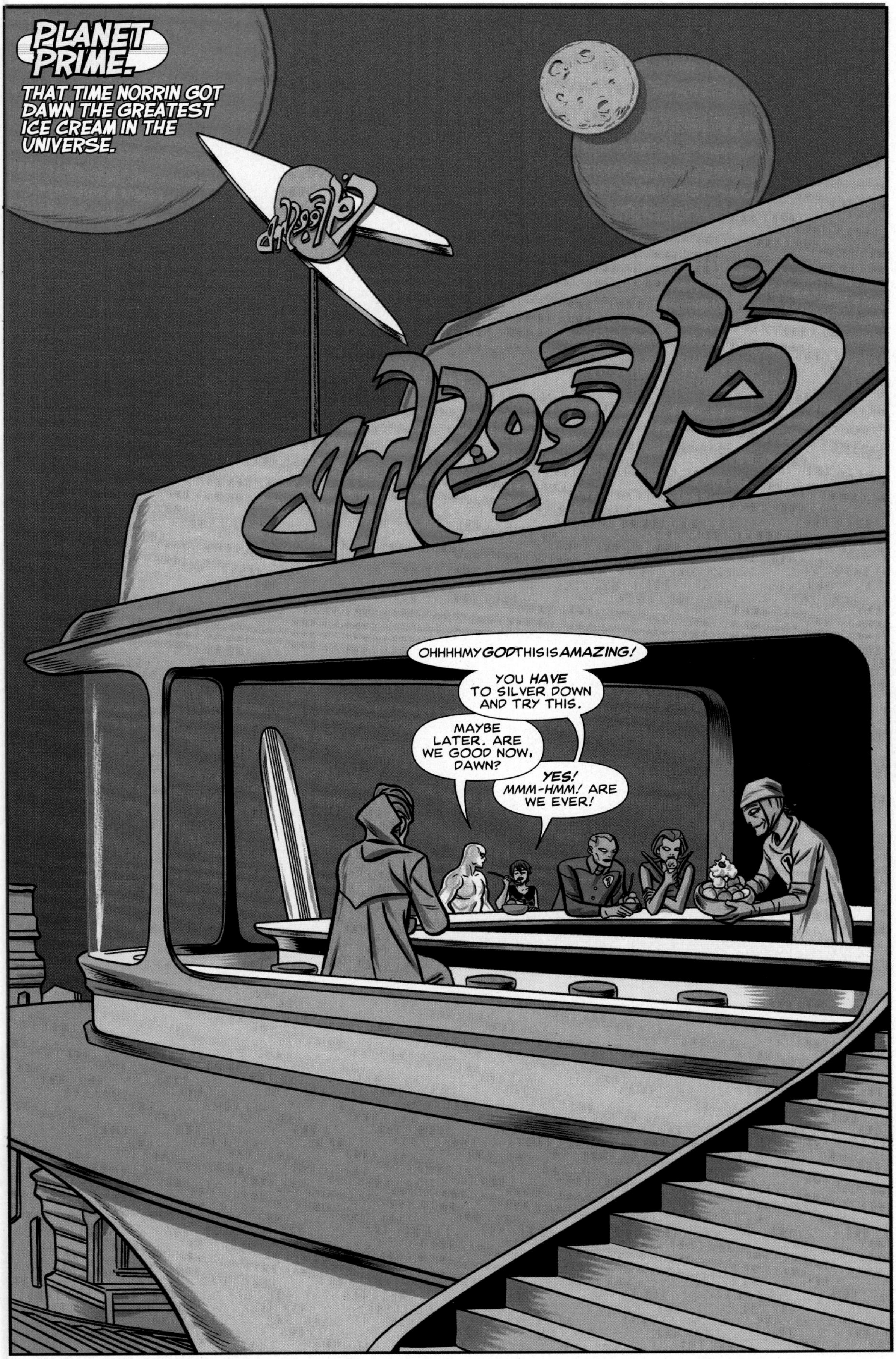
PLANET PRIME.
THAT TIME NORRIN GOT DAWN THE GREATEST ICE CREAM IN THE UNIVERSE.
OHHHHMYGODTHISISAMAZING!
YOU HAVE TO SILVER DOWN AND TRY THIS.
MAYBE LATER. ARE WE GOOD NOW, DAWN?
YES! MMM-HMM! ARE WE EVER!

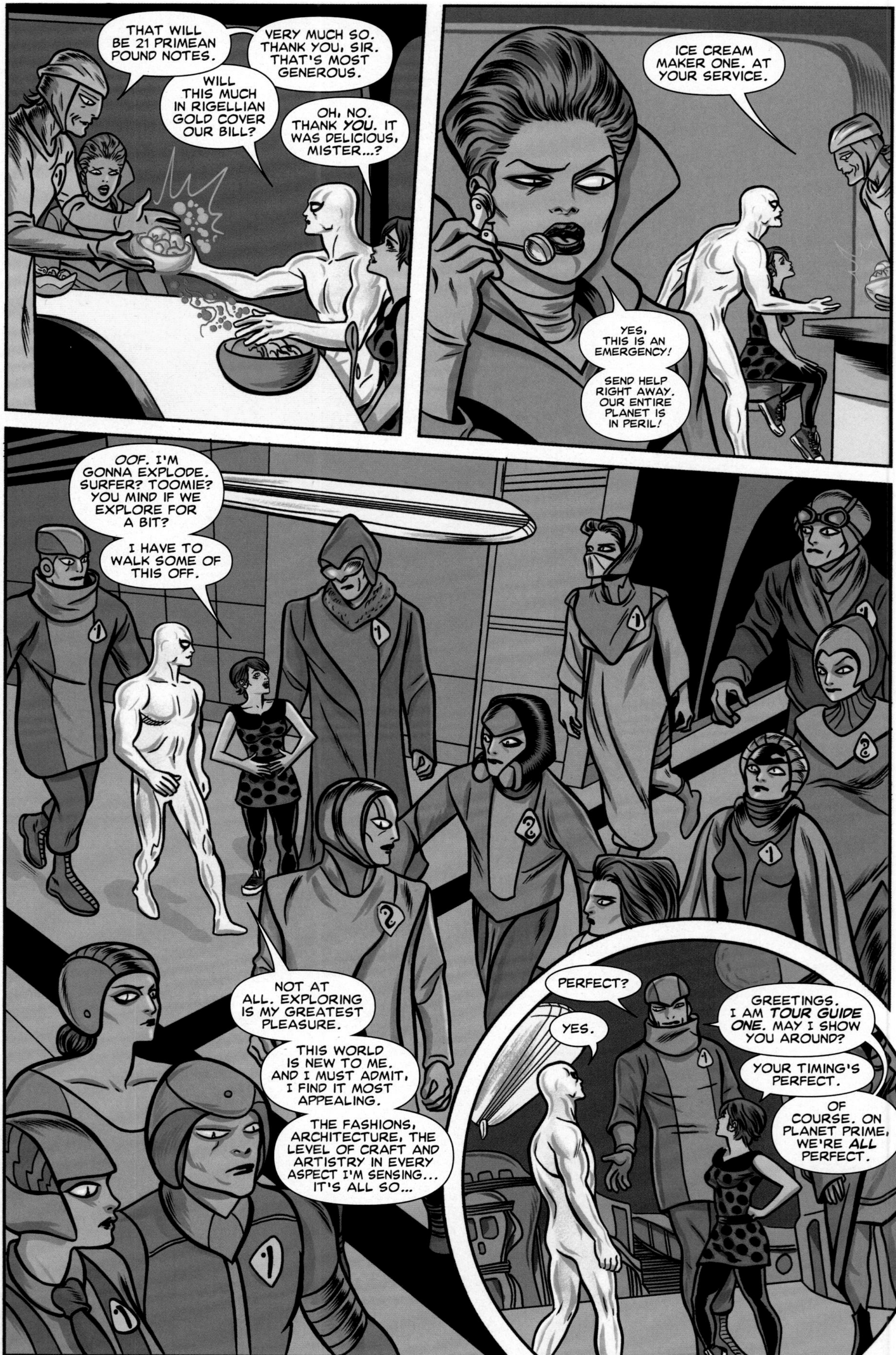
THAT WILL BE 21 PRIMEAN POUND NOTES.
VERY MUCH SO. THANK YOU, SIR. THAT'S MOST GENEROUS.
WILL THIS MUCH IN RIGELLIAN GOLD COVER OUR BILL?
OH, NO. THANK *YOU*. IT WAS DELICIOUS, MISTER...?
ICE CREAM MAKER ONE. AT YOUR SERVICE.
YES, THIS IS AN EMERGENCY!
SEND HELP RIGHT AWAY. OUR ENTIRE PLANET IS IN PERIL!
OOF. I'M GONNA EXPLODE. SURFER? TOOMIE? YOU MIND IF WE EXPLORE FOR A BIT?
I HAVE TO WALK SOME OF THIS OFF.
NOT AT ALL. EXPLORING IS MY GREATEST PLEASURE.
THIS WORLD IS NEW TO ME. AND I MUST ADMIT, I FIND IT MOST APPEALING.
THE FASHIONS, ARCHITECTURE, THE LEVEL OF CRAFT AND ARTISTRY IN EVERY ASPECT I'M SENSING... IT'S ALL SO...
PERFECT?
YES.
GREETINGS. I AM *TOUR GUIDE ONE*. MAY I SHOW YOU AROUND?
YOUR TIMING'S PERFECT.
OF COURSE. ON PLANET PRIME, WE'RE *ALL* PERFECT.

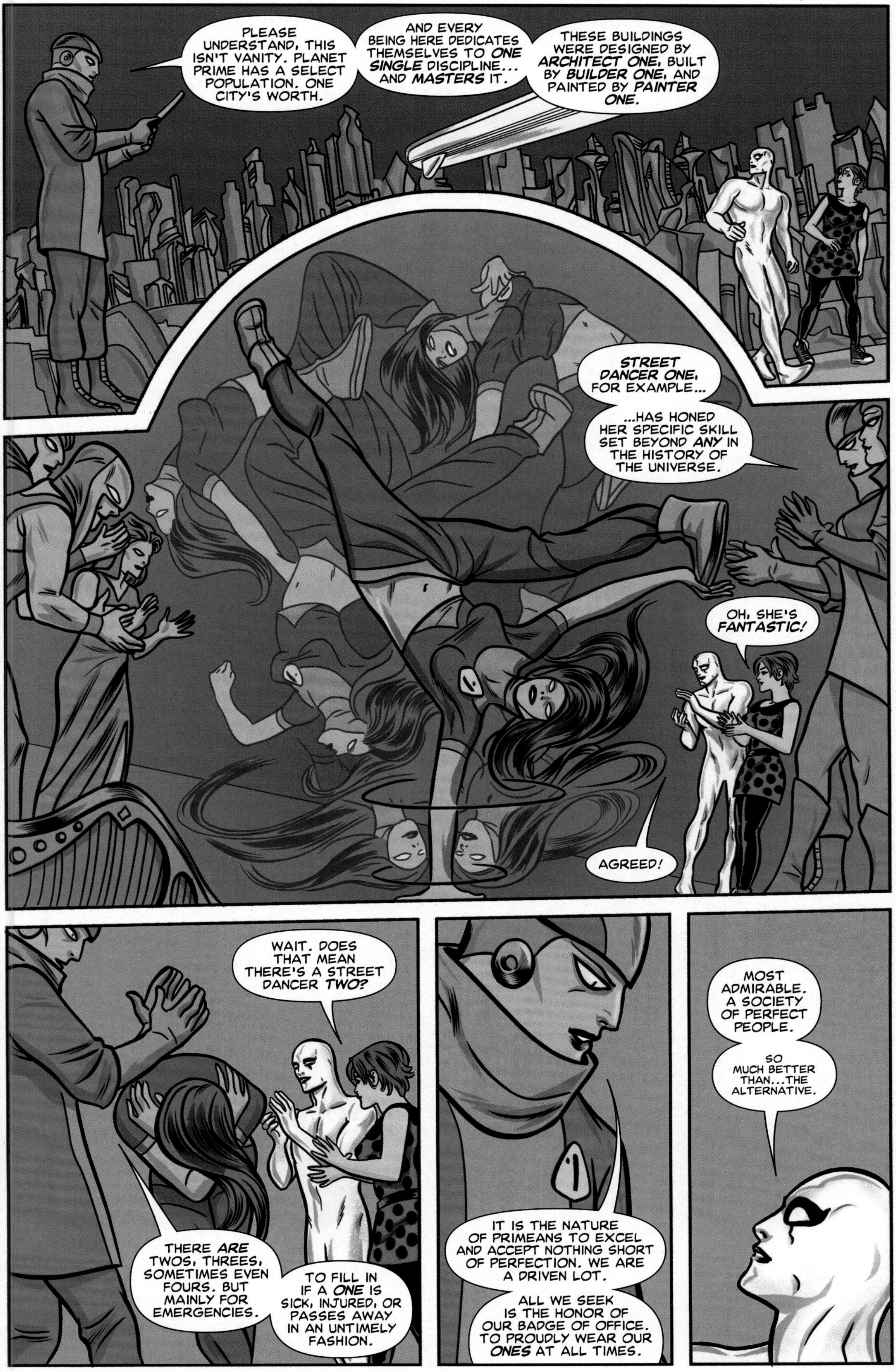
PLEASE UNDERSTAND, THIS ISN'T VANITY. PLANET PRIME HAS A SELECT POPULATION. ONE CITY'S WORTH.
AND EVERY BEING HERE DEDICATES THEMSELVES TO *ONE SINGLE* DISCIPLINE... AND *MASTERS* IT.
THESE BUILDINGS WERE DESIGNED BY *ARCHITECT ONE*, BUILT BY *BUILDER ONE*, AND PAINTED BY *PAINTER ONE*.
STREET DANCER ONE, FOR EXAMPLE...
...HAS HONED HER SPECIFIC SKILL SET BEYOND *ANY* IN THE HISTORY OF THE UNIVERSE.
OH, SHE'S *FANTASTIC!*
AGREED!
WAIT. DOES THAT MEAN THERE'S A STREET DANCER *TWO?*
THERE *ARE* TWOS, THREES, SOMETIMES EVEN FOURS. BUT MAINLY FOR EMERGENCIES.
TO FILL IN IF A *ONE* IS SICK, INJURED, OR PASSES AWAY IN AN UNTIMELY FASHION.
IT IS THE NATURE OF PRIMEANS TO EXCEL AND ACCEPT NOTHING SHORT OF PERFECTION. WE ARE A DRIVEN LOT.
ALL WE SEEK IS THE HONOR OF OUR BADGE OF OFFICE. TO PROUDLY WEAR OUR *ONES* AT ALL TIMES.
MOST ADMIRABLE. A SOCIETY OF PERFECT PEOPLE.
SO MUCH BETTER THAN...THE ALTERNATIVE.

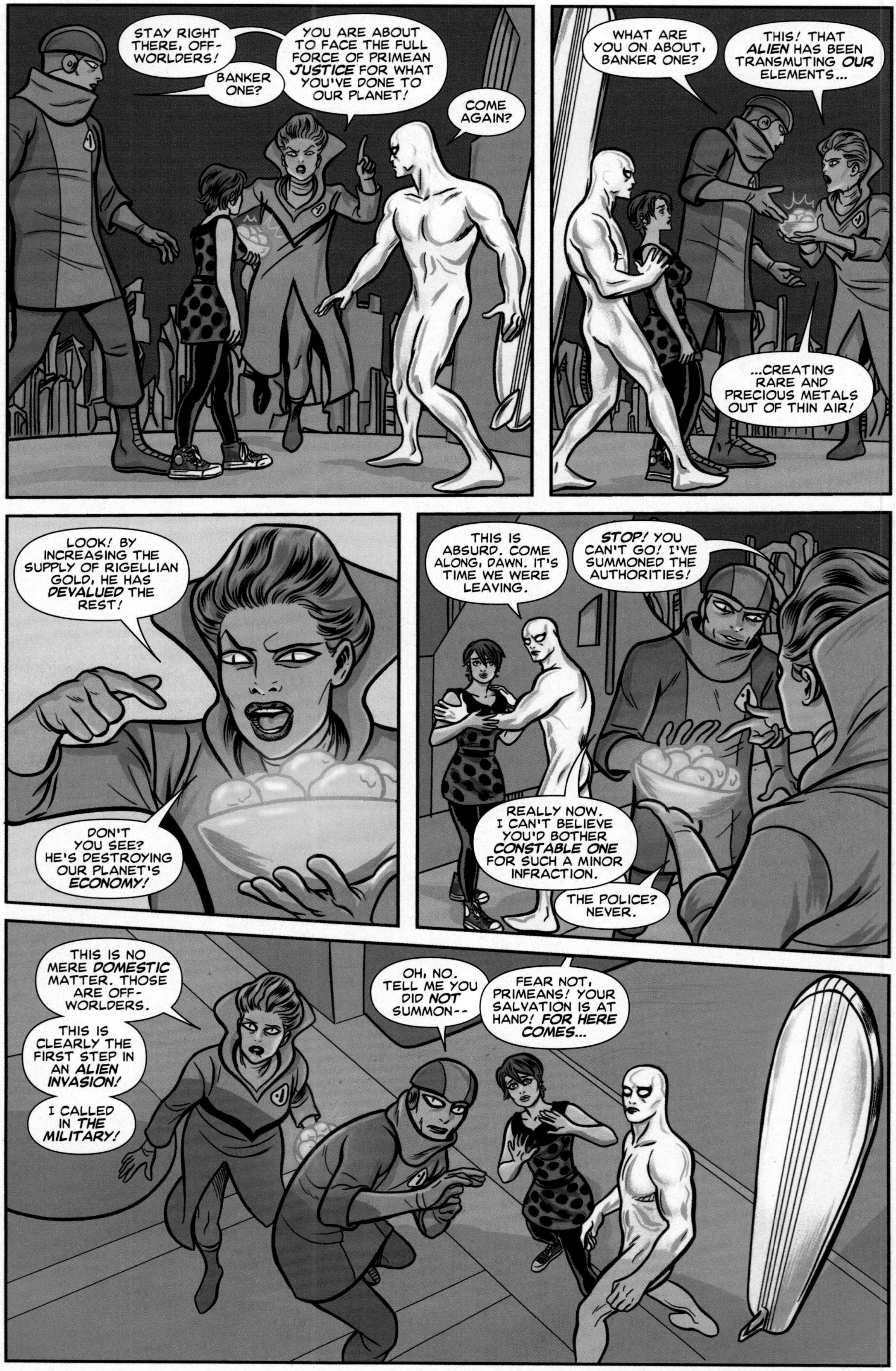
STAY RIGHT THERE, OFF-WORLDERS!
YOU ARE ABOUT TO FACE THE FULL FORCE OF PRIMEAN JUSTICE FOR WHAT YOU'VE DONE TO OUR PLANET!
BANKER ONE?
COME AGAIN?
WHAT ARE YOU ON ABOUT, BANKER ONE?
THIS! THAT ALIEN HAS BEEN TRANSMUTING OUR ELEMENTS...
...CREATING RARE AND PRECIOUS METALS OUT OF THIN AIR!
LOOK! BY INCREASING THE SUPPLY OF RIGELLIAN GOLD, HE HAS DEVALUED THE REST!
DON'T YOU SEE? HE'S DESTROYING OUR PLANET'S ECONOMY!
THIS IS ABSURD. COME ALONG, DAWN. IT'S TIME WE WERE LEAVING.
STOP! YOU CAN'T GO! I'VE SUMMONED THE AUTHORITIES!
REALLY NOW. I CAN'T BELIEVE YOU'D BOTHER CONSTABLE ONE FOR SUCH A MINOR INFRACTION.
THE POLICE? NEVER.
THIS IS NO MERE DOMESTIC MATTER. THOSE ARE OFF-WORLDERS.
THIS IS CLEARLY THE FIRST STEP IN AN ALIEN INVASION!
I CALLED IN THE MILITARY!
OH, NO. TELL ME YOU DID NOT SUMMON--
FEAR NOT, PRIMEANS! YOUR SALVATION IS AT HAND! FOR HERE COMES...

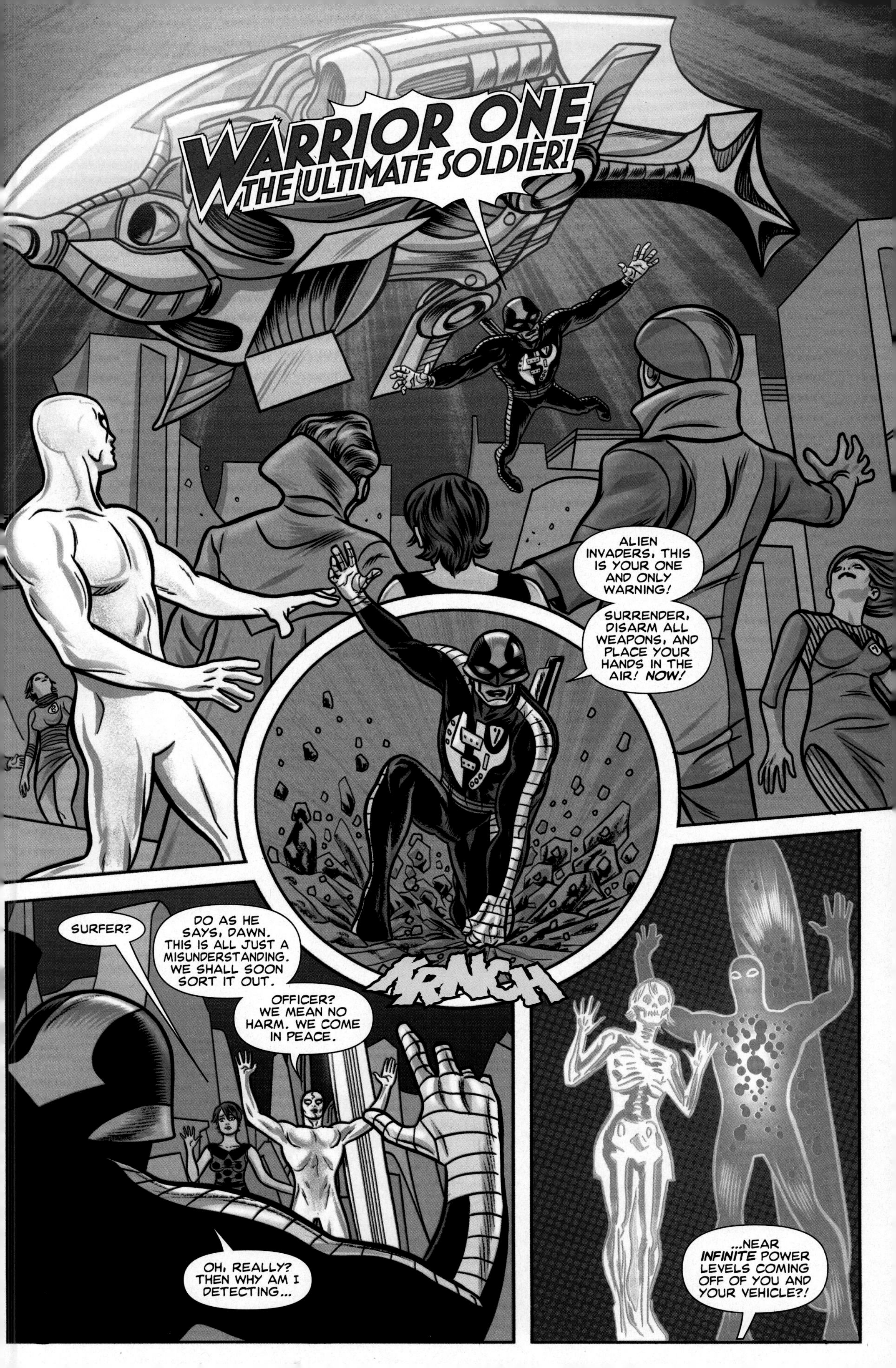
WARRIOR ONE THE ULTIMATE SOLDIER!
ALIEN INVADERS, THIS IS YOUR ONE AND ONLY WARNING!
SURRENDER, DISARM ALL WEAPONS, AND PLACE YOUR HANDS IN THE AIR! NOW!
KRNCH
SURFER?
DO AS HE SAYS, DAWN. THIS IS ALL JUST A MISUNDERSTANDING. WE SHALL SOON SORT IT OUT.
OFFICER? WE MEAN NO HARM. WE COME IN PEACE.
OH, REALLY? THEN WHY AM I DETECTING...
...NEAR INFINITE POWER LEVELS COMING OFF OF YOU AND YOUR VEHICLE?!

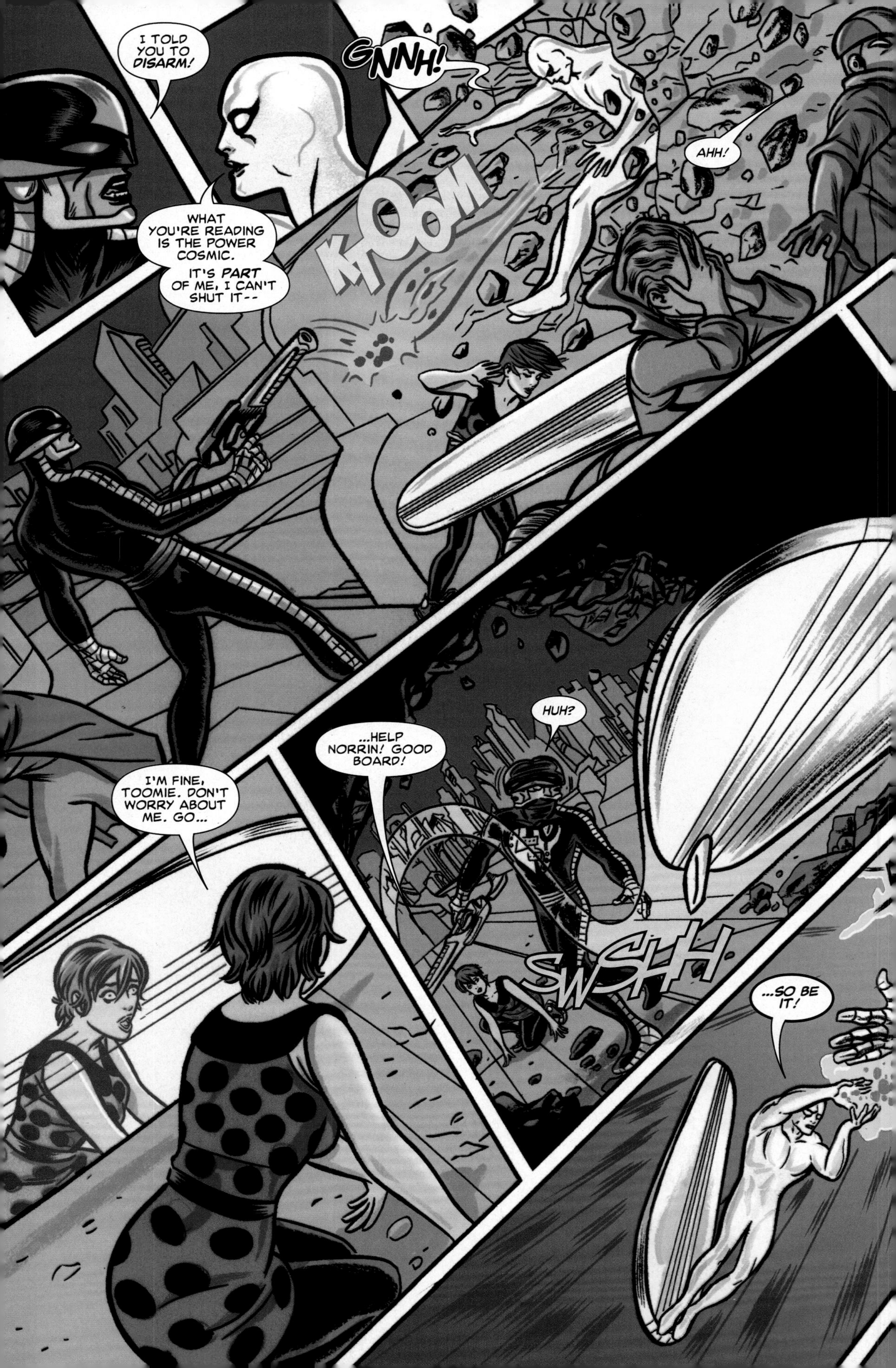
I TOLD YOU TO DISARM!
WHAT YOU'RE READING IS THE POWER COSMIC.
IT'S PART OF ME, I CAN'T SHUT IT--
GNNH!
KTOOOM
AHH!
I'M FINE, TOOMIE. DON'T WORRY ABOUT ME. GO...
...HELP NORRIN! GOOD BOARD!
HUH?
SWSHH
...SO BE IT!

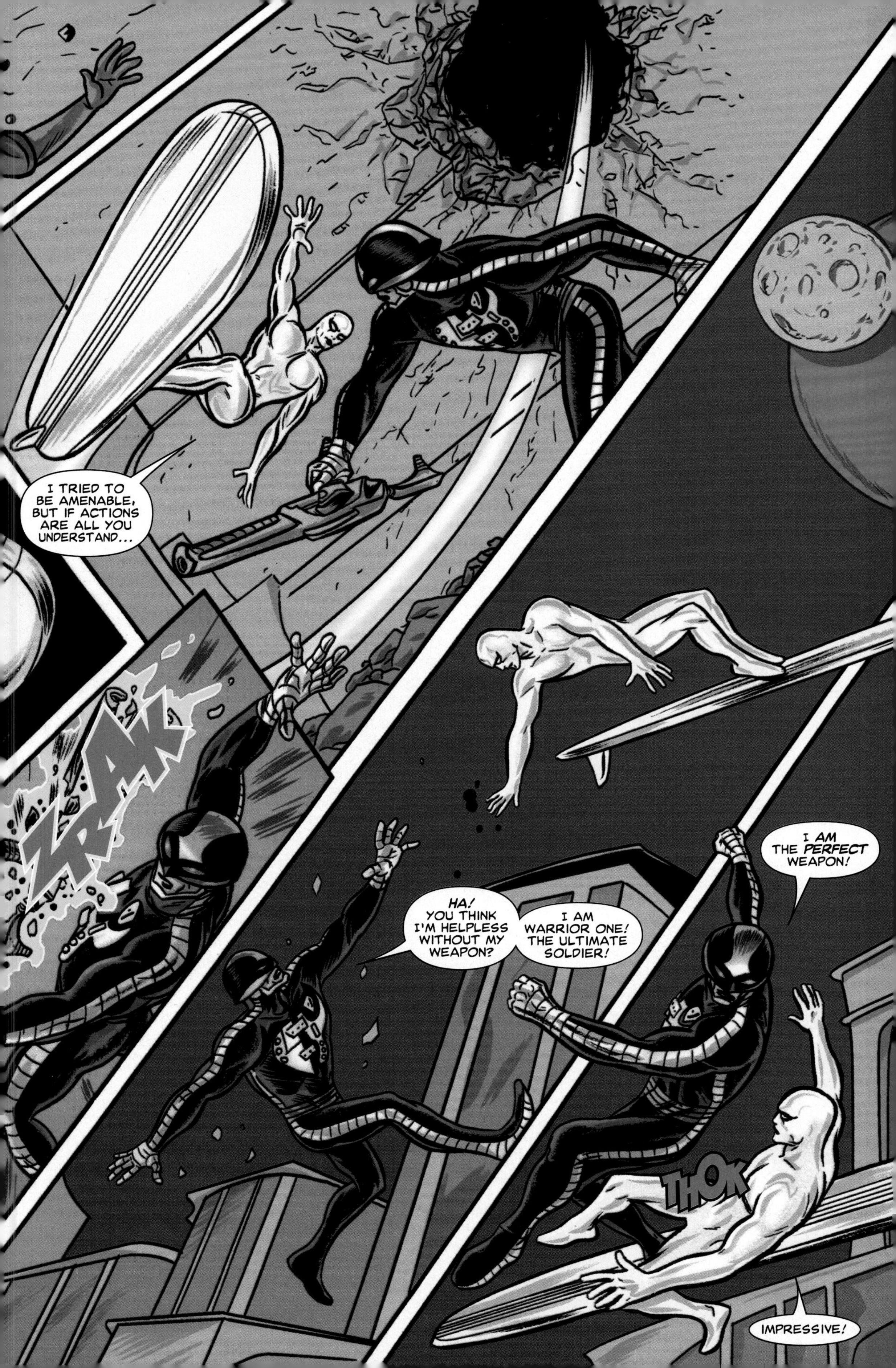
I TRIED TO BE AMENABLE, BUT IF ACTIONS ARE ALL YOU UNDERSTAND...
ZRAK
HA! YOU THINK I'M HELPLESS WITHOUT MY WEAPON?
I AM WARRIOR ONE! THE ULTIMATE SOLDIER!
I AM THE PERFECT WEAPON!
THOK
IMPRESSIVE!

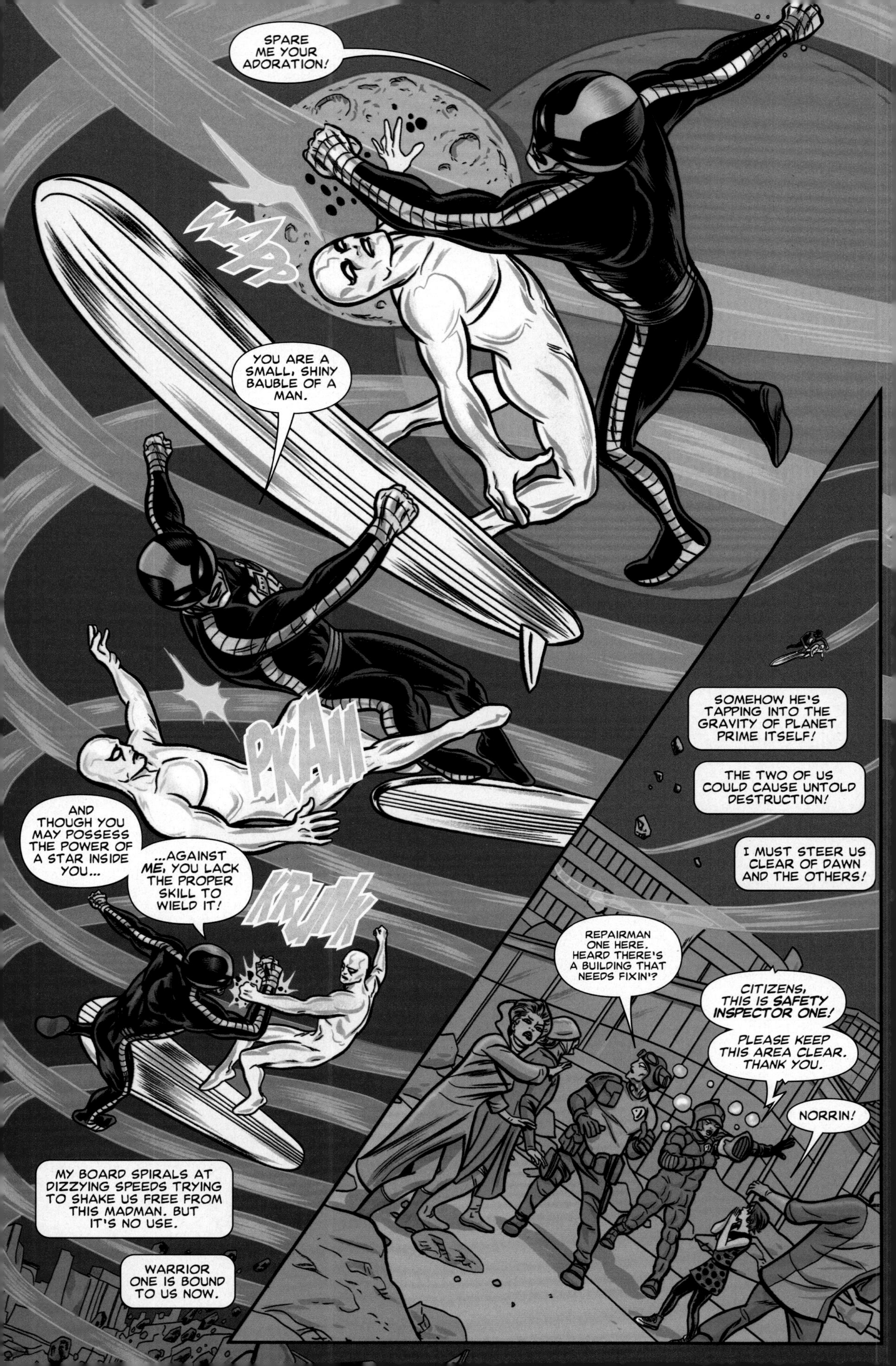
SPARE ME YOUR ADORATION!
WAPP
YOU ARE A SMALL, SHINY BAUBLE OF A MAN.
PKAM
AND THOUGH YOU MAY POSSESS THE POWER OF A STAR INSIDE YOU...
...AGAINST ME, YOU LACK THE PROPER SKILL TO WIELD IT!
KRUNK
MY BOARD SPIRALS AT DIZZYING SPEEDS TRYING TO SHAKE US FREE FROM THIS MADMAN. BUT IT'S NO USE.
WARRIOR ONE IS BOUND TO US NOW.
SOMEHOW HE'S TAPPING INTO THE GRAVITY OF PLANET PRIME ITSELF!
THE TWO OF US COULD CAUSE UNTOLD DESTRUCTION!
I MUST STEER US CLEAR OF DAWN AND THE OTHERS!
REPAIRMAN ONE HERE. HEARD THERE'S A BUILDING THAT NEEDS FIXIN'?
CITIZENS, THIS IS SAFETY INSPECTOR ONE!
PLEASE KEEP THIS AREA CLEAR. THANK YOU.
NORRIN!

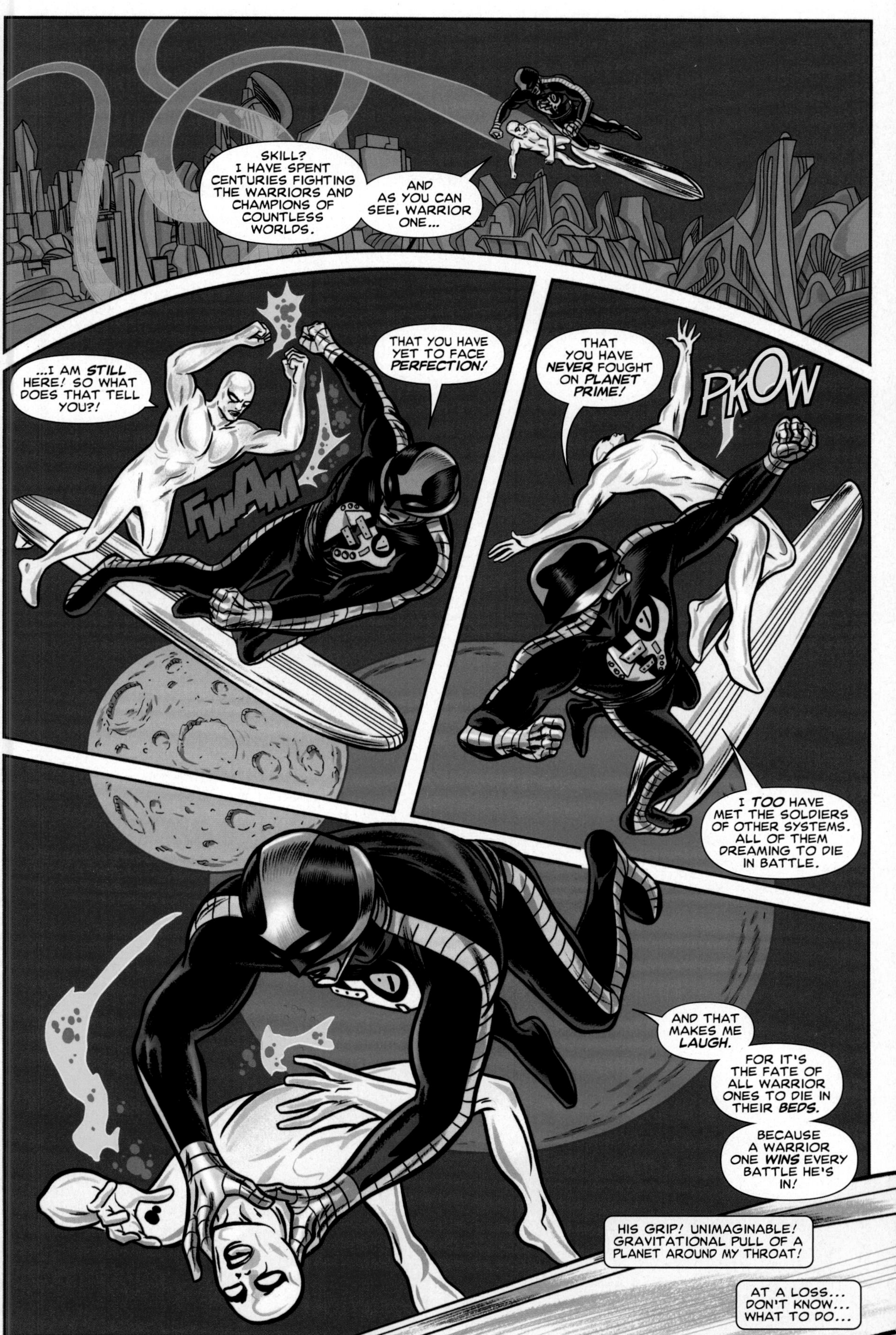
SKILL? I HAVE SPENT CENTURIES FIGHTING THE WARRIORS AND CHAMPIONS OF COUNTLESS WORLDS.
AND AS YOU CAN SEE, WARRIOR ONE...
...I AM STILL HERE! SO WHAT DOES THAT TELL YOU?!
THAT YOU HAVE YET TO FACE PERFECTION!
FWAM
THAT YOU HAVE NEVER FOUGHT ON PLANET PRIME!
PKOW
I TOO HAVE MET THE SOLDIERS OF OTHER SYSTEMS. ALL OF THEM DREAMING TO DIE IN BATTLE.
AND THAT MAKES ME LAUGH.
FOR IT'S THE FATE OF ALL WARRIOR ONES TO DIE IN THEIR BEDS.
BECAUSE A WARRIOR ONE WINS EVERY BATTLE HE'S IN!
HIS GRIP! UNIMAGINABLE! GRAVITATIONAL PULL OF A PLANET AROUND MY THROAT!
AT A LOSS... DON'T KNOW... WHAT TO DO...

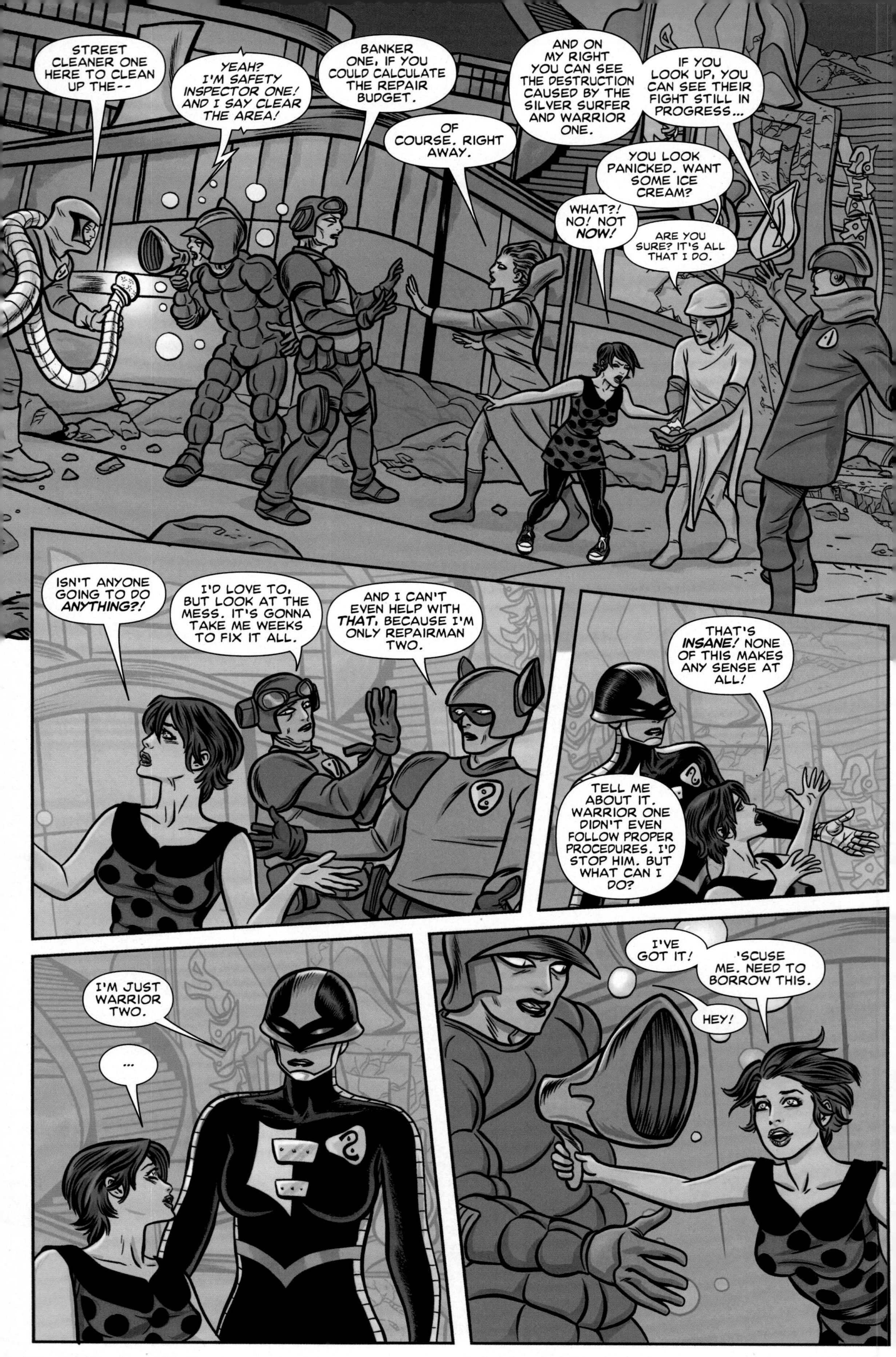
STREET CLEANER ONE HERE TO CLEAN UP THE--
YEAH? I'M SAFETY INSPECTOR ONE! AND I SAY CLEAR THE AREA!
BANKER ONE, IF YOU COULD CALCULATE THE REPAIR BUDGET.
OF COURSE. RIGHT AWAY.
AND ON MY RIGHT YOU CAN SEE THE DESTRUCTION CAUSED BY THE SILVER SURFER AND WARRIOR ONE.
IF YOU LOOK UP, YOU CAN SEE THEIR FIGHT STILL IN PROGRESS...
YOU LOOK PANICKED. WANT SOME ICE CREAM?
WHAT?! NO! NOT NOW!
ARE YOU SURE? IT'S ALL THAT I DO.
ISN'T ANYONE GOING TO DO ANYTHING?!
I'D LOVE TO, BUT LOOK AT THE MESS. IT'S GONNA TAKE ME WEEKS TO FIX IT ALL.
AND I CAN'T EVEN HELP WITH THAT, BECAUSE I'M ONLY REPAIRMAN TWO.
THAT'S INSANE! NONE OF THIS MAKES ANY SENSE AT ALL!
TELL ME ABOUT IT. WARRIOR ONE DIDN'T EVEN FOLLOW PROPER PROCEDURES. I'D STOP HIM. BUT WHAT CAN I DO?
I'M JUST WARRIOR TWO.
...
I'VE GOT IT!
'SCUSE ME. NEED TO BORROW THIS.
HEY!

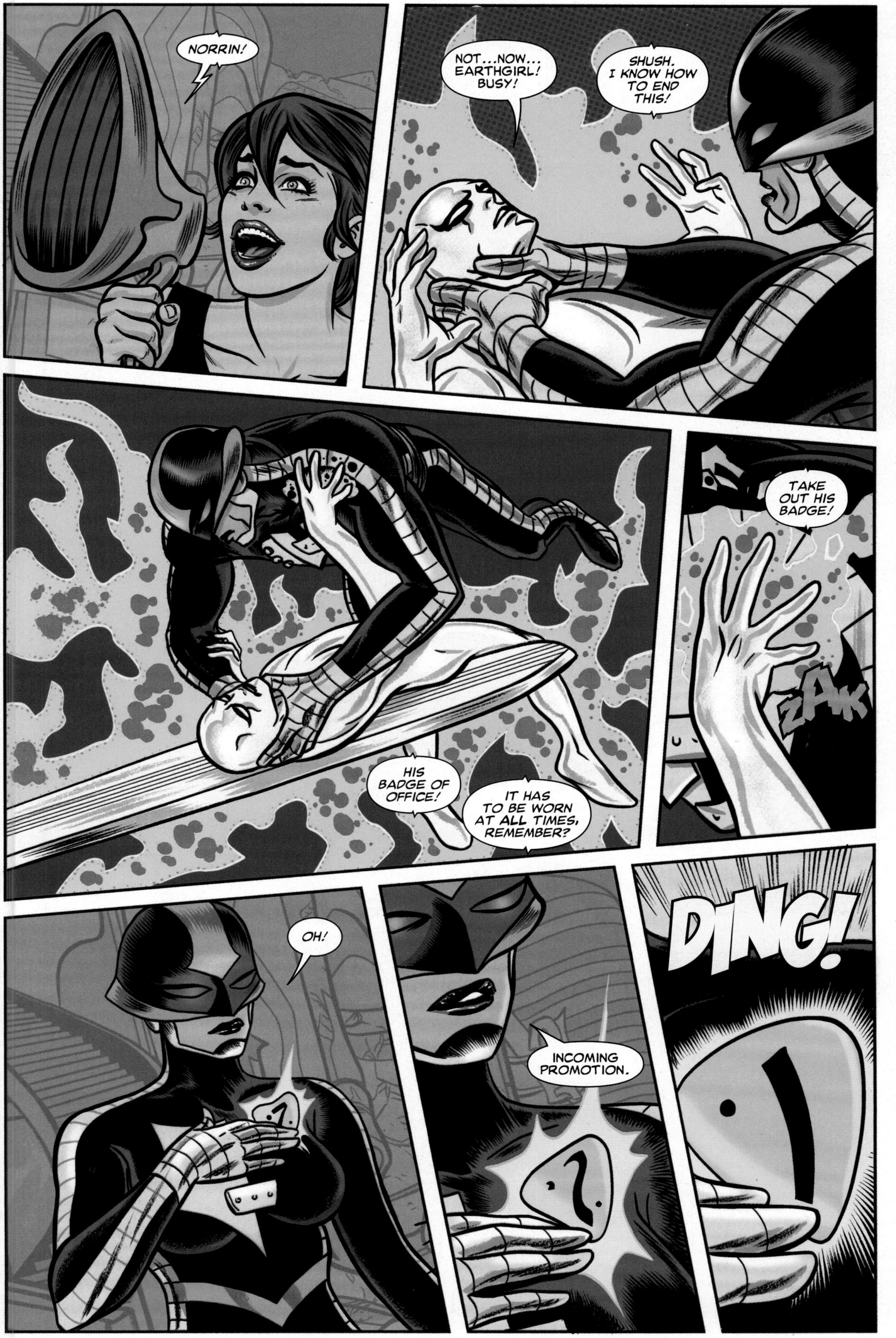
NORRIN!
NOT...NOW... EARTHGIRL! BUSY!
SHUSH. I KNOW HOW TO END THIS!
HIS BADGE OF OFFICE!
IT HAS TO BE WORN AT ALL TIMES, REMEMBER?
TAKE OUT HIS BADGE!
ZAK
OH!
INCOMING PROMOTION.
DING!

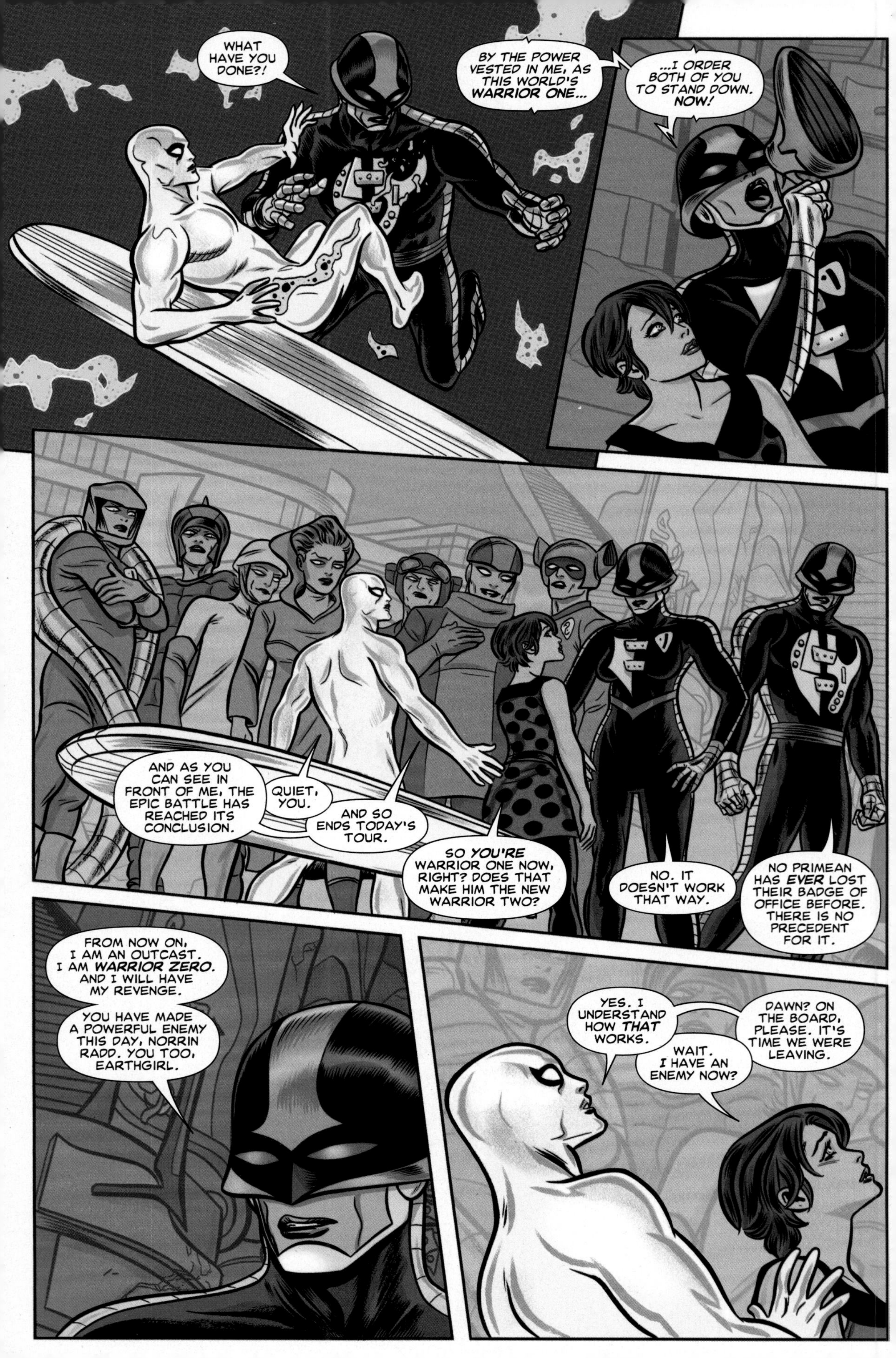
WHAT HAVE YOU DONE?!
BY THE POWER VESTED IN ME, AS THIS WORLD'S WARRIOR ONE...
...I ORDER BOTH OF YOU TO STAND DOWN. NOW!
AND AS YOU CAN SEE IN FRONT OF ME, THE EPIC BATTLE HAS REACHED ITS CONCLUSION.
QUIET, YOU.
AND SO ENDS TODAY'S TOUR.
SO YOU'RE WARRIOR ONE NOW, RIGHT? DOES THAT MAKE HIM THE NEW WARRIOR TWO?
NO. IT DOESN'T WORK THAT WAY.
NO PRIMEAN HAS EVER LOST THEIR BADGE OF OFFICE BEFORE. THERE IS NO PRECEDENT FOR IT.
FROM NOW ON, I AM AN OUTCAST. I AM WARRIOR ZERO. AND I WILL HAVE MY REVENGE.
YOU HAVE MADE A POWERFUL ENEMY THIS DAY, NORRIN RADD. YOU TOO, EARTHGIRL.
YES. I UNDERSTAND HOW THAT WORKS.
DAWN? ON THE BOARD, PLEASE. IT'S TIME WE WERE LEAVING.
WAIT. I HAVE AN ENEMY NOW?

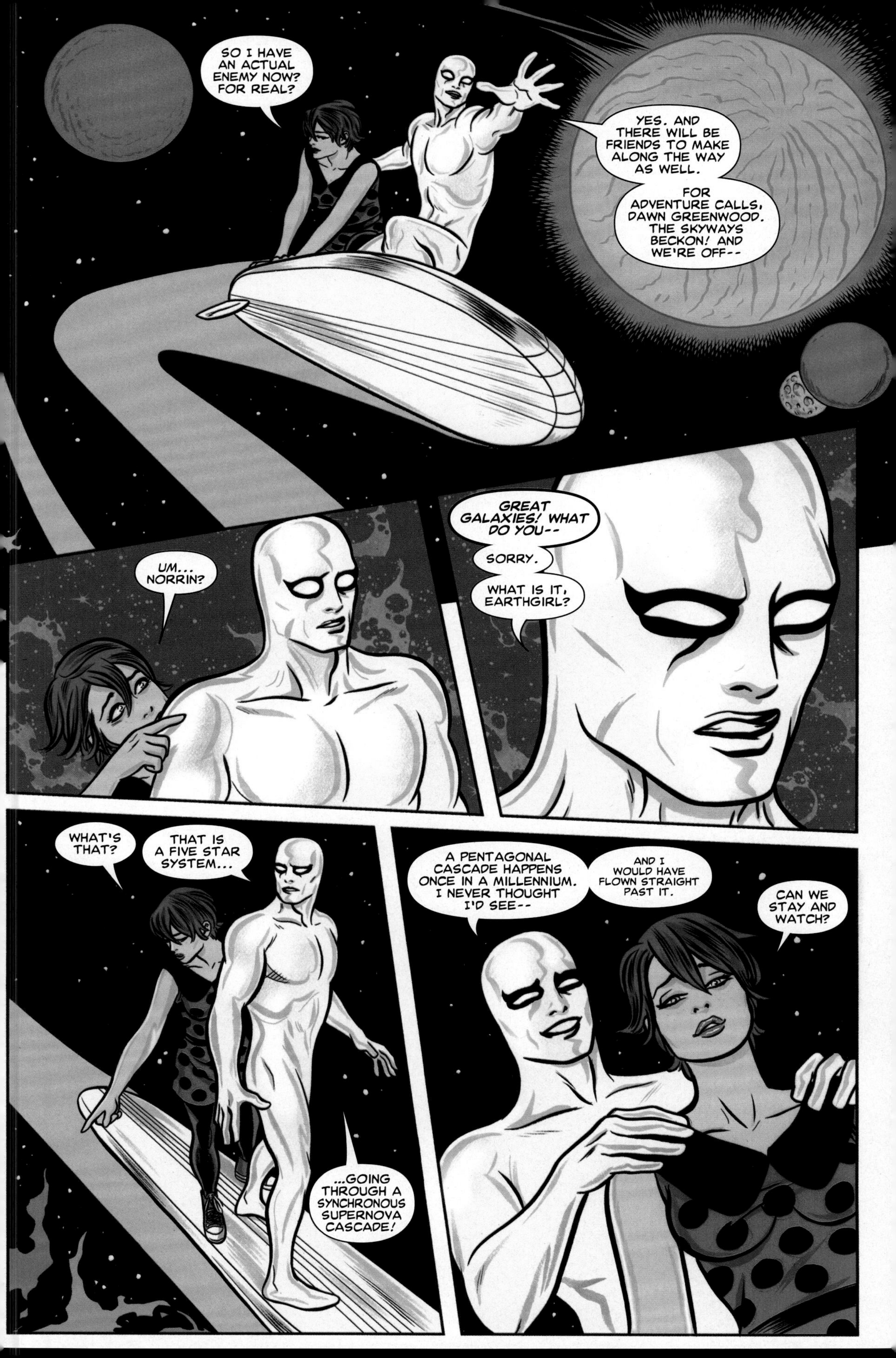
SO I HAVE AN ACTUAL ENEMY NOW? FOR REAL?
YES. AND THERE WILL BE FRIENDS TO MAKE ALONG THE WAY AS WELL.
FOR ADVENTURE CALLS, DAWN GREENWOOD. THE SKYWAYS BECKON! AND WE'RE OFF--
UM... NORRIN?
GREAT GALAXIES! WHAT DO YOU--
SORRY.
WHAT IS IT, EARTHGIRL?
WHAT'S THAT?
THAT IS A FIVE STAR SYSTEM...
...GOING THROUGH A SYNCHRONOUS SUPERNOVA CASCADE!
A PENTAGONAL CASCADE HAPPENS ONCE IN A MILLENNIUM. I NEVER THOUGHT I'D SEE--
AND I WOULD HAVE FLOWN STRAIGHT PAST IT.
CAN WE STAY AND WATCH?

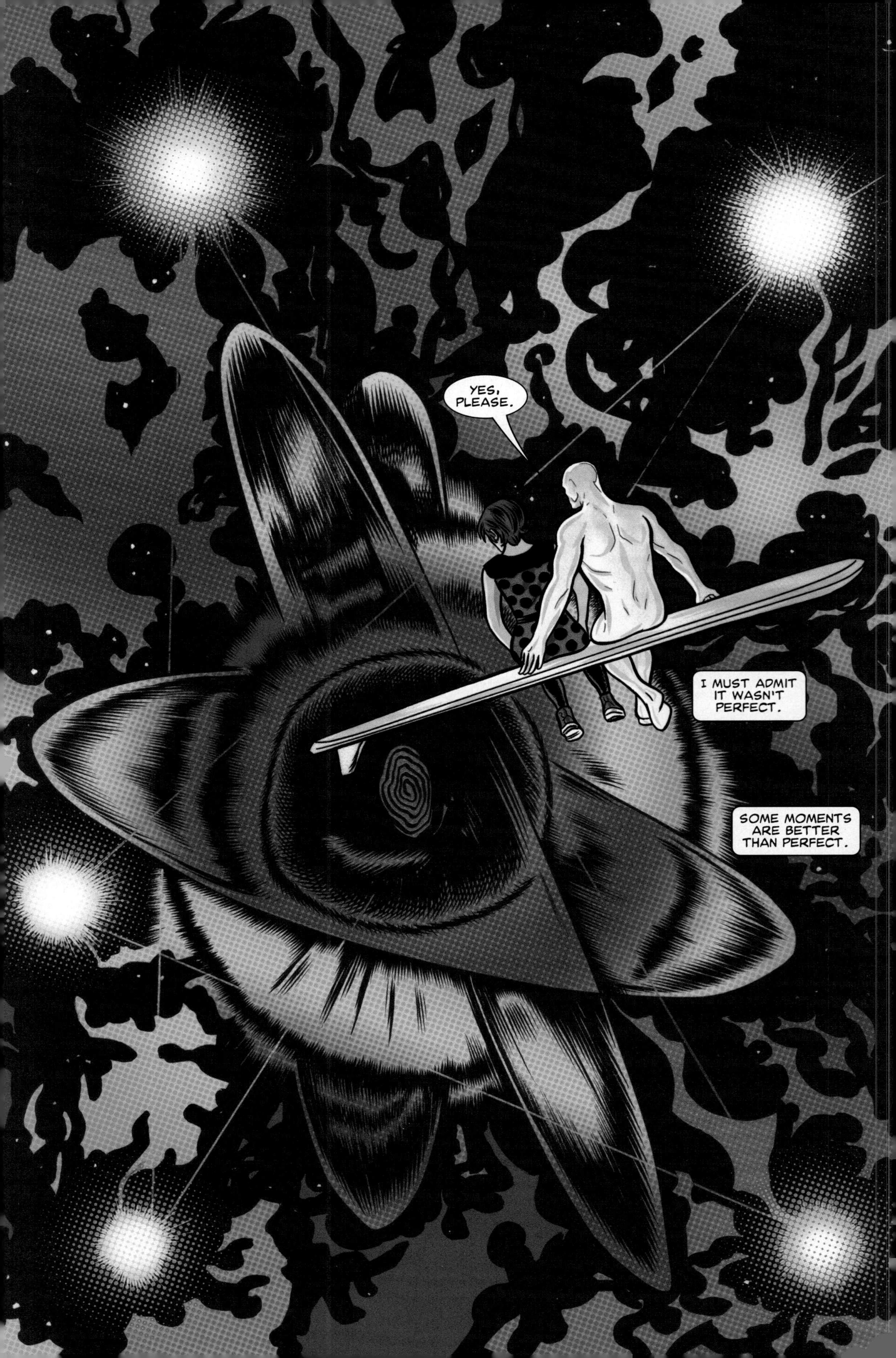
YES, PLEASE.
I MUST ADMIT IT WASN'T PERFECT.
SOME MOMENTS ARE BETTER THAN PERFECT.

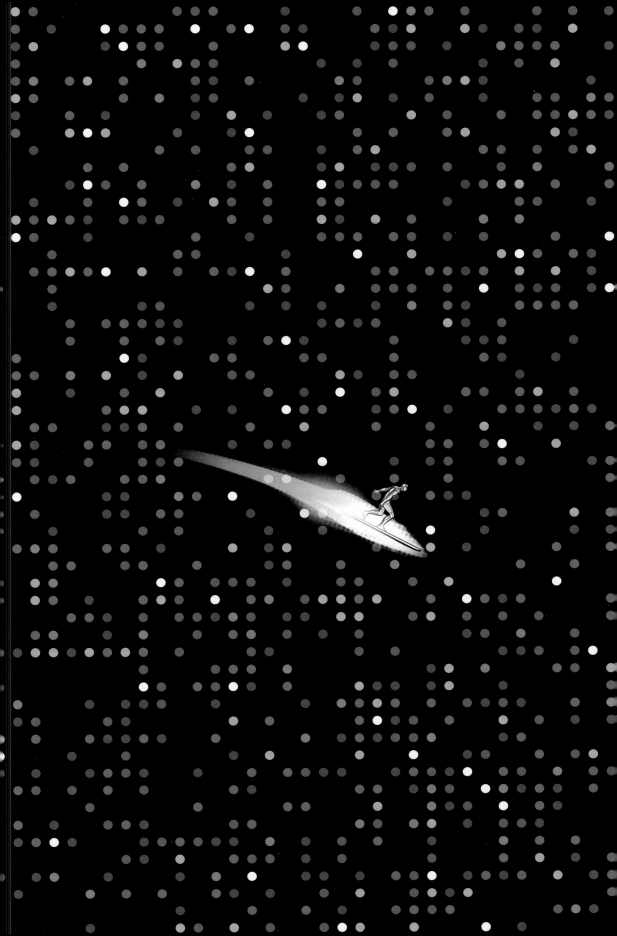

7

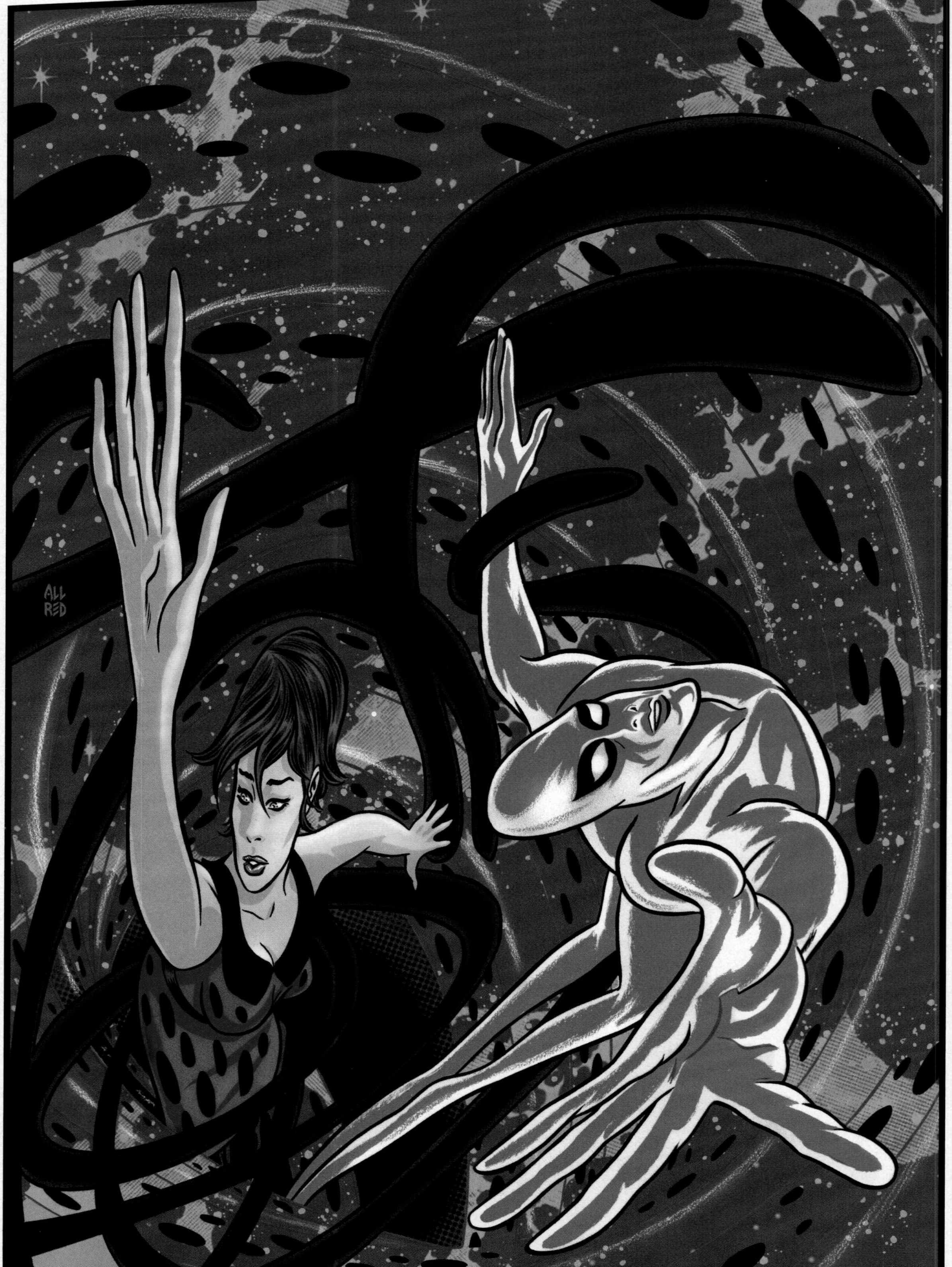
ALL
RED

WE ARE SAILORS ON AN ENDLESS SEA OF NIGHT

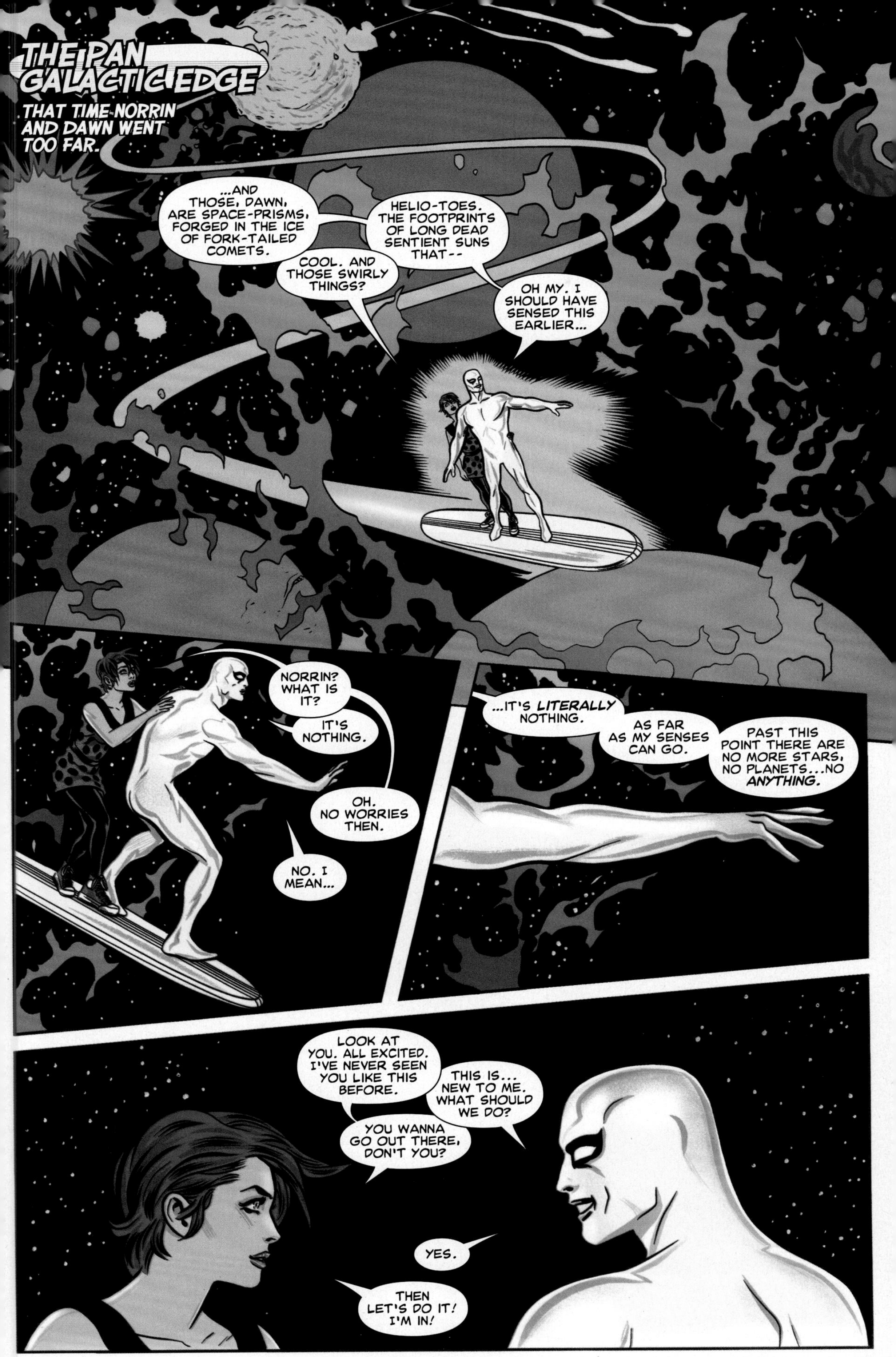
THE PAN GALACTIC EDGE
THAT TIME NORRIN AND DAWN WENT TOO FAR.
...AND THOSE, DAWN, ARE SPACE-PRISMS, FORGED IN THE ICE OF FORK-TAILED COMETS.
COOL. AND THOSE SWIRLY THINGS?
HELIO-TOES. THE FOOTPRINTS OF LONG DEAD SENTIENT SUNS THAT--
OH MY. I SHOULD HAVE SENSED THIS EARLIER...
NORRIN? WHAT IS IT?
IT'S NOTHING.
OH. NO WORRIES THEN.
NO. I MEAN...
...IT'S *LITERALLY* NOTHING.
AS FAR AS MY SENSES CAN GO.
PAST THIS POINT THERE ARE NO MORE STARS, NO PLANETS...NO *ANYTHING.*
LOOK AT YOU. ALL EXCITED. I'VE NEVER SEEN YOU LIKE THIS BEFORE.
THIS IS... NEW TO ME. WHAT SHOULD WE DO?
YOU WANNA GO OUT THERE, DON'T YOU?
YES.
THEN LET'S DO IT! I'M IN!

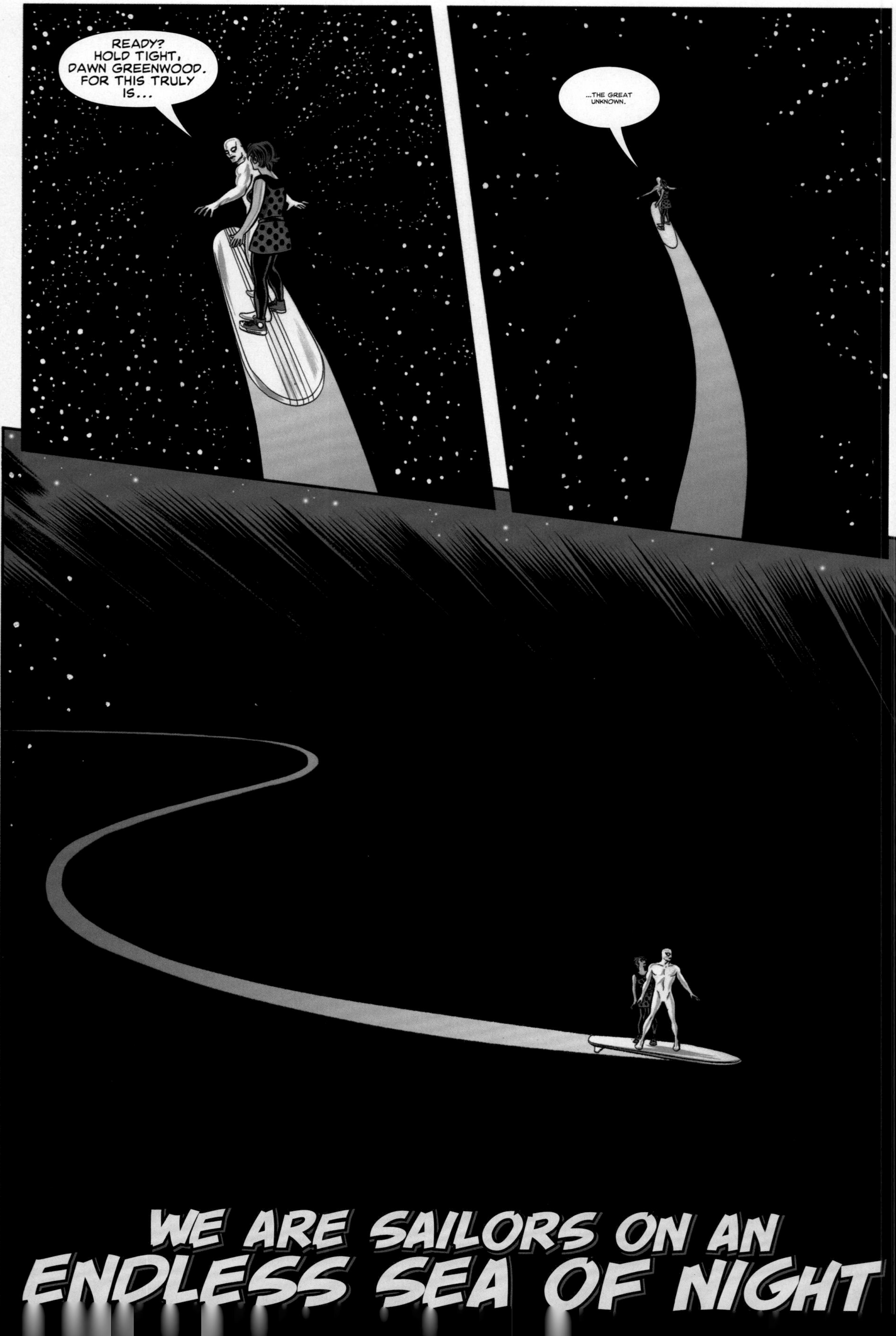
READY? HOLD TIGHT, DAWN GREENWOOD. FOR THIS TRULY IS...
...THE GREAT UNKNOWN.
WE ARE SAILORS ON AN
ENDLESS SEA OF NIGHT

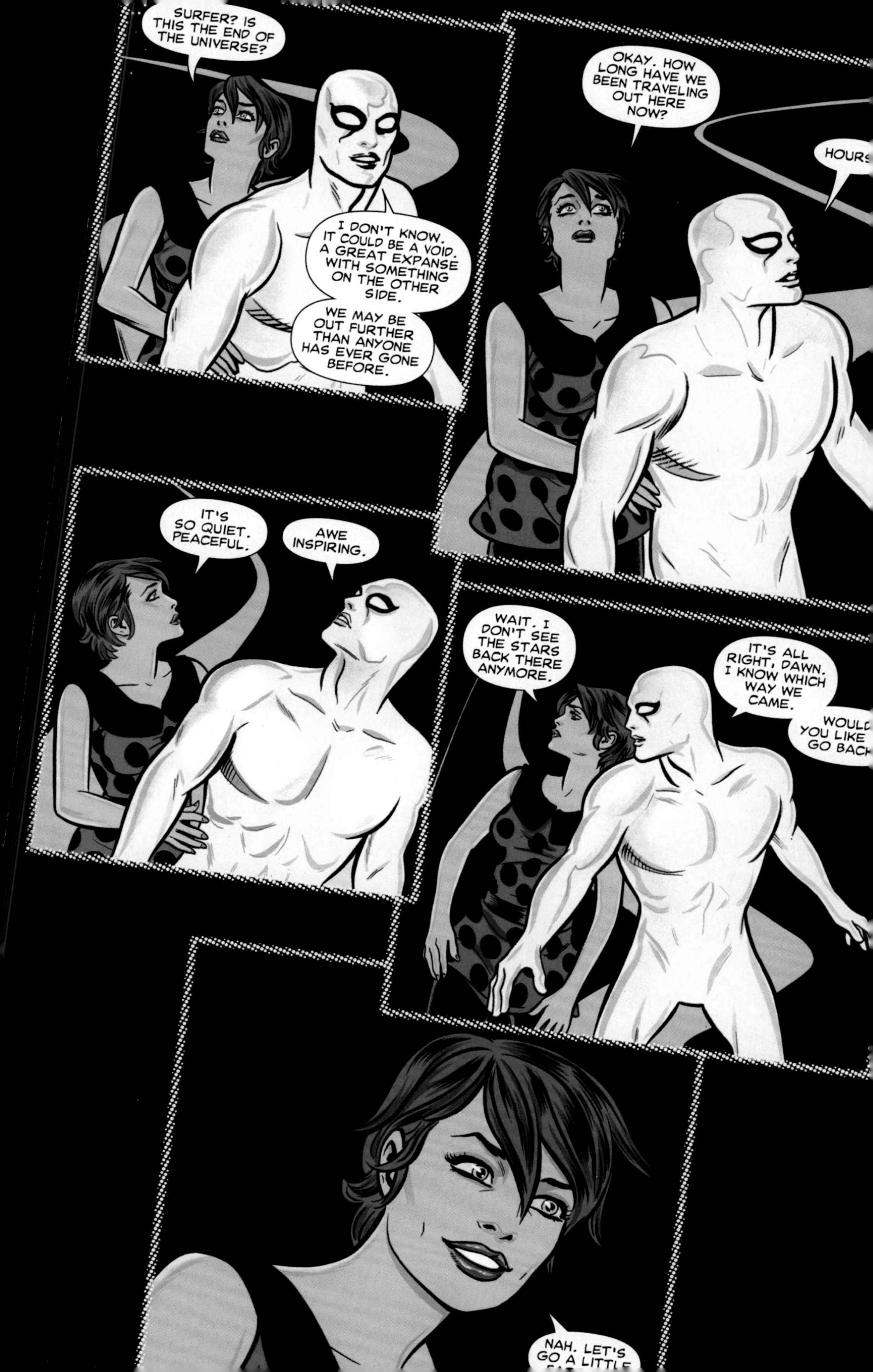
SURFER? IS THIS THE END OF THE UNIVERSE?
I DON'T KNOW. IT COULD BE A VOID. A GREAT EXPANSE WITH SOMETHING ON THE OTHER SIDE.
WE MAY BE OUT FURTHER THAN ANYONE HAS EVER GONE BEFORE.
OKAY. HOW LONG HAVE WE BEEN TRAVELING OUT HERE NOW?
IT'S SO QUIET. PEACEFUL.
AWE INSPIRING.
WAIT. I DON'T SEE THE STARS BACK THERE ANYMORE.
IT'S ALL RIGHT, DAWN. I KNOW WHICH WAY WE CAME.
NAH. LET'S

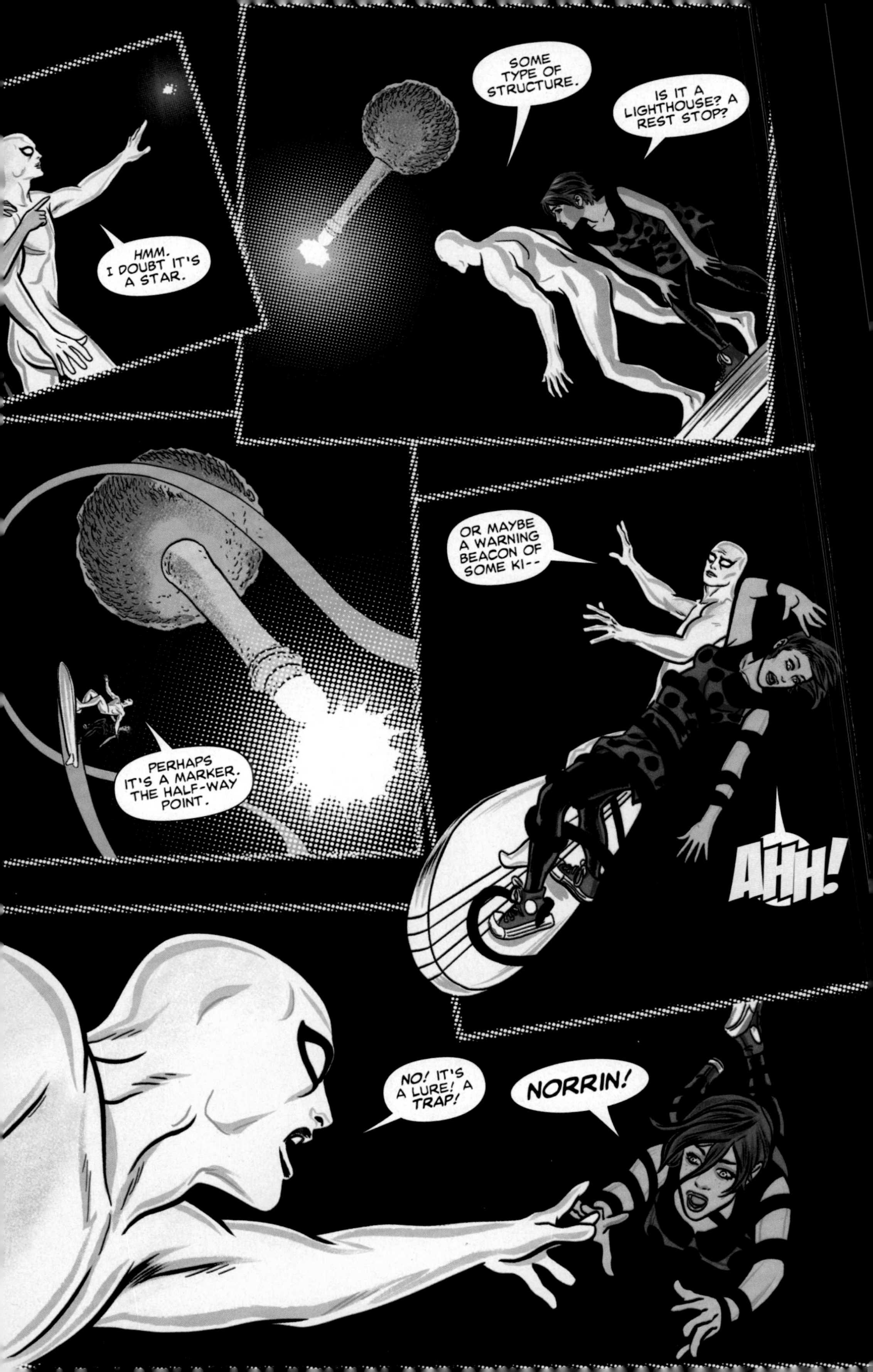
HMM. I DOUBT IT'S A STAR.
SOME TYPE OF STRUCTURE.
IS IT A LIGHTHOUSE? A REST STOP?
PERHAPS IT'S A MARKER. THE HALF-WAY POINT.
OR MAYBE A WARNING BEACON OF SOME KI--
AHH!
NO! IT'S A LURE! A TRAP!
NORRIN!

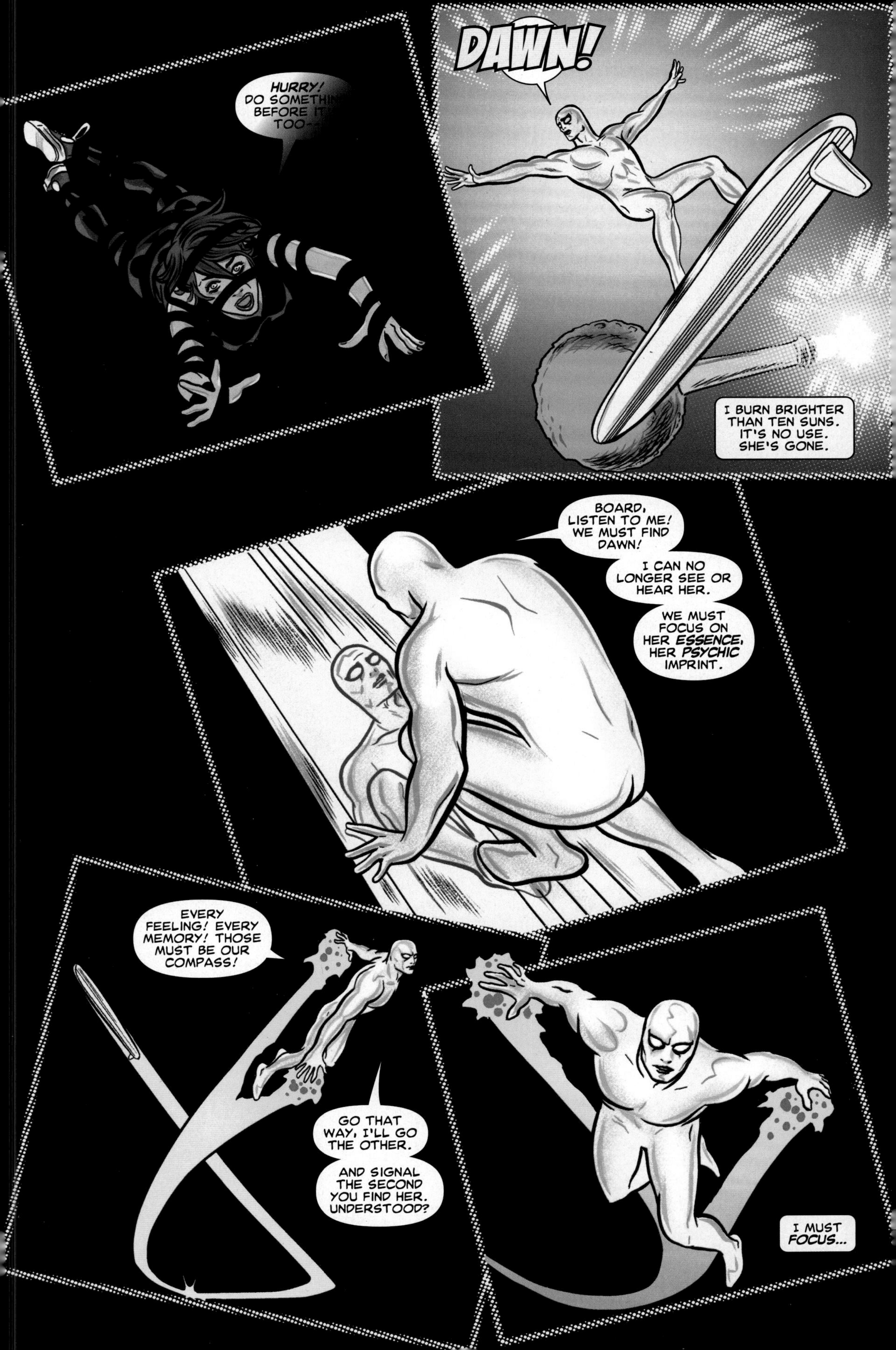

HURRY! DO SOMETHIN BEFORE IT TOO--
DAWN!
I BURN BRIGHTER THAN TEN SUNS. IT'S NO USE. SHE'S GONE.
BOARD, LISTEN TO ME! WE MUST FIND DAWN!
I CAN NO LONGER SEE OR HEAR HER.
WE MUST FOCUS ON HER *ESSENCE*, HER *PSYCHIC* IMPRINT.
EVERY FEELING! EVERY MEMORY! THOSE MUST BE OUR COMPASS!
GO THAT WAY, I'LL GO THE OTHER.
AND SIGNAL THE SECOND YOU FIND HER. UNDERSTOOD?
I MUST *FOCUS*...

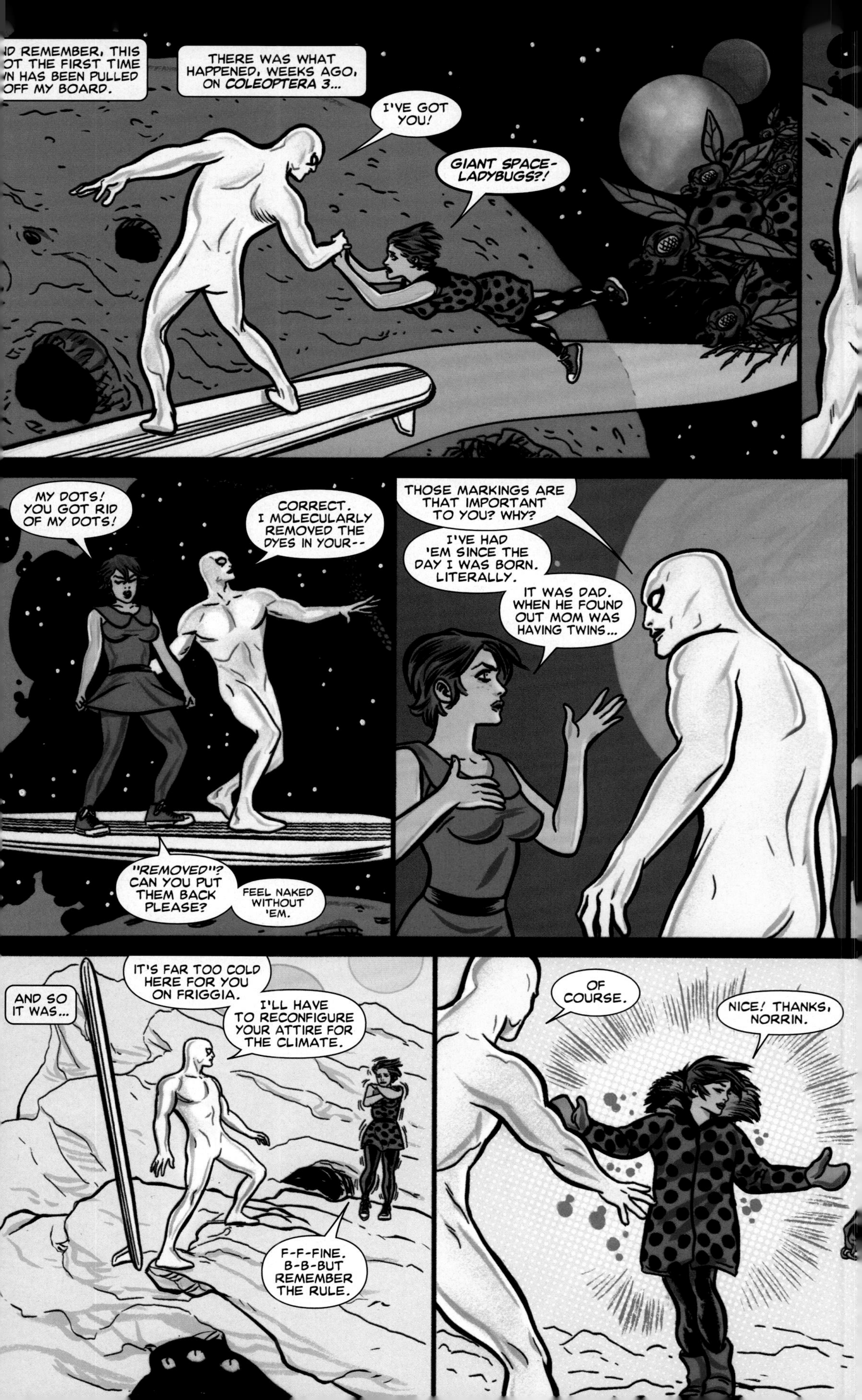
ND REMEMBER, THIS
OT THE FIRST TIME
WN HAS BEEN PULLED
OFF MY BOARD.
THERE WAS WHAT HAPPENED, WEEKS AGO, ON COLEOPTERA 3...
I'VE GOT YOU!
GIANT SPACE-LADYBUGS?!
MY DOTS! YOU GOT RID OF MY DOTS!
CORRECT. I MOLECULARLY REMOVED THE DYES IN YOUR--
"REMOVED"? CAN YOU PUT THEM BACK PLEASE?
FEEL NAKED WITHOUT 'EM.
THOSE MARKINGS ARE THAT IMPORTANT TO YOU? WHY?
I'VE HAD 'EM SINCE THE DAY I WAS BORN. LITERALLY.
IT WAS DAD. WHEN HE FOUND OUT MOM WAS HAVING TWINS...
AND SO IT WAS...
IT'S FAR TOO COLD HERE FOR YOU ON FRIGGIA.
I'LL HAVE TO RECONFIGURE YOUR ATTIRE FOR THE CLIMATE.
F-F-FINE. B-B-BUT REMEMBER THE RULE.
OF COURSE.
NICE! THANKS, NORRIN.

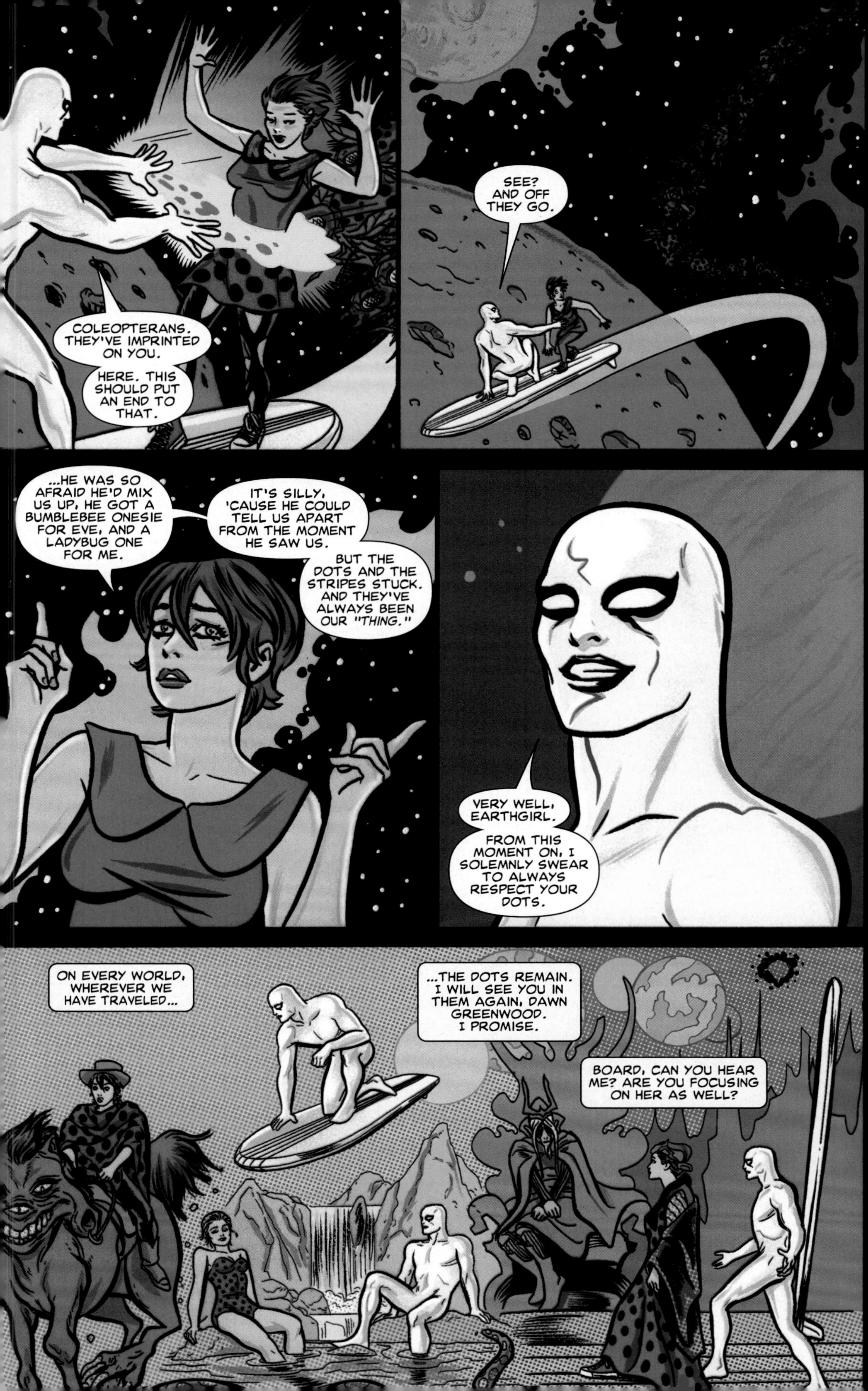

COLEOPTERANS. THEY'VE IMPRINTED ON YOU.
HERE. THIS SHOULD PUT AN END TO THAT.
SEE? AND OFF THEY GO.
...HE WAS SO AFRAID HE'D MIX US UP, HE GOT A BUMBLEBEE ONESIE FOR EVE, AND A LADYBUG ONE FOR ME.
IT'S SILLY, 'CAUSE HE COULD TELL US APART FROM THE MOMENT HE SAW US.
BUT THE DOTS AND THE STRIPES STUCK. AND THEY'VE ALWAYS BEEN OUR "THING."
VERY WELL, EARTHGIRL.
FROM THIS MOMENT ON, I SOLEMNLY SWEAR TO ALWAYS RESPECT YOUR DOTS.
ON EVERY WORLD, WHEREVER WE HAVE TRAVELED...
...THE DOTS REMAIN. I WILL SEE YOU IN THEM AGAIN, DAWN GREENWOOD. I PROMISE.
BOARD, CAN YOU HEAR ME? ARE YOU FOCUSING ON HER AS WELL?

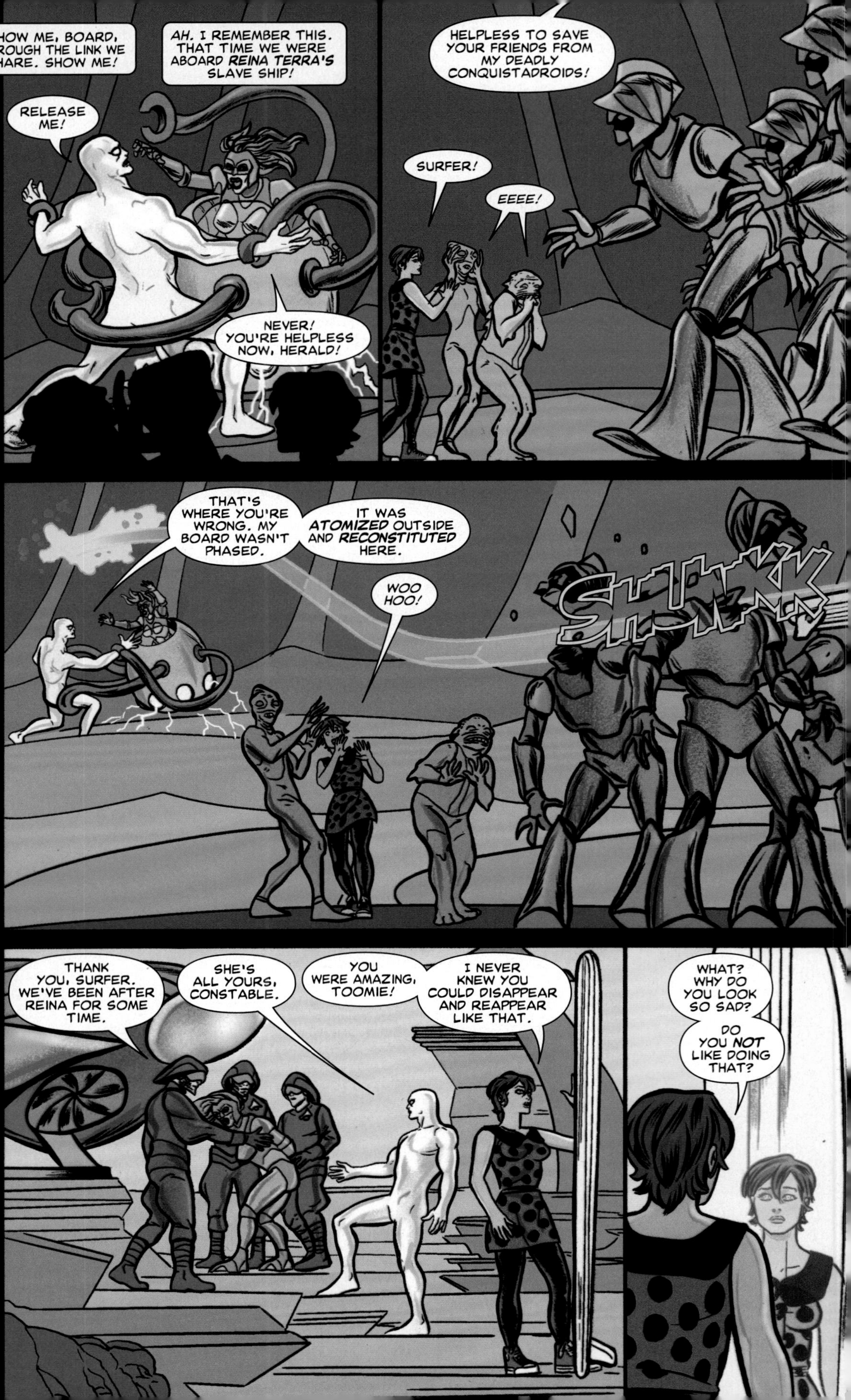
SHOW ME, BOARD, THROUGH THE LINK WE SHARE. SHOW ME!
AH. I REMEMBER THIS. THAT TIME WE WERE ABOARD REINA TERRA'S SLAVE SHIP!
RELEASE ME!
NEVER! YOU'RE HELPLESS NOW, HERALD!
HELPLESS TO SAVE YOUR FRIENDS FROM MY DEADLY CONQUISTADROIDS!
SURFER!
EEEE!
THAT'S WHERE YOU'RE WRONG. MY BOARD WASN'T PHASED.
IT WAS ATOMIZED OUTSIDE AND RECONSTITUTED HERE.
WOO HOO!
SHUNKK
THANK YOU, SURFER. WE'VE BEEN AFTER REINA FOR SOME TIME.
SHE'S ALL YOURS, CONSTABLE.
YOU WERE AMAZING, TOOMIE!
I NEVER KNEW YOU COULD DISAPPEAR AND REAPPEAR LIKE THAT.
WHAT? WHY DO YOU LOOK SO SAD?
DO YOU NOT LIKE DOING THAT?

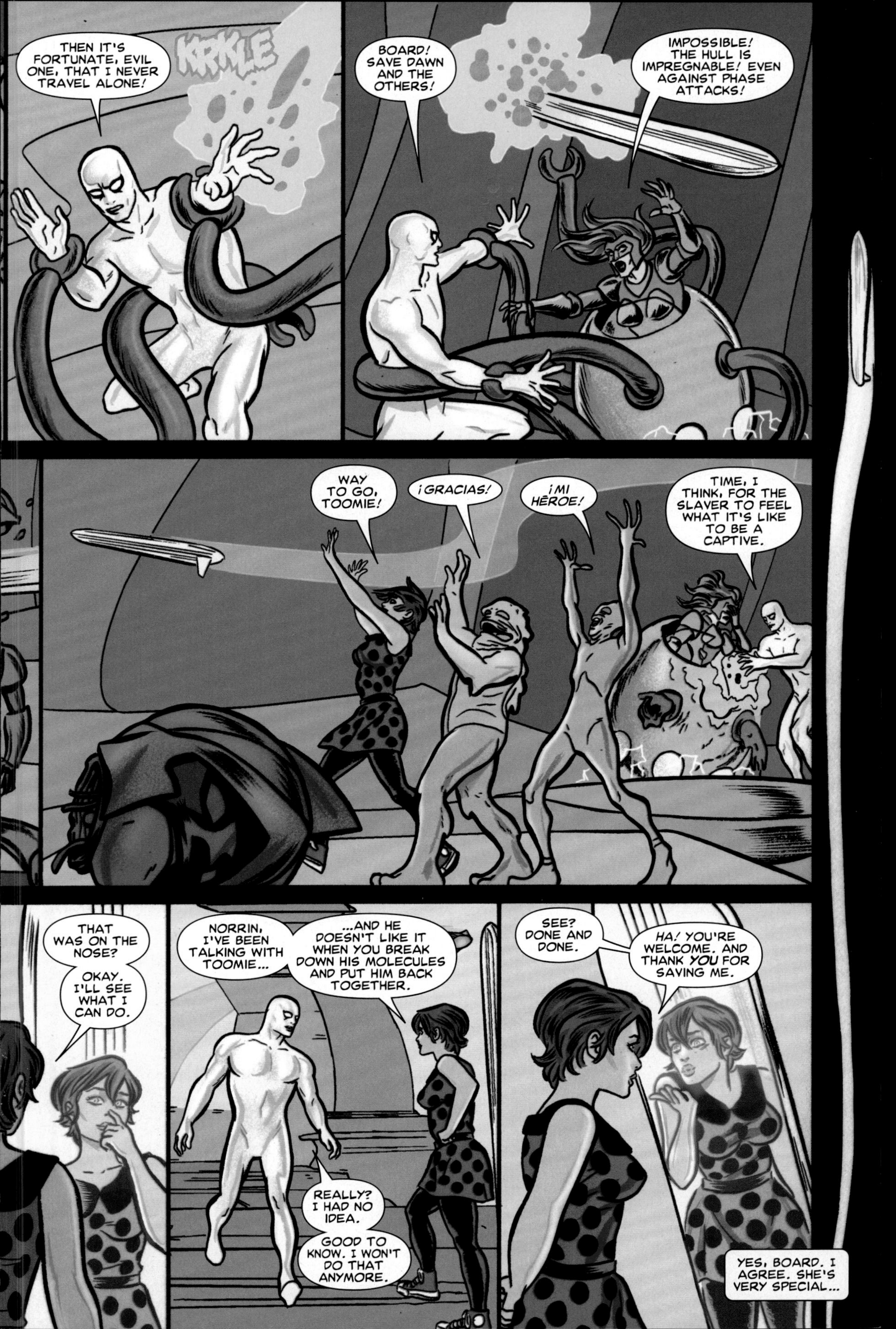
THEN IT'S FORTUNATE, EVIL ONE, THAT I NEVER TRAVEL ALONE!
KRKLE
BOARD! SAVE DAWN AND THE OTHERS!
IMPOSSIBLE! THE HULL IS IMPREGNABLE! EVEN AGAINST PHASE ATTACKS!
WAY TO GO, TOOMIE!
¡GRACIAS!
¡MI HÉROE!
TIME, I THINK, FOR THE SLAVER TO FEEL WHAT IT'S LIKE TO BE A CAPTIVE.
THAT WAS ON THE NOSE?
OKAY. I'LL SEE WHAT I CAN DO.
NORRIN, I'VE BEEN TALKING WITH TOOMIE...
...AND HE DOESN'T LIKE IT WHEN YOU BREAK DOWN HIS MOLECULES AND PUT HIM BACK TOGETHER.
REALLY? I HAD NO IDEA.
GOOD TO KNOW. I WON'T DO THAT ANYMORE.
SEE? DONE AND DONE.
HA! YOU'RE WELCOME. AND THANK YOU FOR SAVING ME.
YES, BOARD. I AGREE. SHE'S VERY SPECIAL...

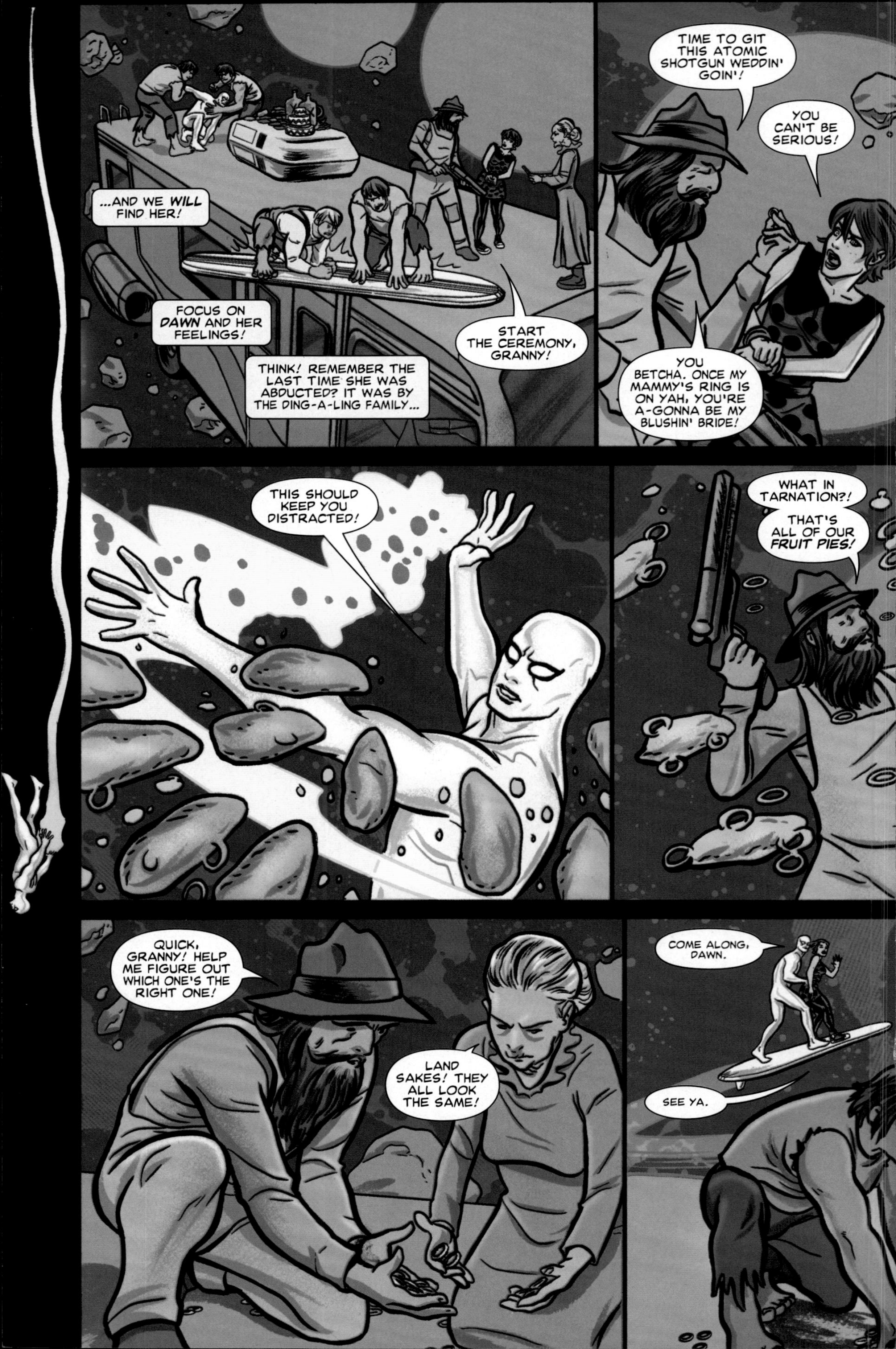

...AND WE WILL FIND HER!
FOCUS ON DAWN AND HER FEELINGS!
THINK! REMEMBER THE LAST TIME SHE WAS ABDUCTED? IT WAS BY THE DING-A-LING FAMILY...
START THE CEREMONY, GRANNY!
TIME TO GIT THIS ATOMIC SHOTGUN WEDDIN' GOIN'!
YOU CAN'T BE SERIOUS!
YOU BETCHA. ONCE MY MAMMY'S RING IS ON YAH, YOU'RE A-GONNA BE MY BLUSHIN' BRIDE!
THIS SHOULD KEEP YOU DISTRACTED!
WHAT IN TARNATION?!
THAT'S ALL OF OUR FRUIT PIES!
QUICK, GRANNY! HELP ME FIGURE OUT WHICH ONE'S THE RIGHT ONE!
LAND SAKES! THEY ALL LOOK THE SAME!
COME ALONG, DAWN.
SEE YA.

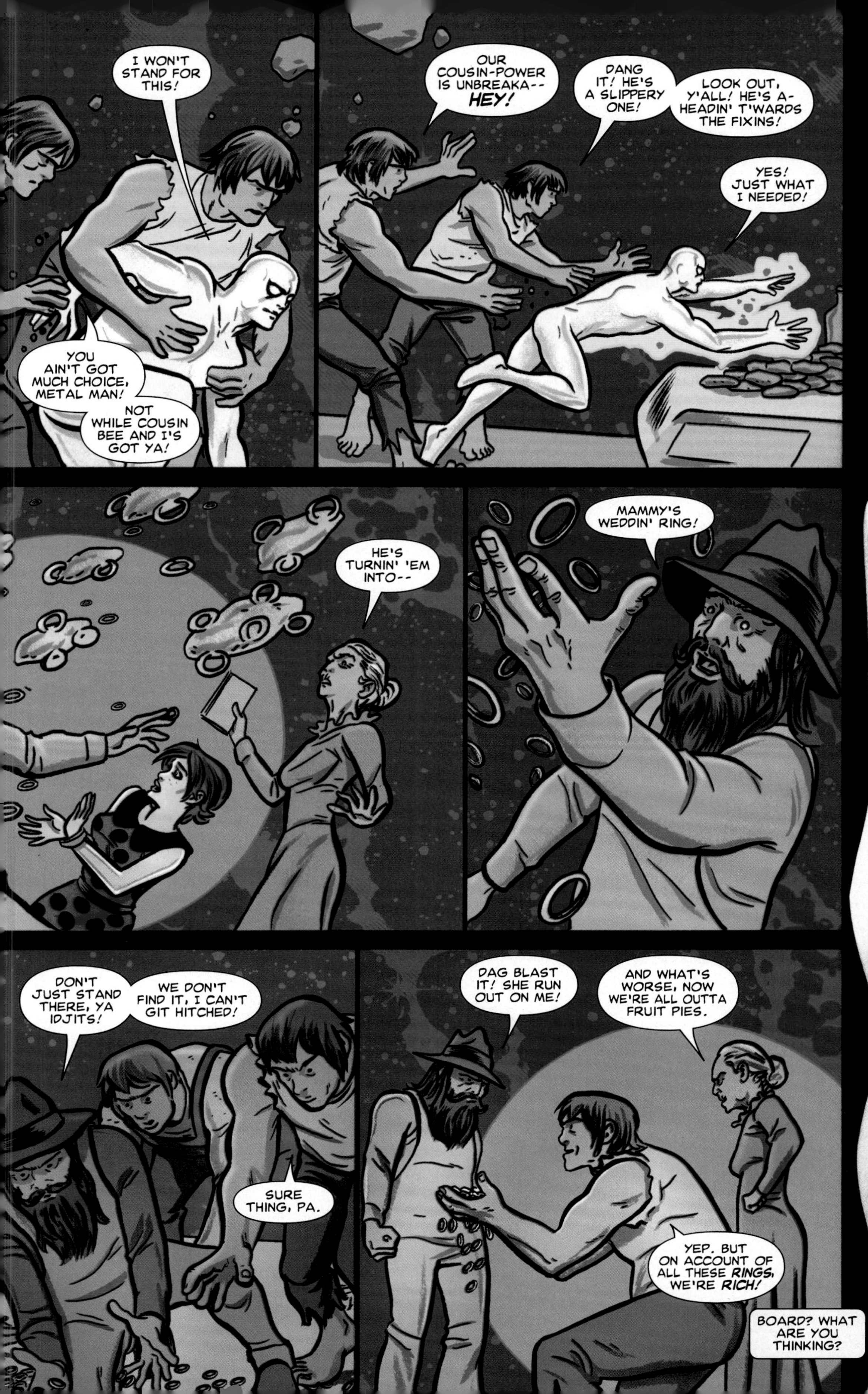
I WON'T STAND FOR THIS!
YOU AIN'T GOT MUCH CHOICE, METAL MAN!
NOT WHILE COUSIN BEE AND I'S GOT YA!
OUR COUSIN-POWER IS UNBREAKA-- HEY!
DANG IT! HE'S A SLIPPERY ONE!
LOOK OUT, Y'ALL! HE'S A-HEADIN' T'WARDS THE FIXINS!
YES! JUST WHAT I NEEDED!
HE'S TURNIN' 'EM INTO--
MAMMY'S WEDDIN' RING!
DON'T JUST STAND THERE, YA IDJITS!
WE DON'T FIND IT, I CAN'T GIT HITCHED!
SURE THING, PA.
DAG BLAST IT! SHE RUN OUT ON ME!
AND WHAT'S WORSE, NOW WE'RE ALL OUTTA FRUIT PIES.
YEP. BUT ON ACCOUNT OF ALL THESE RINGS, WE'RE RICH!
BOARD? WHAT ARE YOU THINKING?

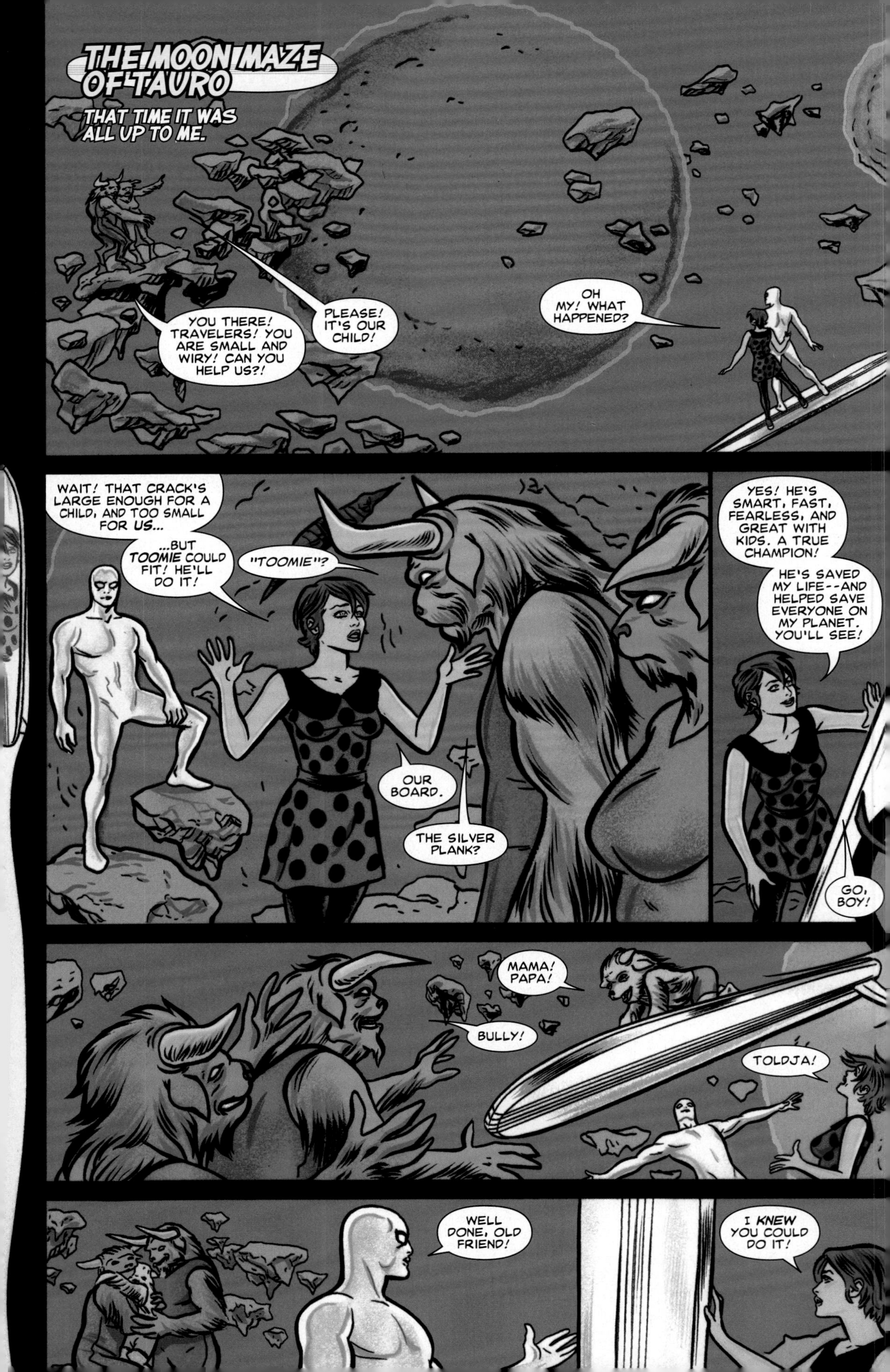
THE MOON MAZE OF TAURO
THAT TIME IT WAS ALL UP TO ME.
YOU THERE! TRAVELERS! YOU ARE SMALL AND WIRY! CAN YOU HELP US?!
PLEASE! IT'S OUR CHILD!
OH MY! WHAT HAPPENED?
WAIT! THAT CRACK'S LARGE ENOUGH FOR A CHILD, AND TOO SMALL FOR US...
...BUT TOOMIE COULD FIT! HE'LL DO IT!
"TOOMIE"?
OUR BOARD.
THE SILVER PLANK?
YES! HE'S SMART, FAST, FEARLESS, AND GREAT WITH KIDS. A TRUE CHAMPION!
HE'S SAVED MY LIFE--AND HELPED SAVE EVERYONE ON MY PLANET. YOU'LL SEE!
GO, BOY!
MAMA! PAPA!
BULLY!
TOLDJA!
WELL DONE, OLD FRIEND!
I KNEW YOU COULD DO IT!

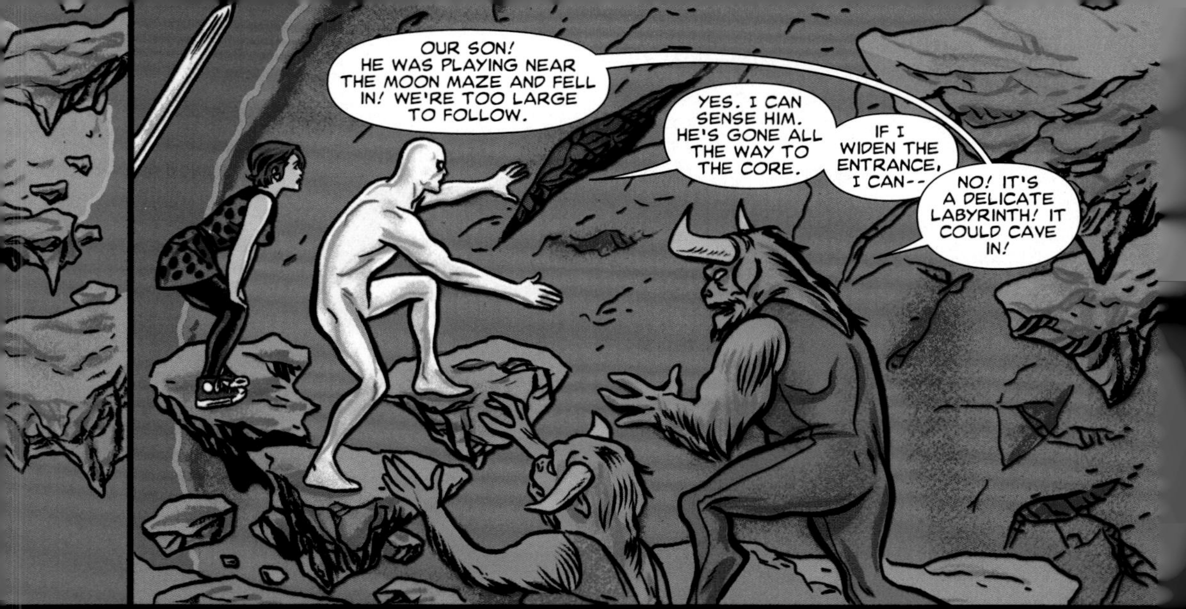
OUR SON! HE WAS PLAYING NEAR THE MOON MAZE AND FELL IN! WE'RE TOO LARGE TO FOLLOW.
YES. I CAN SENSE HIM. HE'S GONE ALL THE WAY TO THE CORE.
IF I WIDEN THE ENTRANCE, I CAN--
NO! IT'S A DELICATE LABYRINTH! IT COULD CAVE IN!

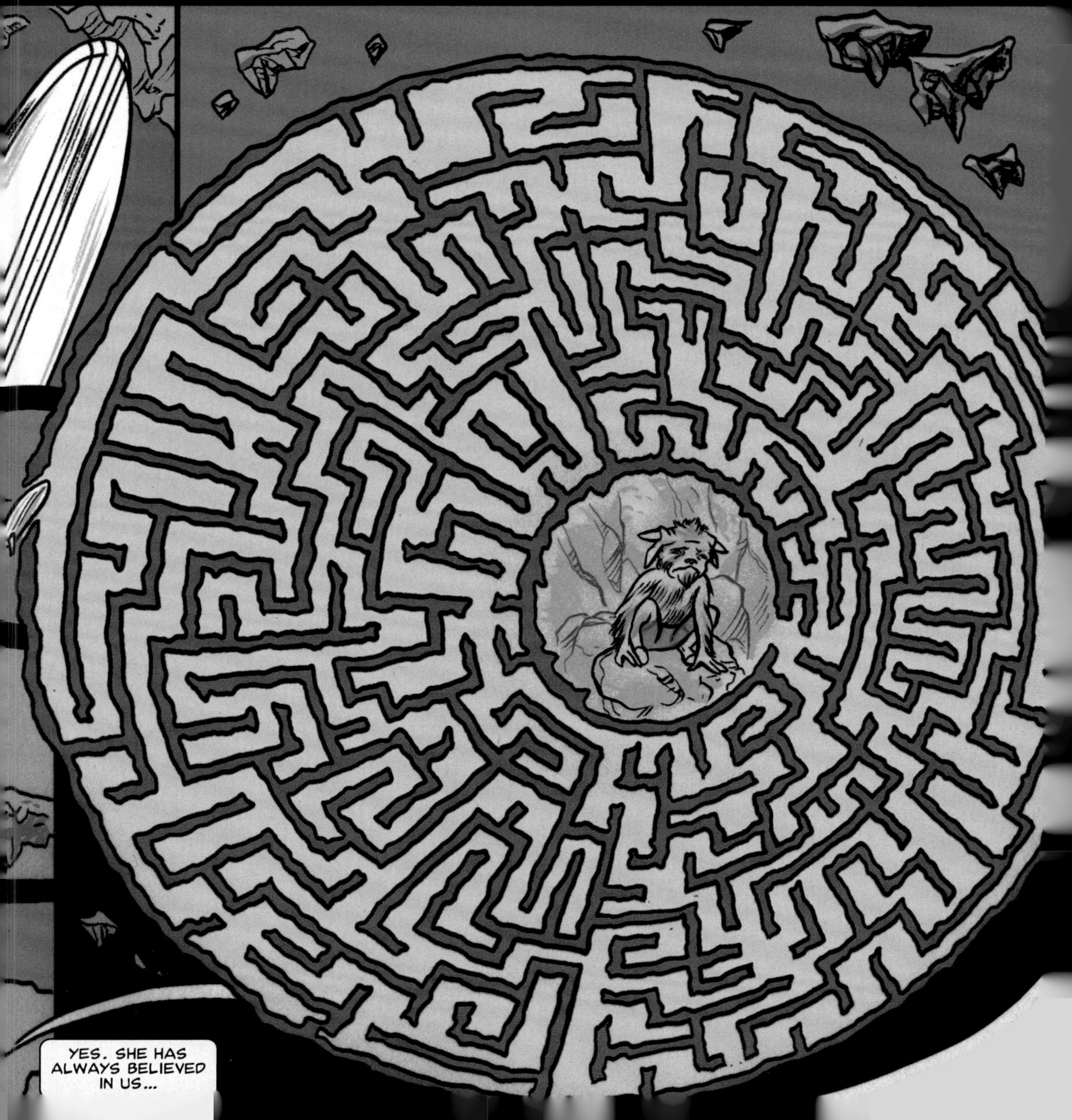
YES. SHE HAS ALWAYS BELIEVED IN US...

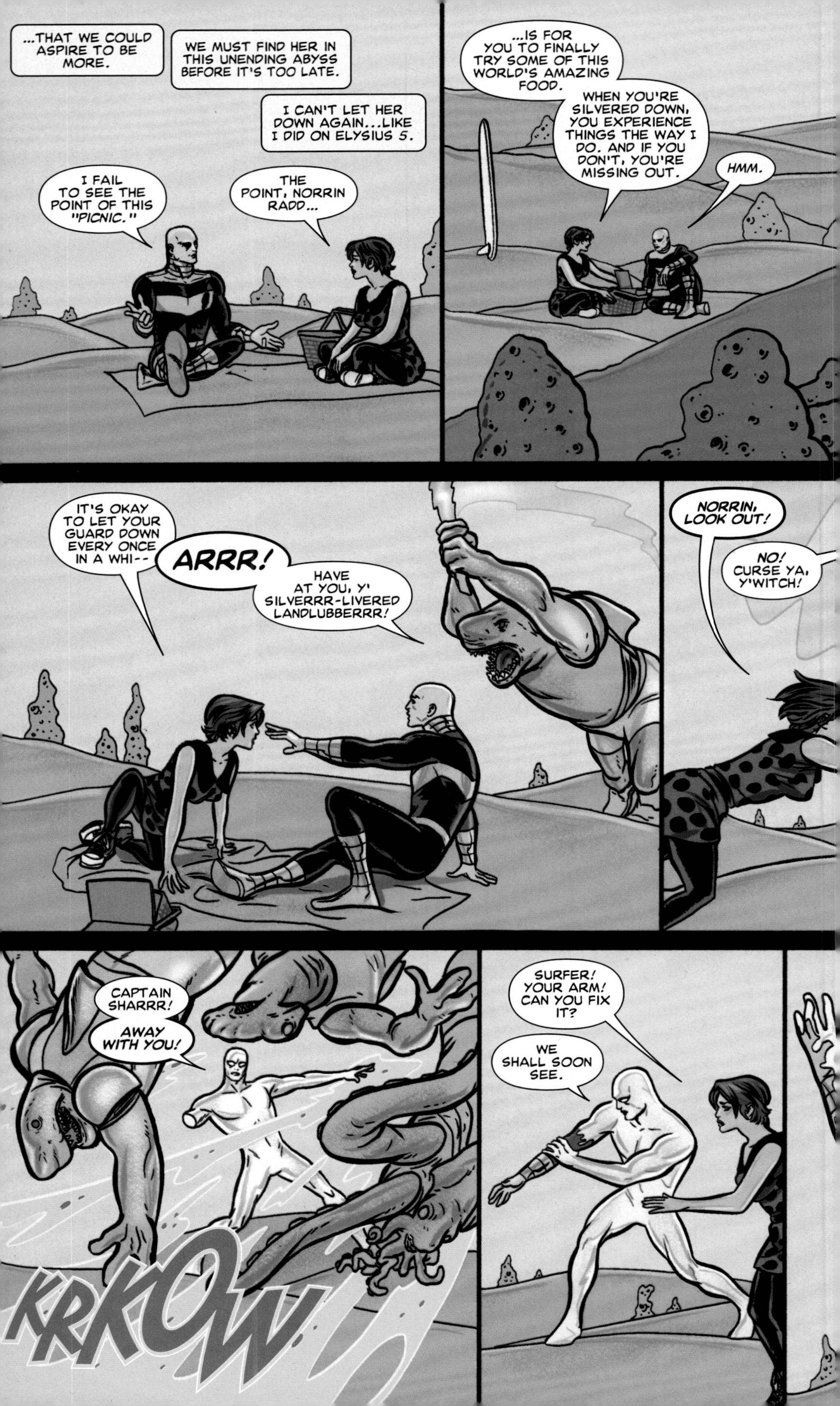
...THAT WE COULD ASPIRE TO BE MORE.
WE MUST FIND HER IN THIS UNENDING ABYSS BEFORE IT'S TOO LATE.
I CAN'T LET HER DOWN AGAIN...LIKE I DID ON ELYSIUS 5.
I FAIL TO SEE THE POINT OF THIS "PICNIC."
THE POINT, NORRIN RADD...
...IS FOR YOU TO FINALLY TRY SOME OF THIS WORLD'S AMAZING FOOD.
WHEN YOU'RE SILVERED DOWN, YOU EXPERIENCE THINGS THE WAY I DO. AND IF YOU DON'T, YOU'RE MISSING OUT.
HMM.
IT'S OKAY TO LET YOUR GUARD DOWN EVERY ONCE IN A WHI--
ARRR!
HAVE AT YOU, Y' SILVERRR-LIVERED LANDLUBBERRR!
NORRIN, LOOK OUT!
NO! CURSE YA, Y'WITCH!
CAPTAIN SHARRR!
AWAY WITH YOU!
KRKOW
SURFER! YOUR ARM! CAN YOU FIX IT?
WE SHALL SOON SEE.

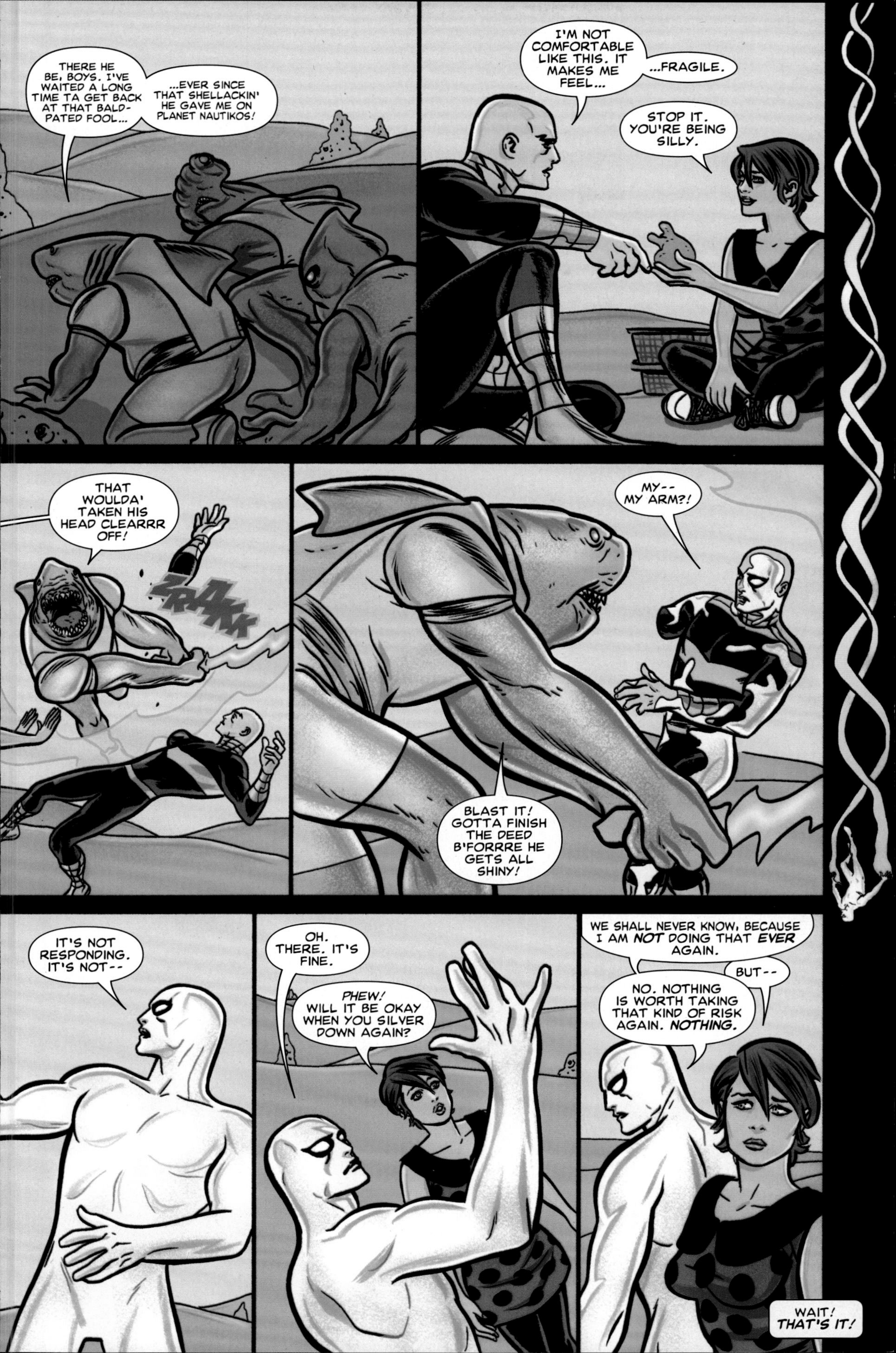
THERE HE BE, BOYS. I'VE WAITED A LONG TIME TA GET BACK AT THAT BALD-PATED FOOL...
...EVER SINCE THAT SHELLACKIN' HE GAVE ME ON PLANET NAUTIKOS!
I'M NOT COMFORTABLE LIKE THIS. IT MAKES ME FEEL...
...FRAGILE.
STOP IT. YOU'RE BEING SILLY.
THAT WOULDA' TAKEN HIS HEAD CLEARRR OFF!
ZRAAKK
MY-- MY ARM?!
BLAST IT! GOTTA FINISH THE DEED B'FORRRE HE GETS ALL SHINY!
IT'S NOT RESPONDING. IT'S NOT--
OH. THERE. IT'S FINE.
PHEW! WILL IT BE OKAY WHEN YOU SILVER DOWN AGAIN?
WE SHALL NEVER KNOW, BECAUSE I AM NOT DOING THAT EVER AGAIN.
BUT--
NO. NOTHING IS WORTH TAKING THAT KIND OF RISK AGAIN. NOTHING.
WAIT! THAT'S IT!

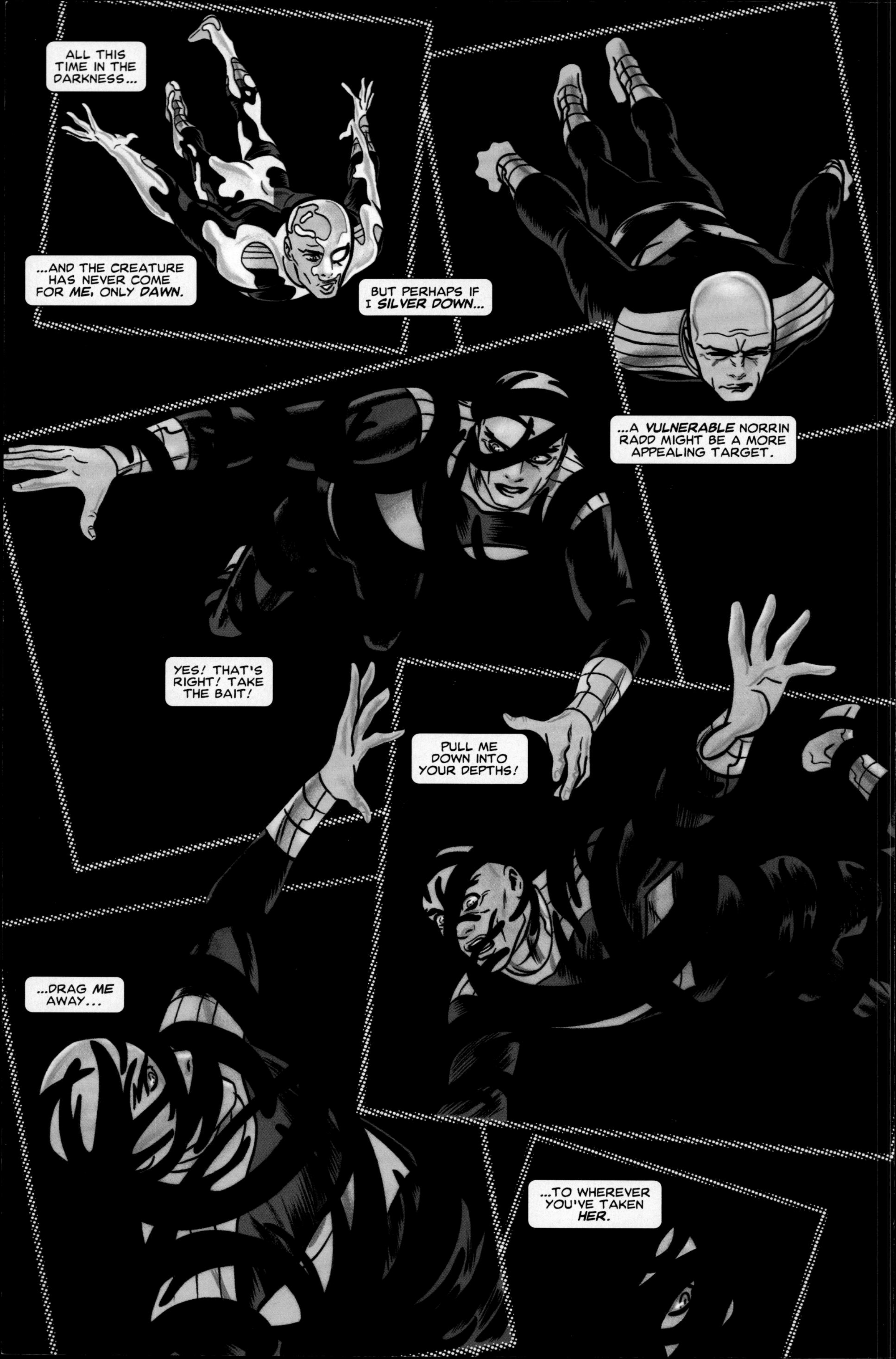
ALL THIS TIME IN THE DARKNESS...
...AND THE CREATURE HAS NEVER COME FOR ME, ONLY DAWN.
BUT PERHAPS IF I SILVER DOWN...
...A VULNERABLE NORRIN RADD MIGHT BE A MORE APPEALING TARGET.
YES! THAT'S RIGHT! TAKE THE BAIT!
PULL ME DOWN INTO YOUR DEPTHS!
...DRAG ME AWAY...
...TO WHEREVER YOU'VE TAKEN HER.

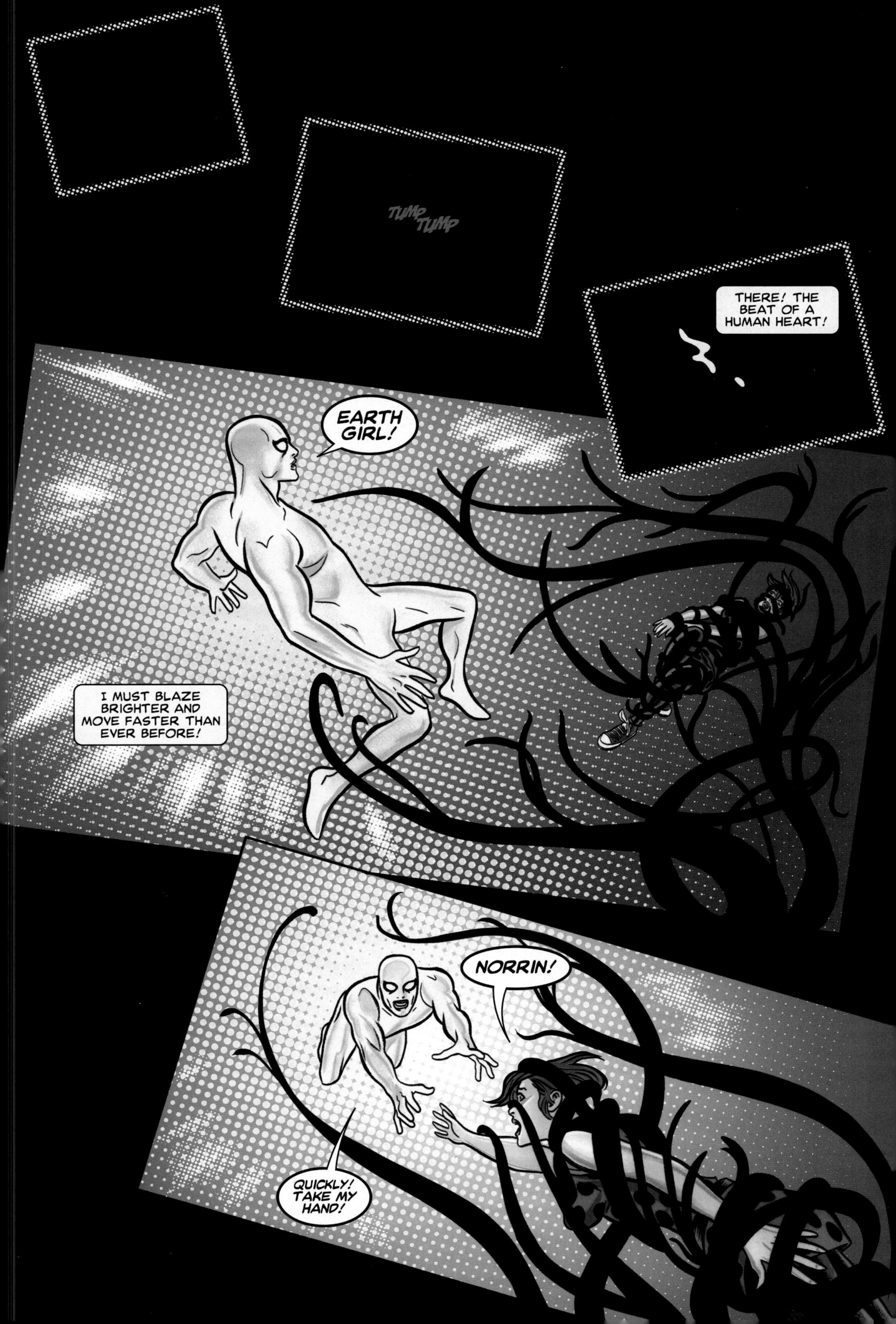
TUMP TUMP
THERE! THE BEAT OF A HUMAN HEART!
EARTH GIRL!
I MUST BLAZE BRIGHTER AND MOVE FASTER THAN EVER BEFORE!
NORRIN!
QUICKLY! TAKE MY HAND!

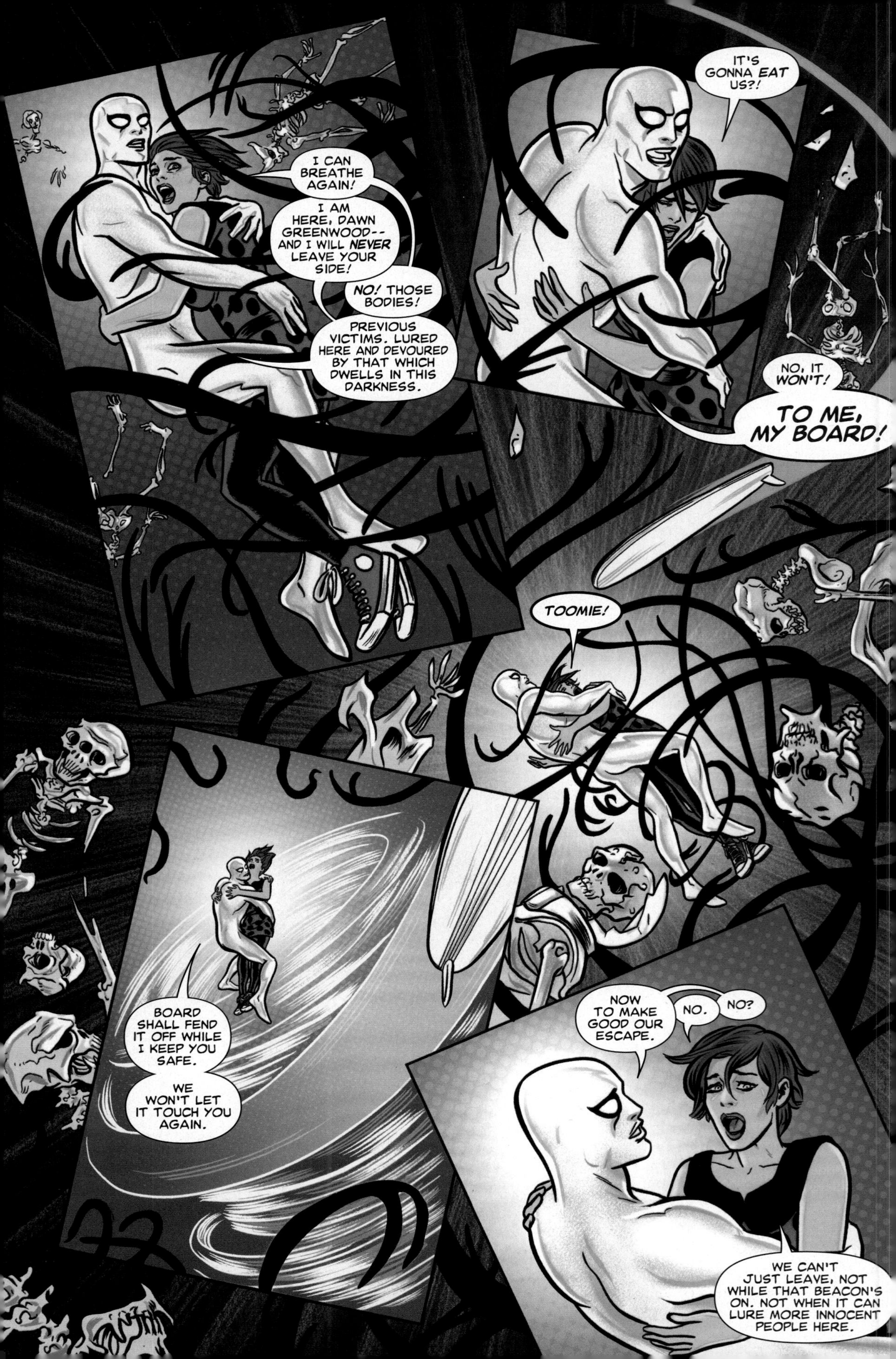
I CAN BREATHE AGAIN!
I AM HERE, DAWN GREENWOOD-- AND I WILL NEVER LEAVE YOUR SIDE!
NO! THOSE BODIES!
PREVIOUS VICTIMS. LURED HERE AND DEVOURED BY THAT WHICH DWELLS IN THIS DARKNESS.
IT'S GONNA EAT US?!
NO, IT WON'T!
TO ME, MY BOARD!
TOOMIE!
BOARD SHALL FEND IT OFF WHILE I KEEP YOU SAFE.
WE WON'T LET IT TOUCH YOU AGAIN.
NOW TO MAKE GOOD OUR ESCAPE.
NO.
NO?
WE CAN'T JUST LEAVE, NOT WHILE THAT BEACON'S ON. NOT WHEN IT CAN LURE MORE INNOCENT PEOPLE HERE.

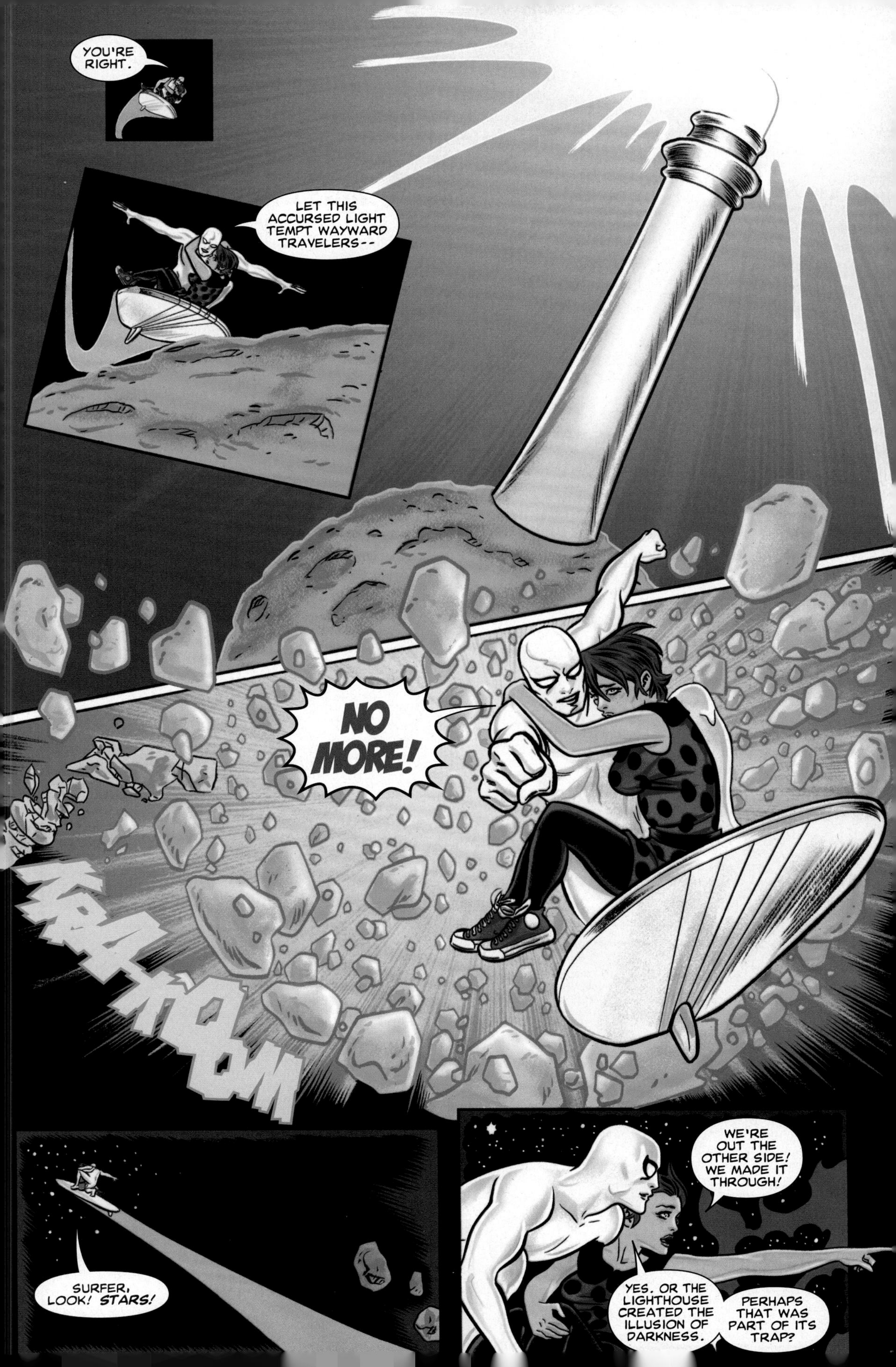

YOU'RE RIGHT.
LET THIS ACCURSED LIGHT TEMPT WAYWARD TRAVELERS--
NO MORE!
SURFER, LOOK! STARS!
WE'RE OUT THE OTHER SIDE! WE MADE IT THROUGH!
YES. OR THE LIGHTHOUSE CREATED THE ILLUSION OF DARKNESS.
PERHAPS THAT WAS PART OF ITS TRAP?

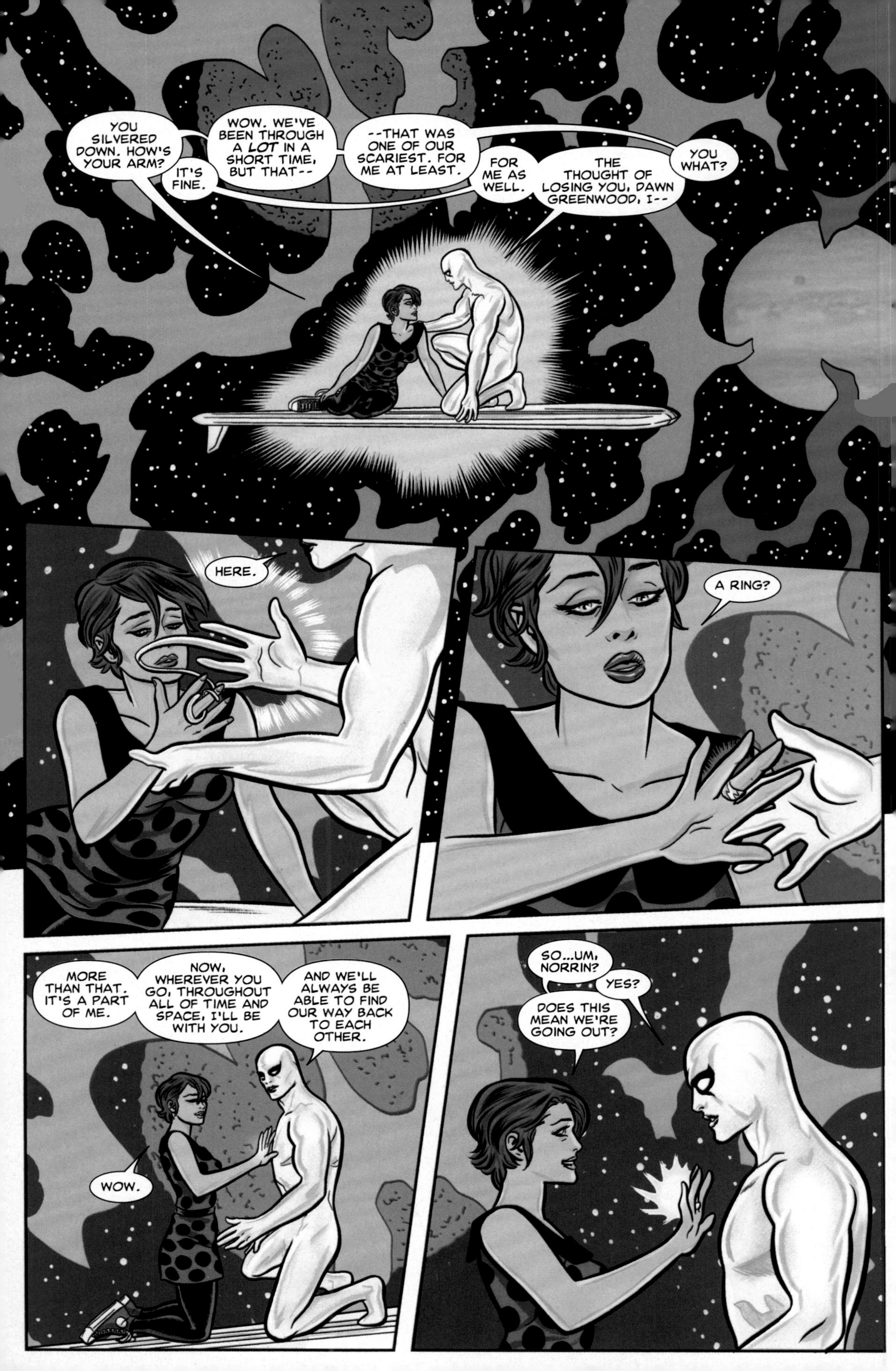
YOU SILVERED DOWN. HOW'S YOUR ARM?
IT'S FINE.
WOW. WE'VE BEEN THROUGH A *LOT* IN A SHORT TIME, BUT THAT--
--THAT WAS ONE OF OUR SCARIEST. FOR ME AT LEAST.
FOR ME AS WELL.
THE THOUGHT OF LOSING YOU, DAWN GREENWOOD, I--
YOU WHAT?
HERE.
A RING?
MORE THAN THAT. IT'S A PART OF ME.
NOW, WHEREVER YOU GO, THROUGHOUT ALL OF TIME AND SPACE, I'LL BE WITH YOU.
AND WE'LL ALWAYS BE ABLE TO FIND OUR WAY BACK TO EACH OTHER.
WOW.
SO...UM, NORRIN?
YES?
DOES THIS MEAN WE'RE GOING OUT?

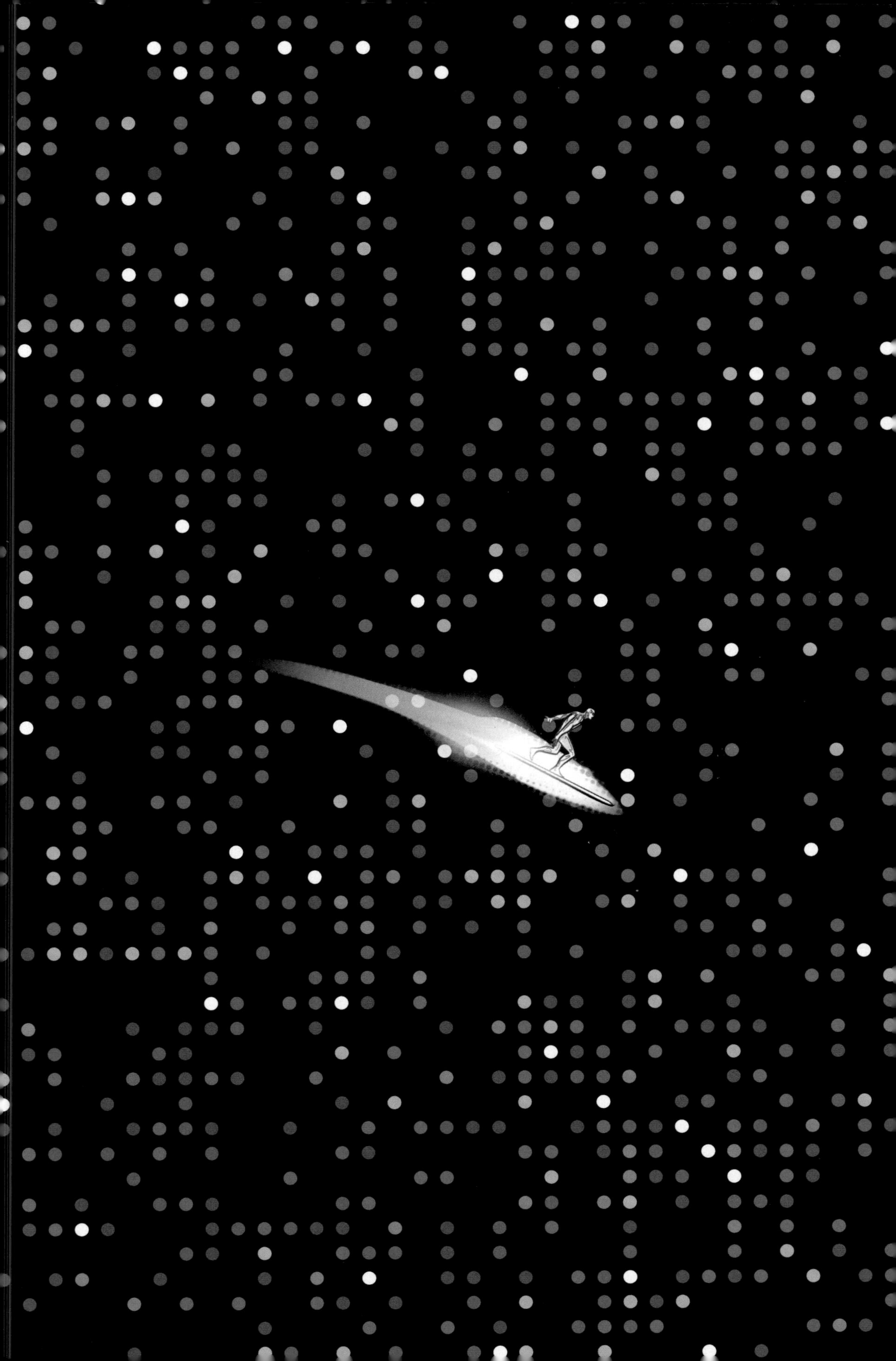

8

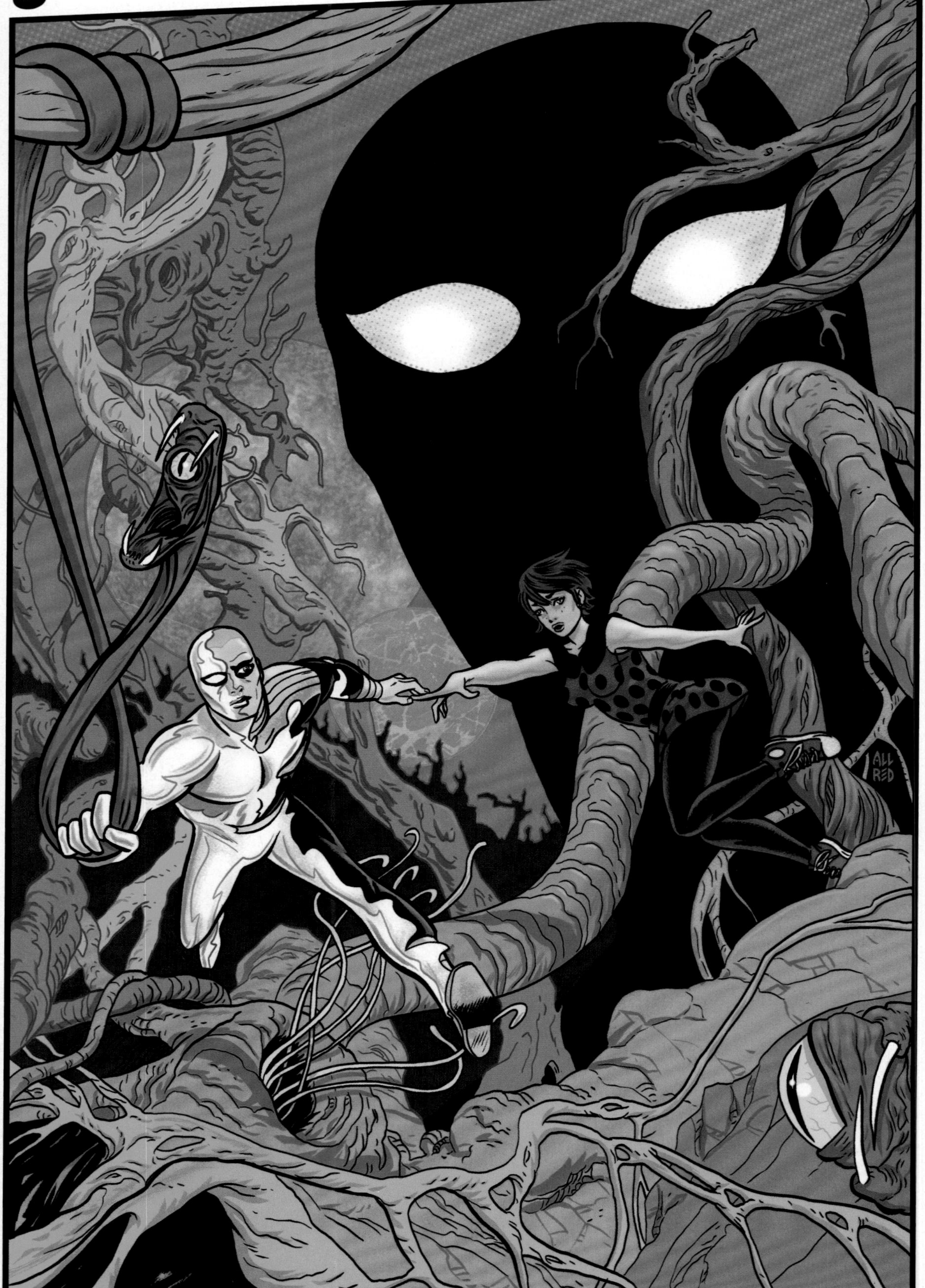
ALL
RED

WORLDS APART

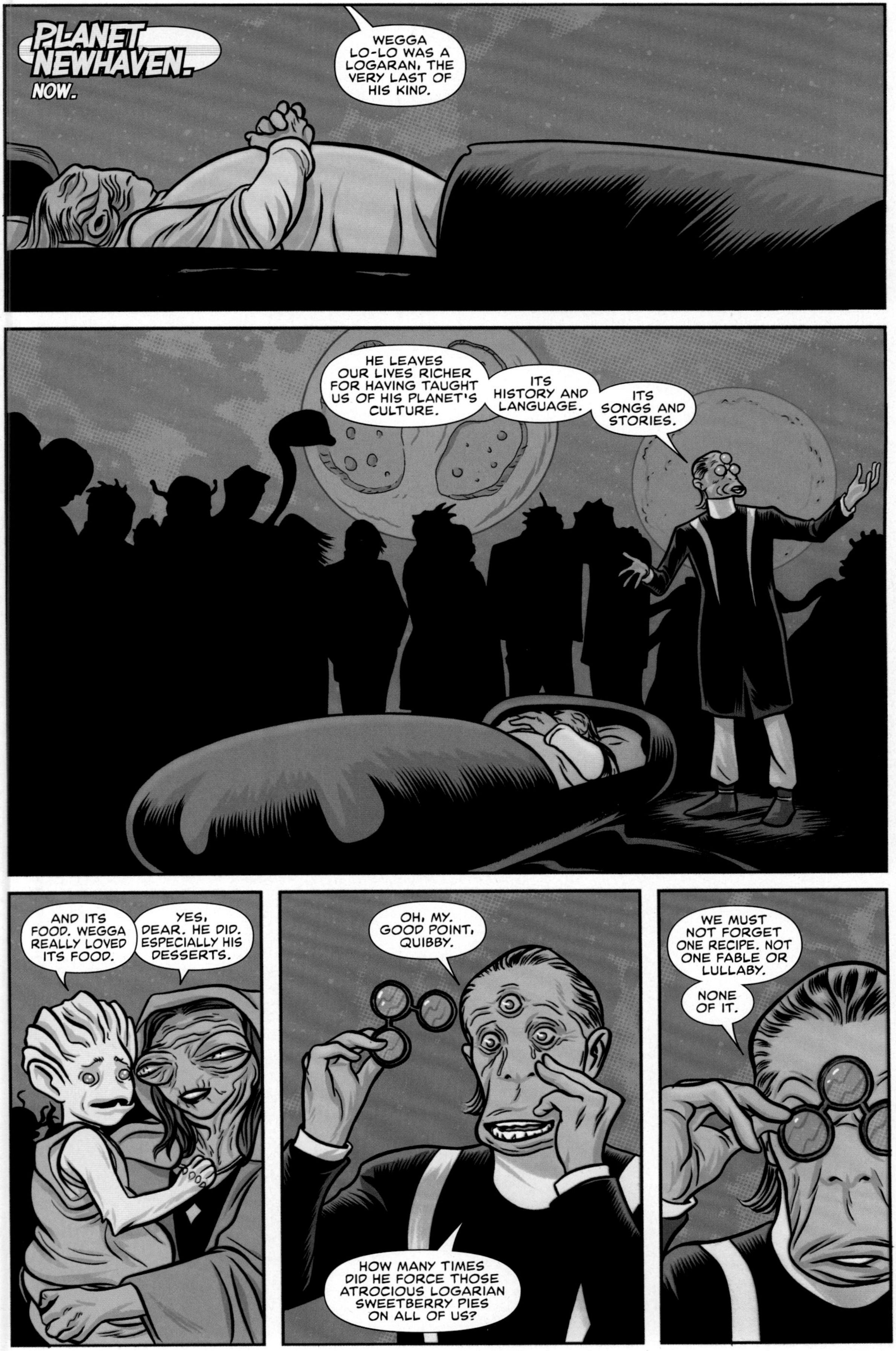
PLANET NEWHAVEN.
NOW.
WEGGA LO-LO WAS A LOGARAN, THE VERY LAST OF HIS KIND.
HE LEAVES OUR LIVES RICHER FOR HAVING TAUGHT US OF HIS PLANET'S CULTURE.
ITS HISTORY AND LANGUAGE.
ITS SONGS AND STORIES.
AND ITS FOOD. WEGGA REALLY LOVED ITS FOOD.
YES, DEAR. HE DID. ESPECIALLY HIS DESSERTS.
OH, MY. GOOD POINT, QUIBBY.
HOW MANY TIMES DID HE FORCE THOSE ATROCIOUS LOGARIAN SWEETBERRY PIES ON ALL OF US?
WE MUST NOT FORGET ONE RECIPE. NOT ONE FABLE OR LULLABY.
NONE OF IT.

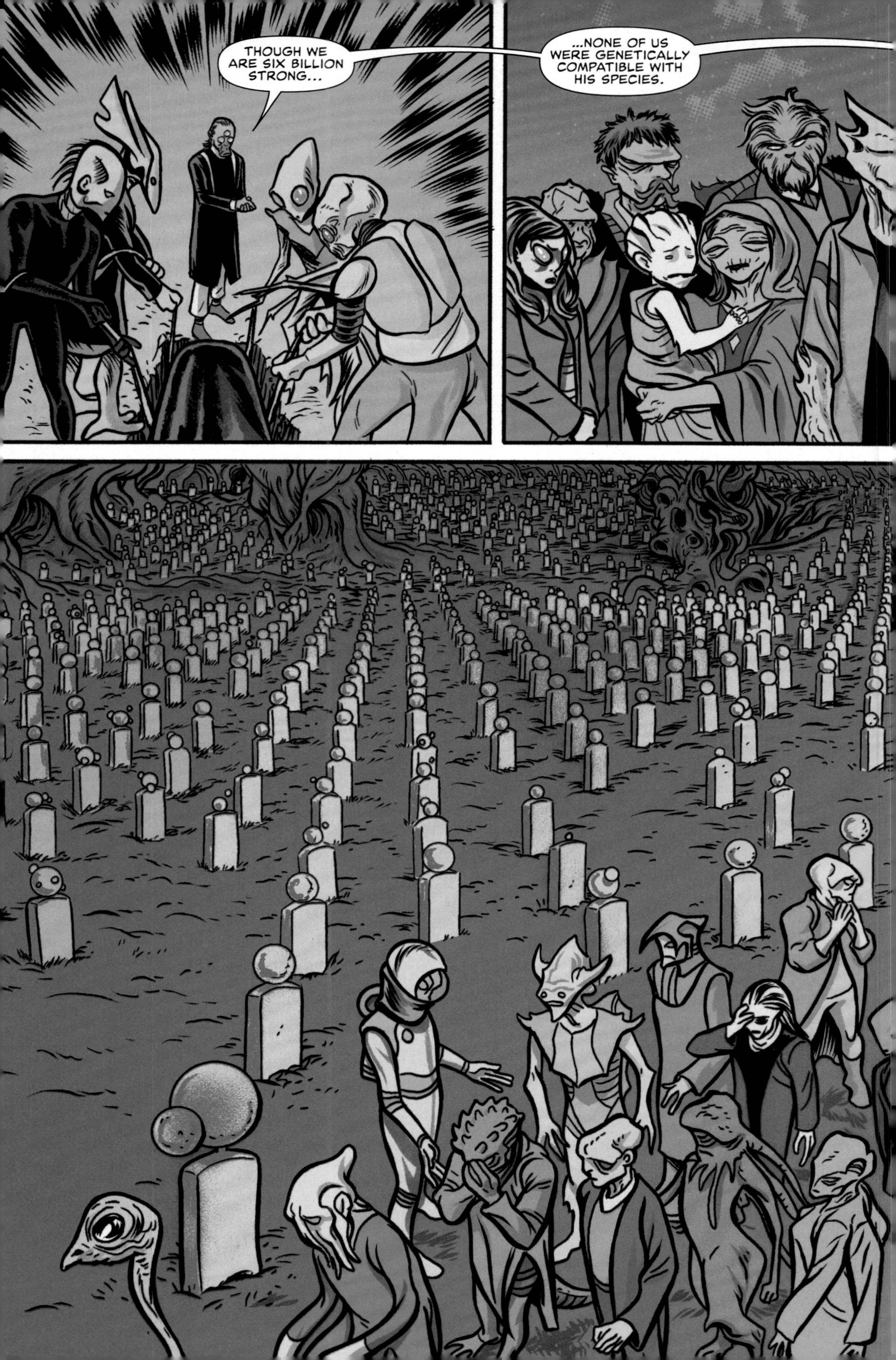
THOUGH WE ARE SIX BILLION STRONG...
...NONE OF US WERE GENETICALLY COMPATIBLE WITH HIS SPECIES.

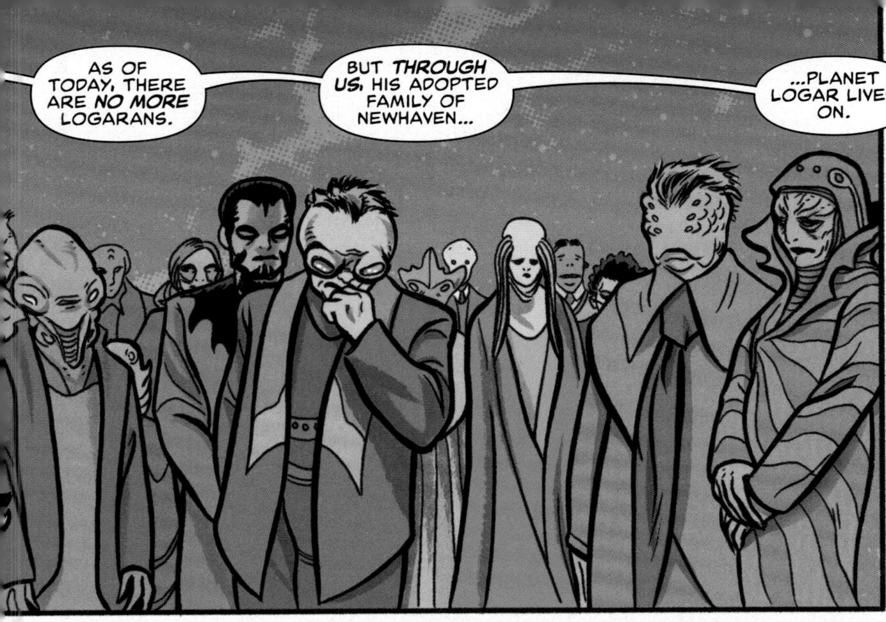
AS OF TODAY, THERE ARE NO MORE LOGARANS.
BUT THROUGH US, HIS ADOPTED FAMILY OF NEWHAVEN...
...PLANET LOGAR LIVES ON.

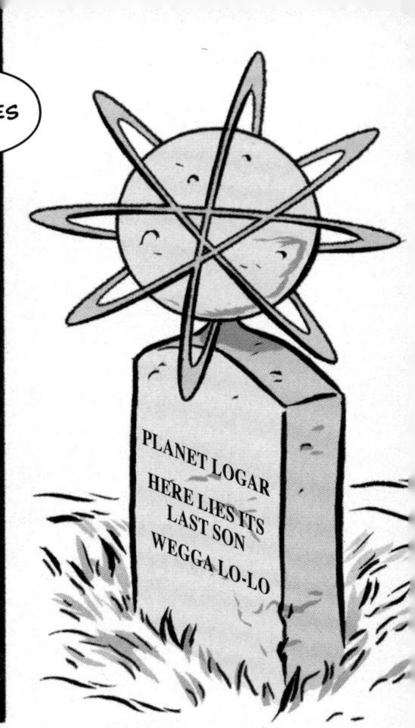
PLANET LOGAR
HERE LIES ITS LAST SON
WEGGA-LO-LO

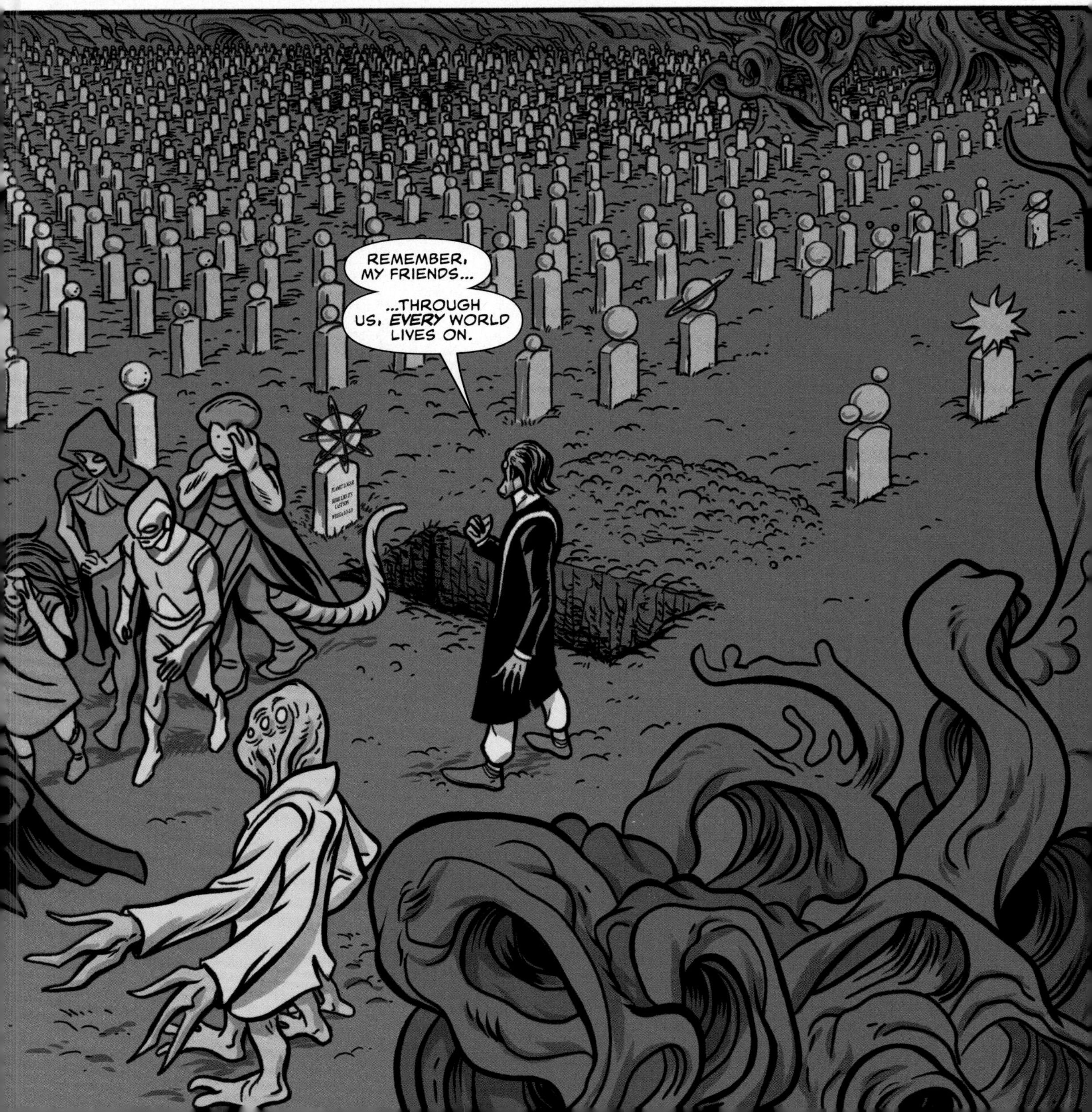
REMEMBER, MY FRIENDS...
...THROUGH US, EVERY WORLD LIVES ON.

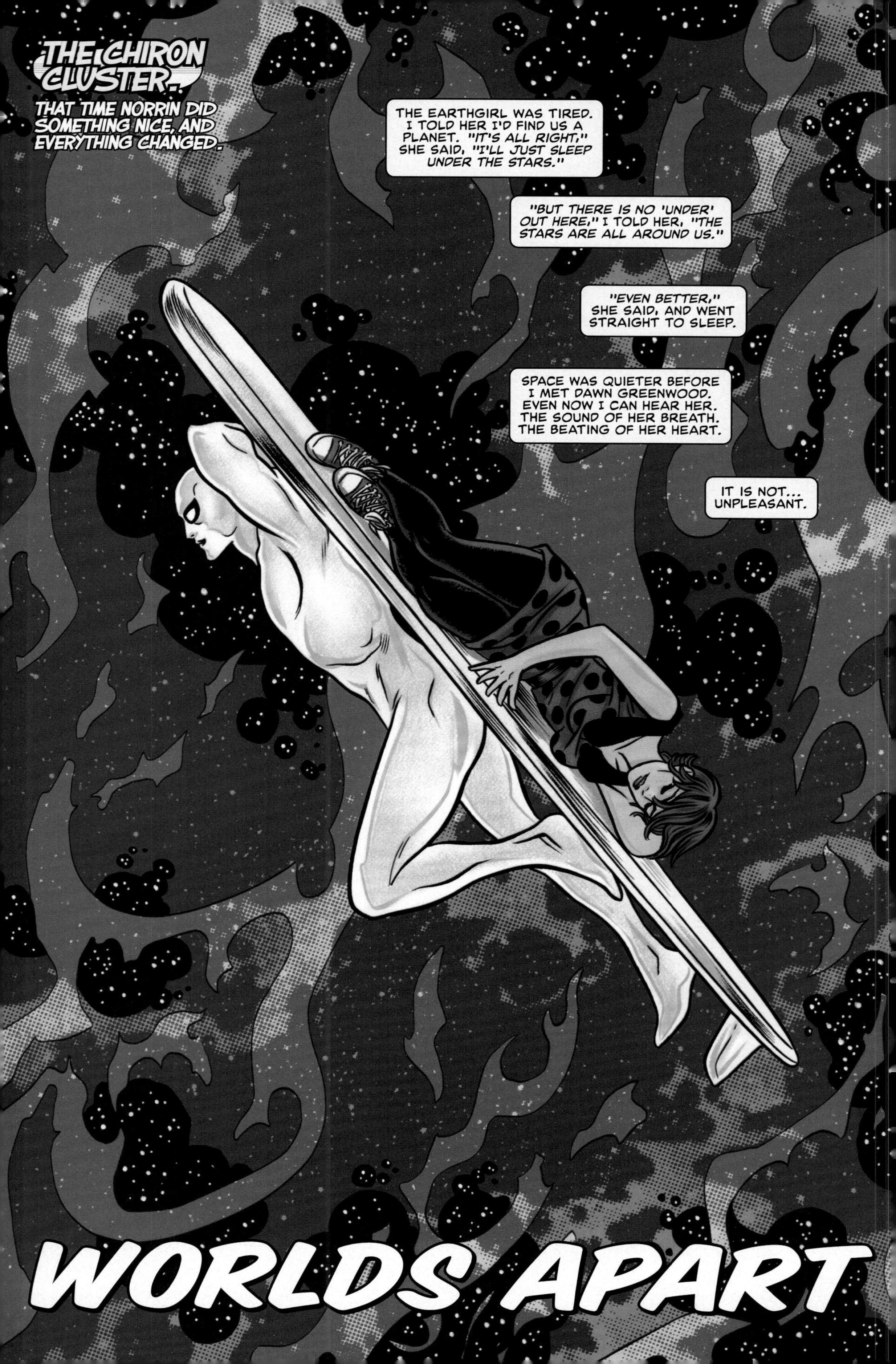
THE CHIRON CLUSTER...
THAT TIME NORRIN DID SOMETHING NICE, AND EVERYTHING CHANGED.
THE EARTHGIRL WAS TIRED. I TOLD HER I'D FIND US A PLANET. "IT'S ALL RIGHT," SHE SAID, "I'LL JUST SLEEP UNDER THE STARS."
"BUT THERE IS NO 'UNDER' OUT HERE," I TOLD HER, "THE STARS ARE ALL AROUND US."
"EVEN BETTER," SHE SAID, AND WENT STRAIGHT TO SLEEP.
SPACE WAS QUIETER BEFORE I MET DAWN GREENWOOD. EVEN NOW I CAN HEAR HER. THE SOUND OF HER BREATH. THE BEATING OF HER HEART.
IT IS NOT... UNPLEASANT.
WORLDS APART

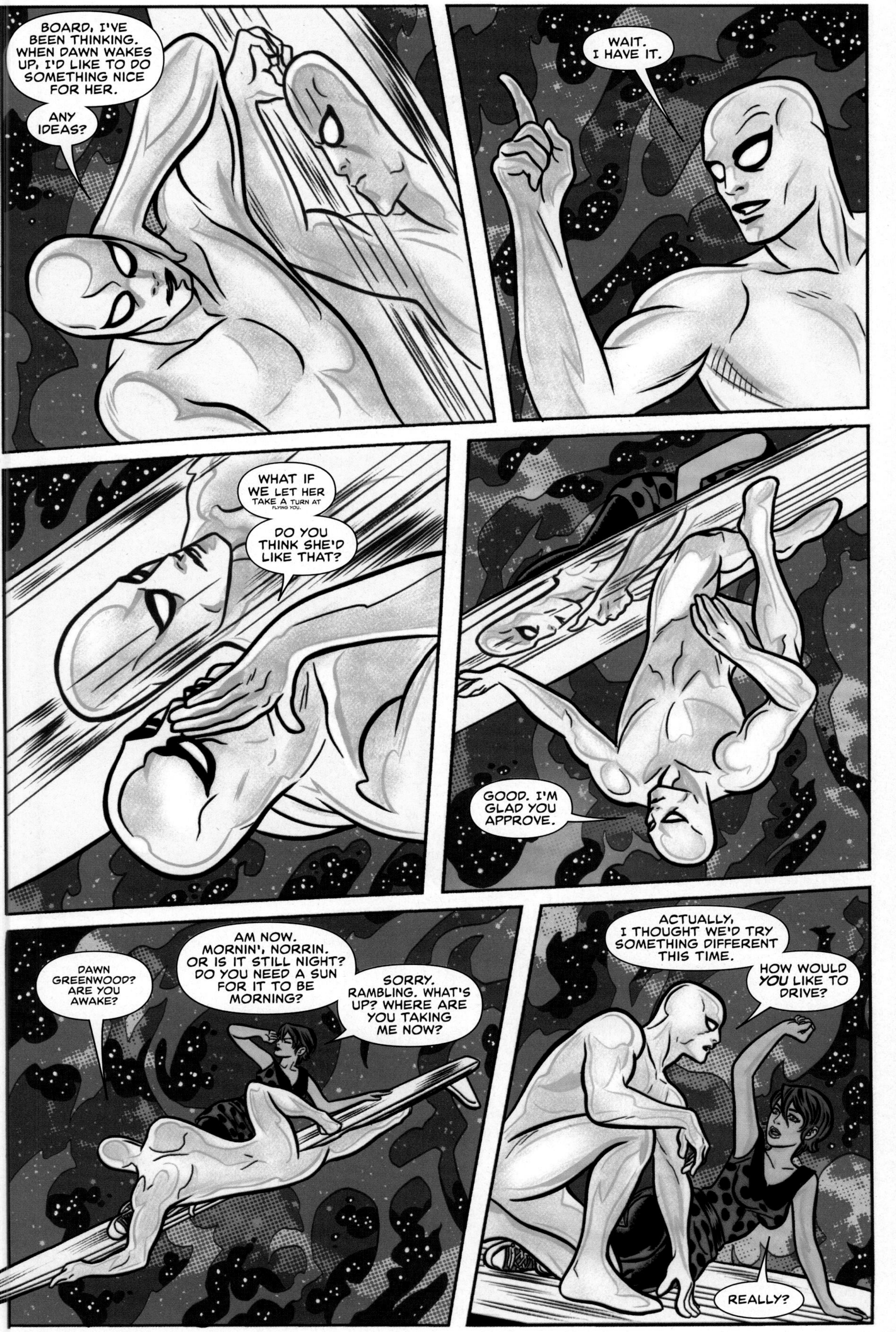
BOARD, I'VE BEEN THINKING. WHEN DAWN WAKES UP, I'D LIKE TO DO SOMETHING NICE FOR HER.
ANY IDEAS?
WAIT. I HAVE IT.
WHAT IF WE LET HER TAKE A TURN AT FLYING YOU.
DO YOU THINK SHE'D LIKE THAT?
GOOD. I'M GLAD YOU APPROVE.
DAWN GREENWOOD? ARE YOU AWAKE?
AM NOW. MORNIN', NORRIN. OR IS IT STILL NIGHT? DO YOU NEED A SUN FOR IT TO BE MORNING?
SORRY. RAMBLING. WHAT'S UP? WHERE ARE YOU TAKING ME NOW?
ACTUALLY, I THOUGHT WE'D TRY SOMETHING DIFFERENT THIS TIME.
HOW WOULD *YOU* LIKE TO DRIVE?
REALLY?

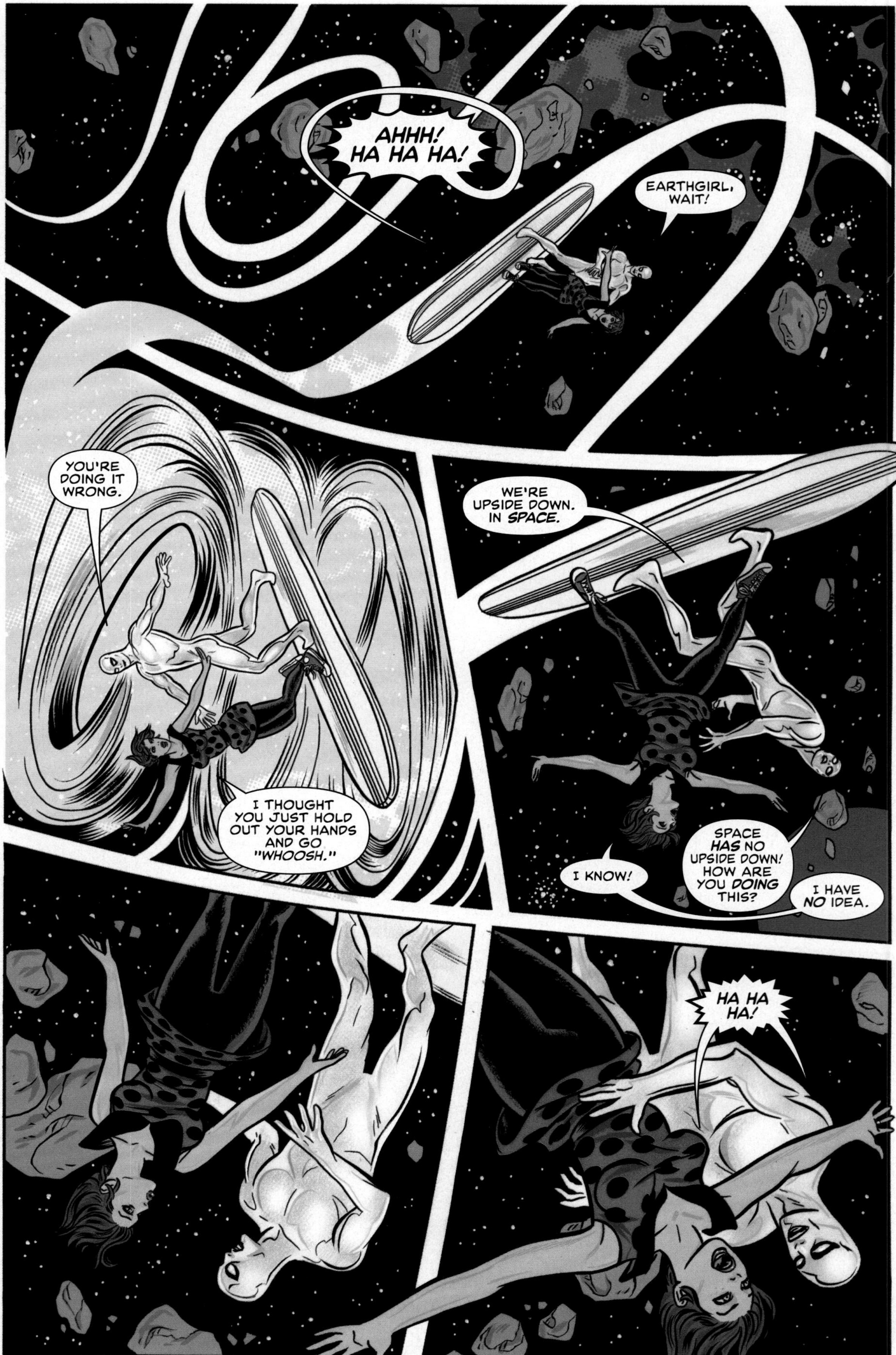

AHHH! HA HA HA!
EARTHGIRL, WAIT!
YOU'RE DOING IT WRONG.
I THOUGHT YOU JUST HOLD OUT YOUR HANDS AND GO "WHOOSH."
WE'RE UPSIDE DOWN. IN SPACE.
SPACE HAS NO UPSIDE DOWN! HOW ARE YOU DOING THIS?
I KNOW!
I HAVE NO IDEA.
HA HA HA!

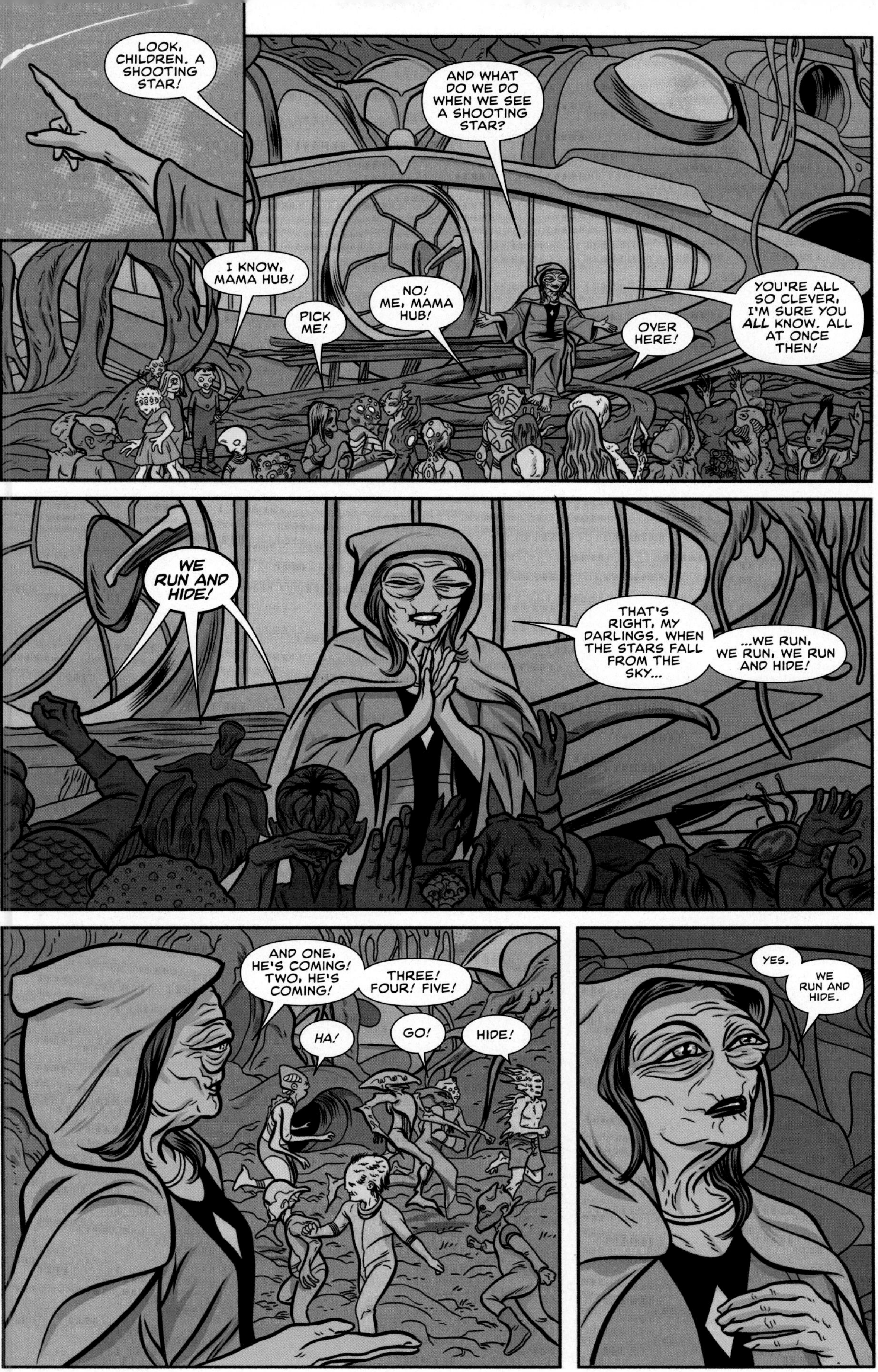

LOOK, CHILDREN. A SHOOTING STAR!
AND WHAT DO WE DO WHEN WE SEE A SHOOTING STAR?
I KNOW, MAMA HUB!
PICK ME!
NO! ME, MAMA HUB!
OVER HERE!
YOU'RE ALL SO CLEVER, I'M SURE YOU **ALL** KNOW. ALL AT ONCE THEN!
WE RUN AND HIDE!
THAT'S RIGHT, MY DARLINGS. WHEN THE STARS FALL FROM THE SKY...
...WE RUN, WE RUN, WE RUN AND HIDE!
AND ONE, HE'S COMING! TWO, HE'S COMING!
THREE! FOUR! FIVE!
HA!
GO!
HIDE!
YES.
WE RUN AND HIDE.

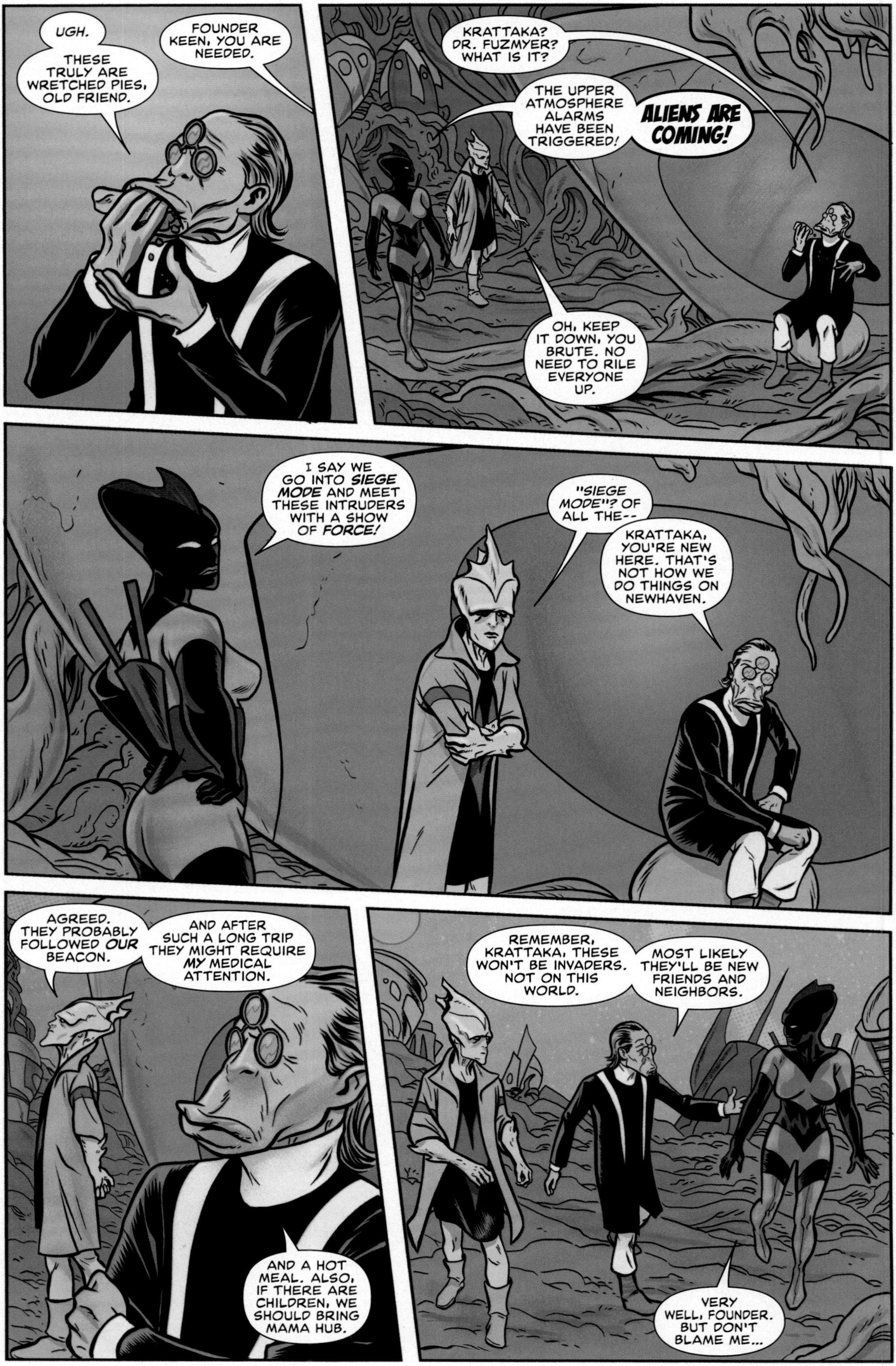
UGH.
THESE TRULY ARE WRETCHED PIES, OLD FRIEND.
FOUNDER KEEN, YOU ARE NEEDED.
KRATTAKA? DR. FUZMYER? WHAT IS IT?
THE UPPER ATMOSPHERE ALARMS HAVE BEEN TRIGGERED!
ALIENS ARE COMING!
OH, KEEP IT DOWN, YOU BRUTE. NO NEED TO RILE EVERYONE UP.
I SAY WE GO INTO SIEGE MODE AND MEET THESE INTRUDERS WITH A SHOW OF FORCE!
"SIEGE MODE"? OF ALL THE--
KRATTAKA, YOU'RE NEW HERE. THAT'S NOT HOW WE DO THINGS ON NEWHAVEN.
AGREED. THEY PROBABLY FOLLOWED OUR BEACON.
AND AFTER SUCH A LONG TRIP THEY MIGHT REQUIRE MY MEDICAL ATTENTION.
AND A HOT MEAL. ALSO, IF THERE ARE CHILDREN, WE SHOULD BRING MAMA HUB.
REMEMBER, KRATTAKA, THESE WON'T BE INVADERS. NOT ON THIS WORLD.
MOST LIKELY THEY'LL BE NEW FRIENDS AND NEIGHBORS.
VERY WELL, FOUNDER. BUT DON'T BLAME ME...

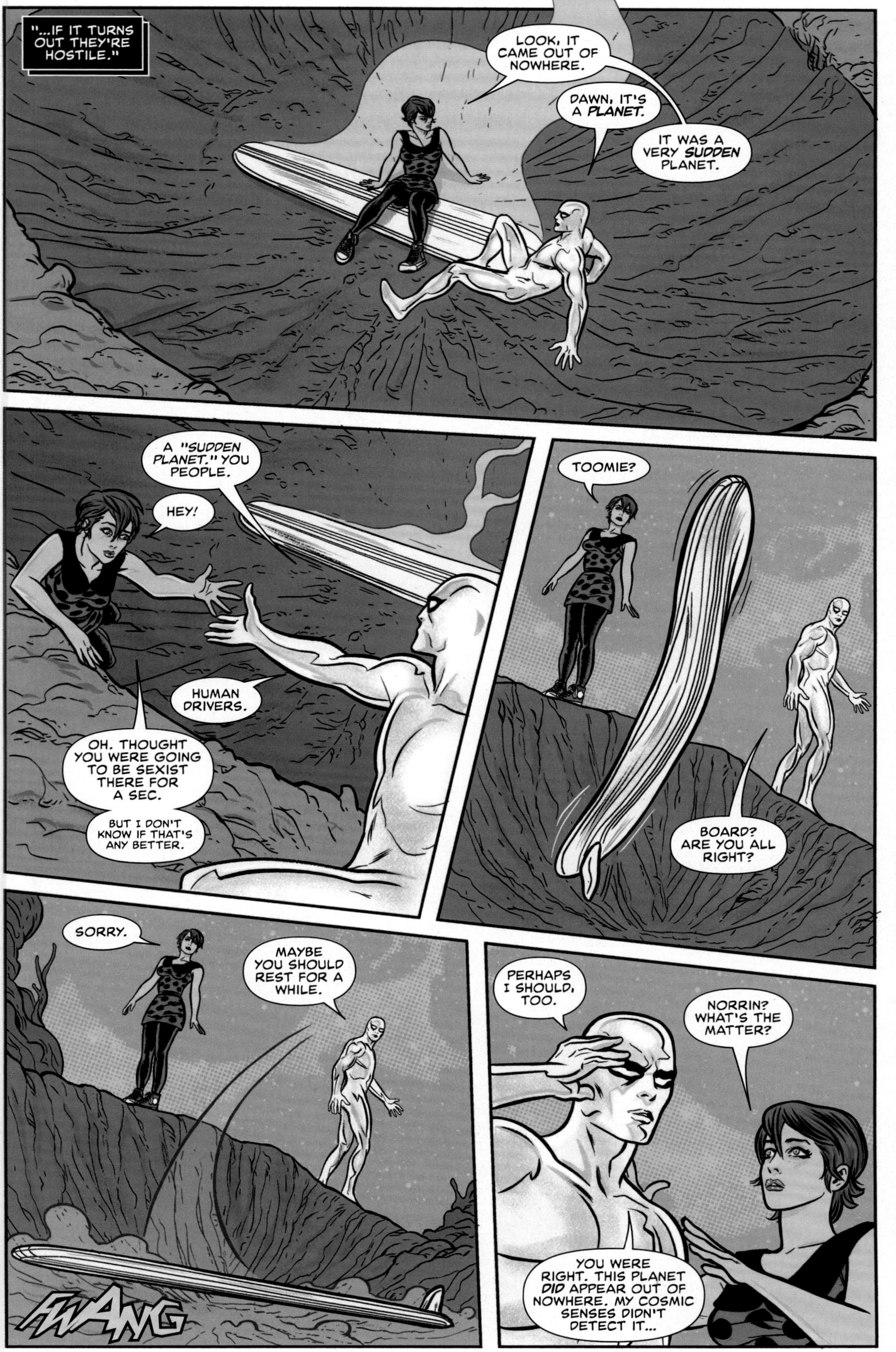
"...IF IT TURNS OUT THEY'RE HOSTILE."
LOOK, IT CAME OUT OF NOWHERE.
DAWN, IT'S A PLANET.
IT WAS A VERY SUDDEN PLANET.
A "SUDDEN PLANET." YOU PEOPLE.
HEY!
HUMAN DRIVERS.
OH. THOUGHT YOU WERE GOING TO BE SEXIST THERE FOR A SEC.
BUT I DON'T KNOW IF THAT'S ANY BETTER.
TOOMIE?
BOARD? ARE YOU ALL RIGHT?
SORRY.
MAYBE YOU SHOULD REST FOR A WHILE.
FWANG
PERHAPS I SHOULD, TOO.
NORRIN? WHAT'S THE MATTER?
YOU WERE RIGHT. THIS PLANET DID APPEAR OUT OF NOWHERE. MY COSMIC SENSES DIDN'T DETECT IT...

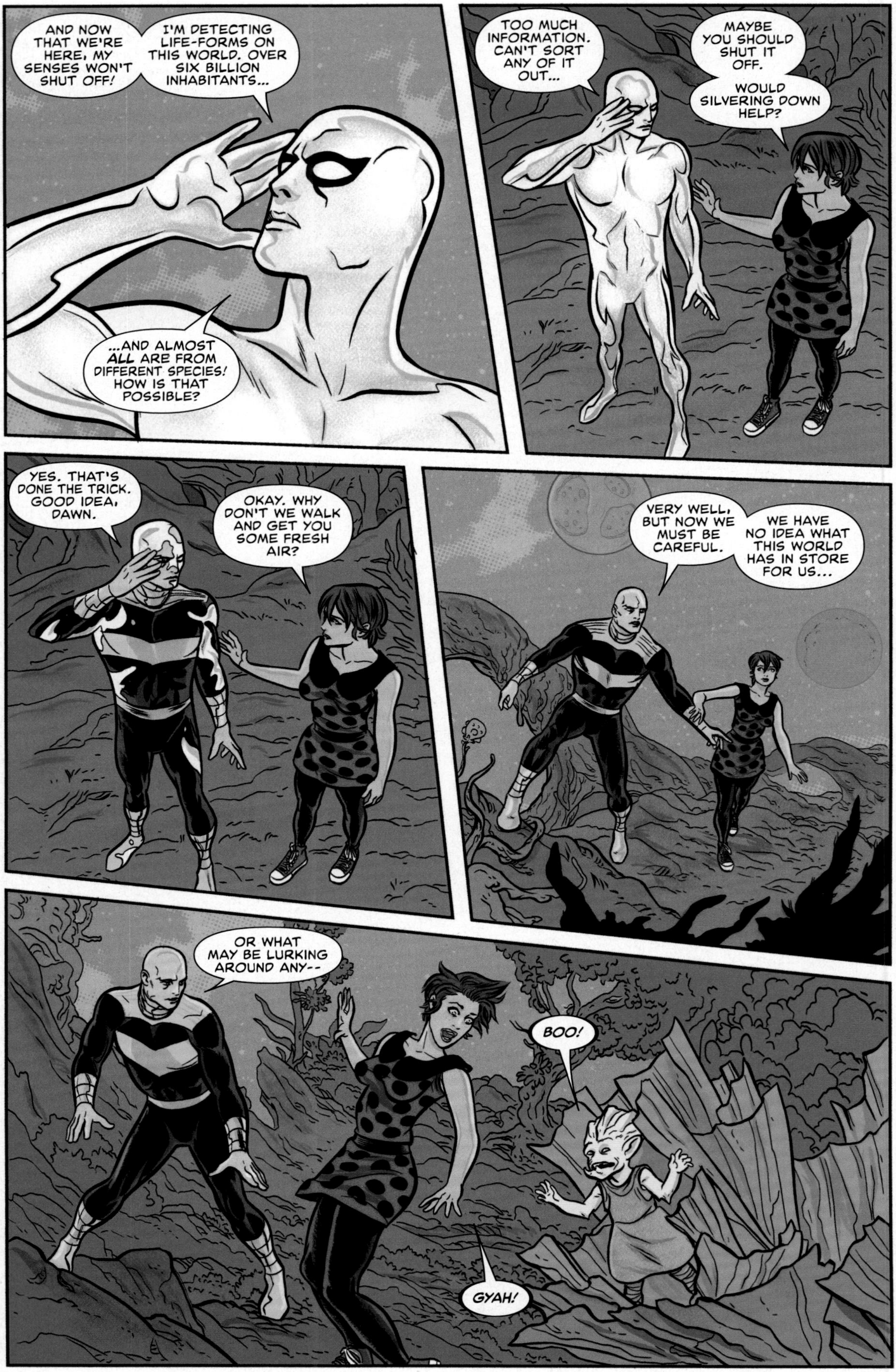
AND NOW THAT WE'RE HERE, MY SENSES WON'T SHUT OFF!
I'M DETECTING LIFE-FORMS ON THIS WORLD. OVER SIX BILLION INHABITANTS...
...AND ALMOST ALL ARE FROM DIFFERENT SPECIES! HOW IS THAT POSSIBLE?
TOO MUCH INFORMATION. CAN'T SORT ANY OF IT OUT...
MAYBE YOU SHOULD SHUT IT OFF.
WOULD SILVERING DOWN HELP?
YES. THAT'S DONE THE TRICK. GOOD IDEA, DAWN.
OKAY. WHY DON'T WE WALK AND GET YOU SOME FRESH AIR?
VERY WELL, BUT NOW WE MUST BE CAREFUL.
WE HAVE NO IDEA WHAT THIS WORLD HAS IN STORE FOR US...
OR WHAT MAY BE LURKING AROUND ANY--
BOO!
GYAH!

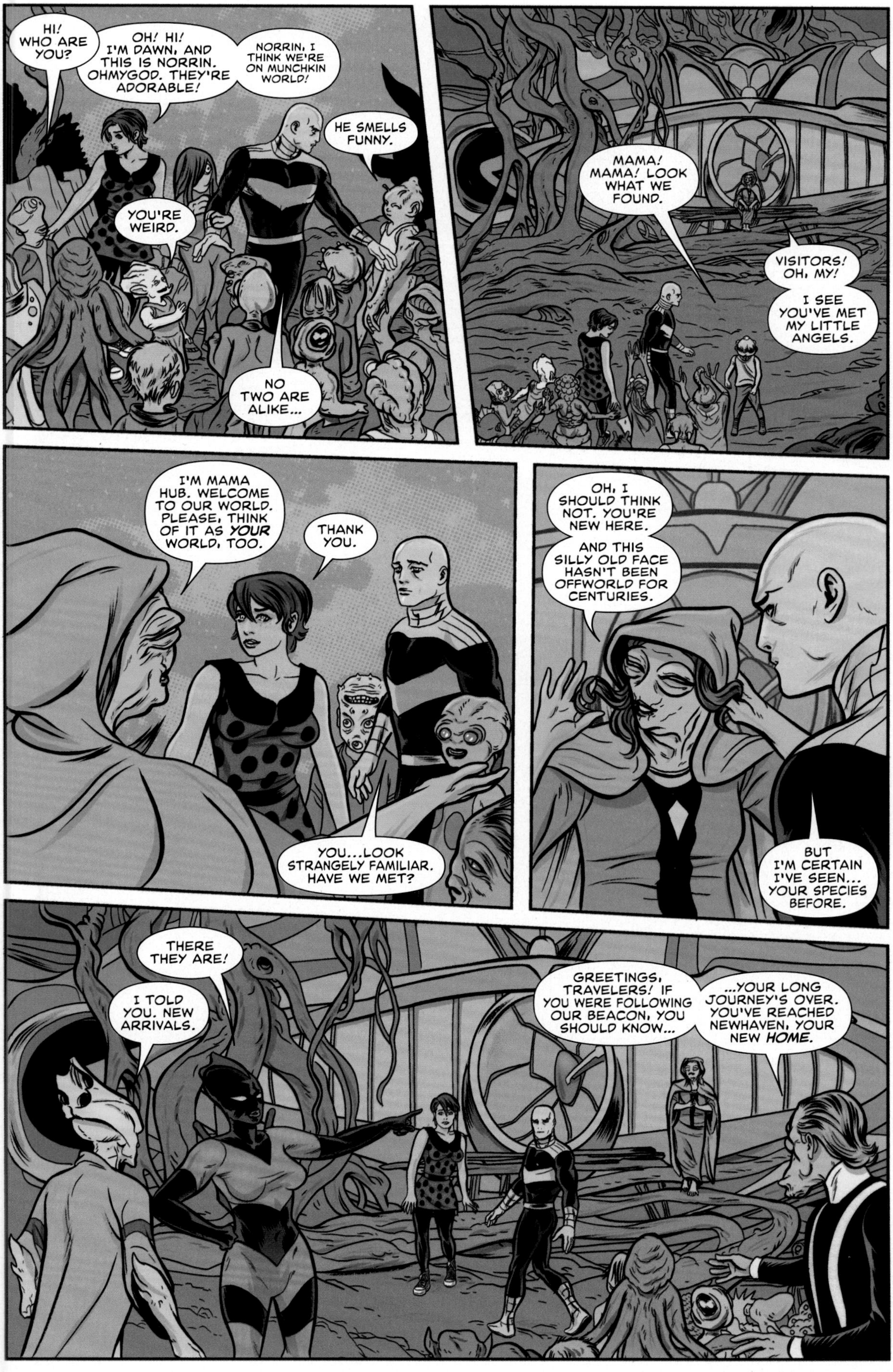
HI! WHO ARE YOU?
OH! HI! I'M DAWN, AND THIS IS NORRIN. OHMYGOD. THEY'RE ADORABLE!
NORRIN, I THINK WE'RE ON MUNCHKIN WORLD!
HE SMELLS FUNNY.
YOU'RE WEIRD.
NO TWO ARE ALIKE...
MAMA! MAMA! LOOK WHAT WE FOUND.
VISITORS! OH, MY!
I SEE YOU'VE MET MY LITTLE ANGELS.
I'M MAMA HUB. WELCOME TO OUR WORLD. PLEASE, THINK OF IT AS YOUR WORLD, TOO.
THANK YOU.
YOU...LOOK STRANGELY FAMILIAR. HAVE WE MET?
OH, I SHOULD THINK NOT. YOU'RE NEW HERE.
AND THIS SILLY OLD FACE HASN'T BEEN OFFWORLD FOR CENTURIES.
BUT I'M CERTAIN I'VE SEEN... YOUR SPECIES BEFORE.
THERE THEY ARE!
I TOLD YOU. NEW ARRIVALS.
GREETINGS, TRAVELERS! IF YOU WERE FOLLOWING OUR BEACON, YOU SHOULD KNOW...
...YOUR LONG JOURNEY'S OVER. YOU'VE REACHED NEWHAVEN, YOUR NEW HOME.

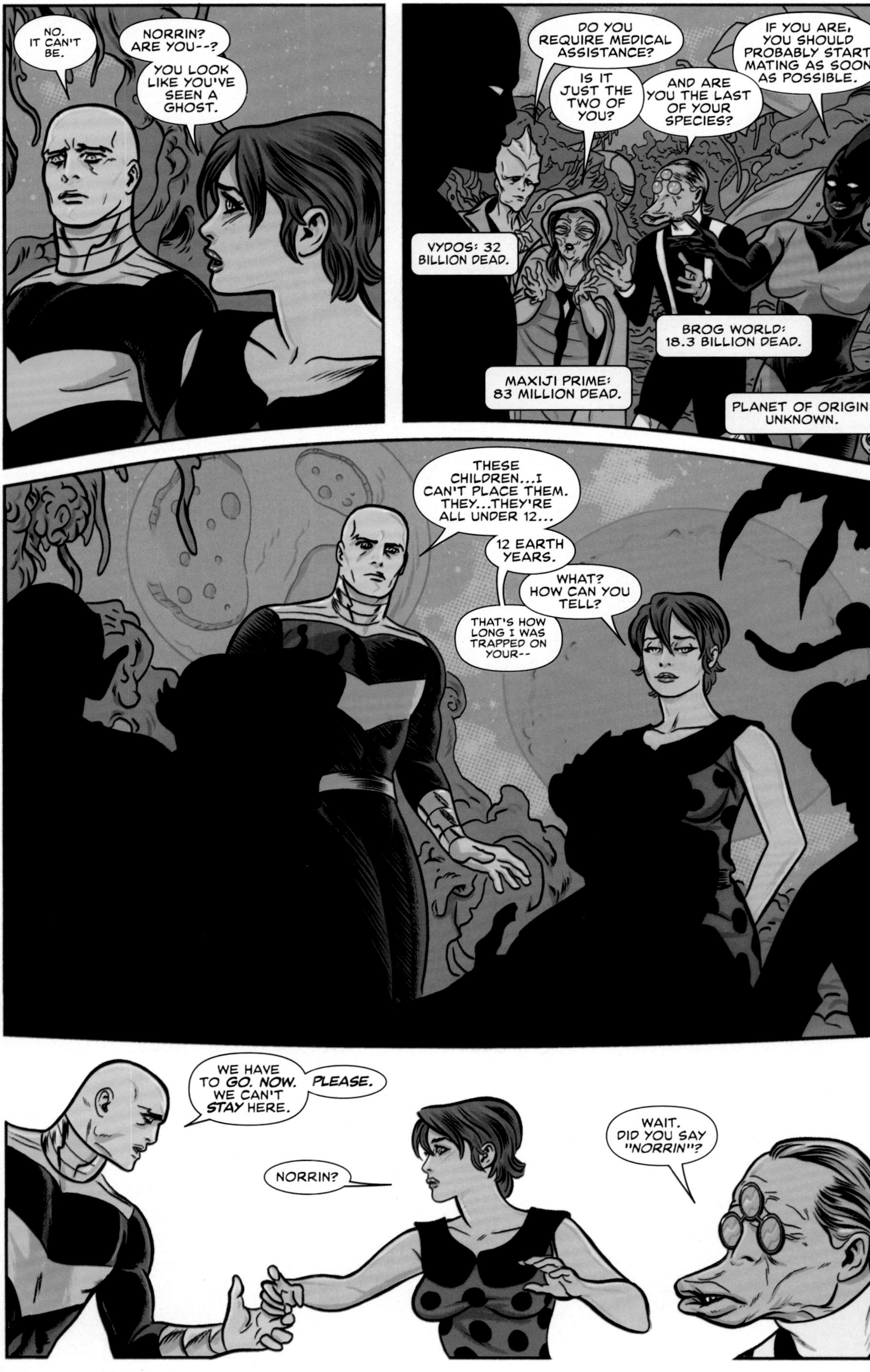
NO. IT CAN'T BE.
NORRIN? ARE YOU--?
YOU LOOK LIKE YOU'VE SEEN A GHOST.
DO YOU REQUIRE MEDICAL ASSISTANCE?
IS IT JUST THE TWO OF YOU?
AND ARE YOU THE LAST OF YOUR SPECIES?
IF YOU ARE, YOU SHOULD PROBABLY START MATING AS SOON AS POSSIBLE.
VYDOS: 32 BILLION DEAD.
MAXIJI PRIME: 83 MILLION DEAD.
BROG WORLD: 18.3 BILLION DEAD.
PLANET OF ORIGIN: UNKNOWN.
THESE CHILDREN...I CAN'T PLACE THEM. THEY...THEY'RE ALL UNDER 12...
12 EARTH YEARS.
WHAT? HOW CAN YOU TELL?
THAT'S HOW LONG I WAS TRAPPED ON YOUR--
WE HAVE TO GO. NOW. WE CAN'T STAY HERE.
PLEASE.
NORRIN?
WAIT. DID YOU SAY "NORRIN"?

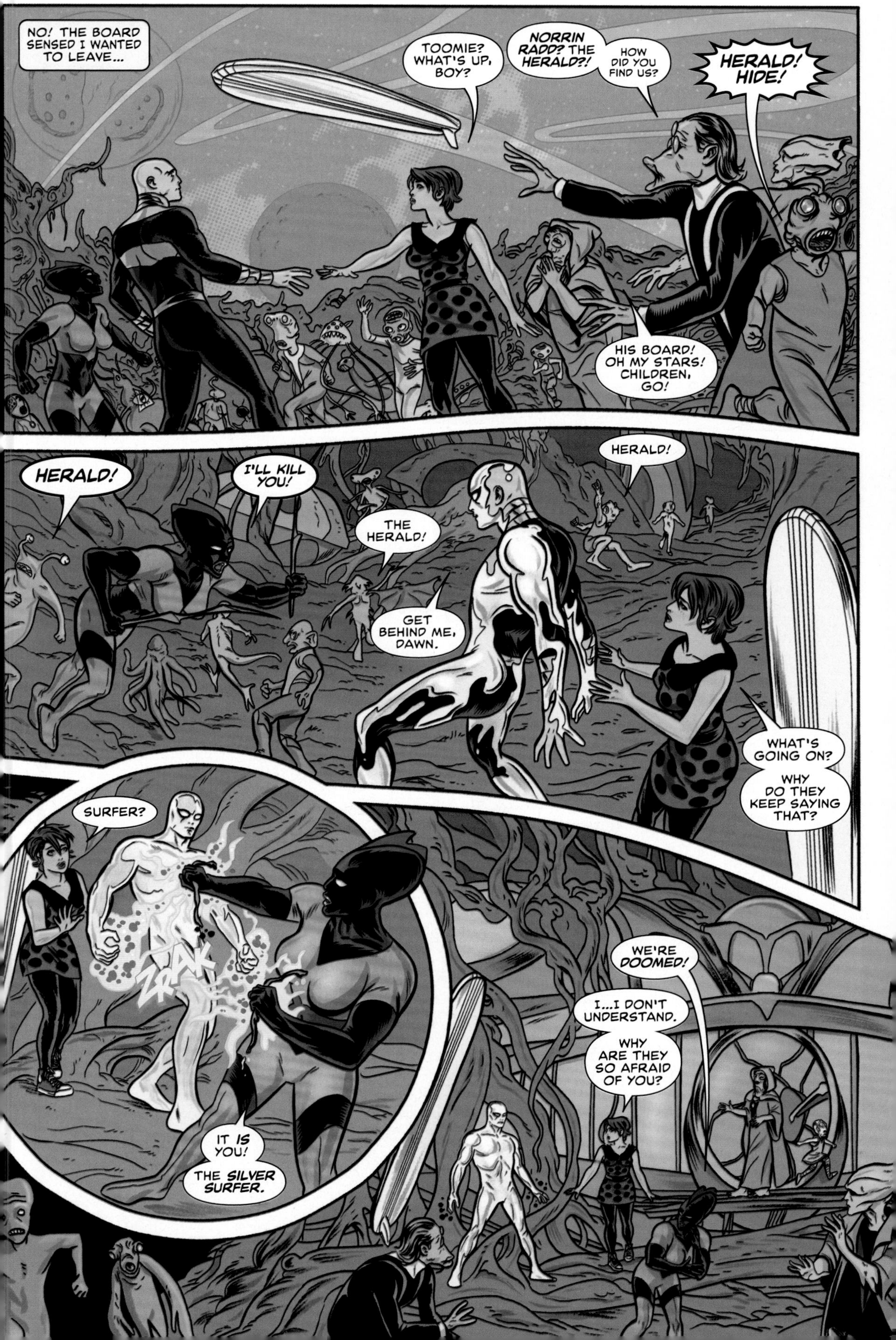
NO! THE BOARD SENSED I WANTED TO LEAVE...
TOOMIE? WHAT'S UP, BOY?
NORRIN RADD? THE HERALD?!
HOW DID YOU FIND US?
HERALD! HIDE!
HIS BOARD! OH MY STARS! CHILDREN, GO!
HERALD!
I'LL KILL YOU!
THE HERALD!
HERALD!
GET BEHIND ME, DAWN.
WHAT'S GOING ON?
WHY DO THEY KEEP SAYING THAT?
SURFER?
IT IS YOU!
THE SILVER SURFER.
WE'RE DOOMED!
I...I DON'T UNDERSTAND.
WHY ARE THEY SO AFRAID OF YOU?

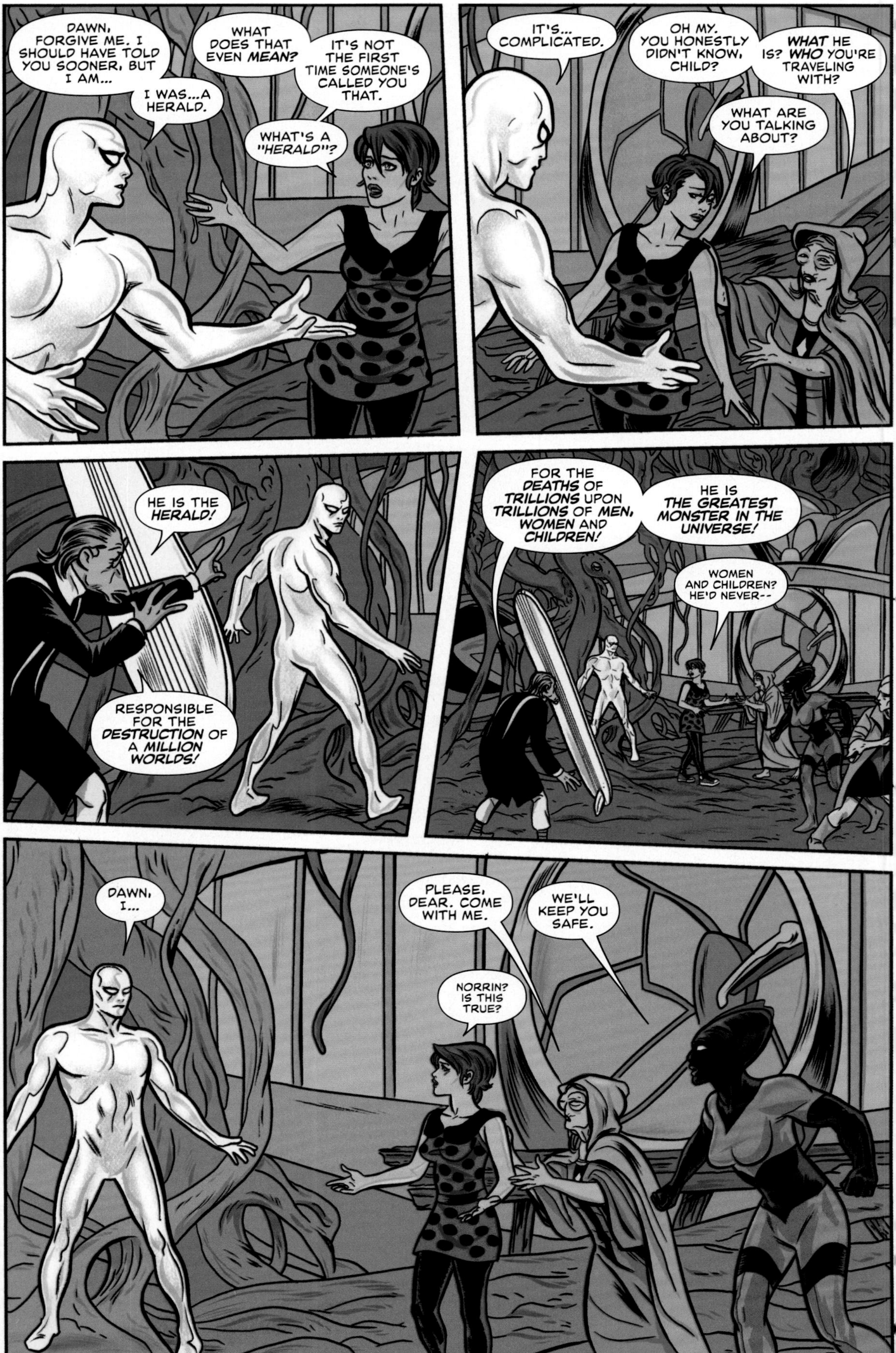
DAWN, FORGIVE ME. I SHOULD HAVE TOLD YOU SOONER, BUT I AM...
I WAS...A HERALD.
WHAT DOES THAT EVEN *MEAN?*
IT'S NOT THE FIRST TIME SOMEONE'S CALLED YOU THAT.
WHAT'S A "HERALD"?
IT'S... COMPLICATED.
OH MY. YOU HONESTLY DIDN'T KNOW, CHILD?
WHAT HE IS? *WHO* YOU'RE TRAVELING WITH?
WHAT ARE YOU TALKING ABOUT?
HE IS THE *HERALD!*
RESPONSIBLE FOR THE *DESTRUCTION* OF A *MILLION WORLDS!*
FOR THE *DEATHS* OF *TRILLIONS* UPON *TRILLIONS* OF *MEN, WOMEN* AND *CHILDREN!*
HE IS *THE GREATEST MONSTER IN THE UNIVERSE!*
WOMEN AND CHILDREN? HE'D NEVER--
DAWN, I...
PLEASE, DEAR. COME WITH ME.
WE'LL KEEP YOU SAFE.
NORRIN? IS THIS TRUE?

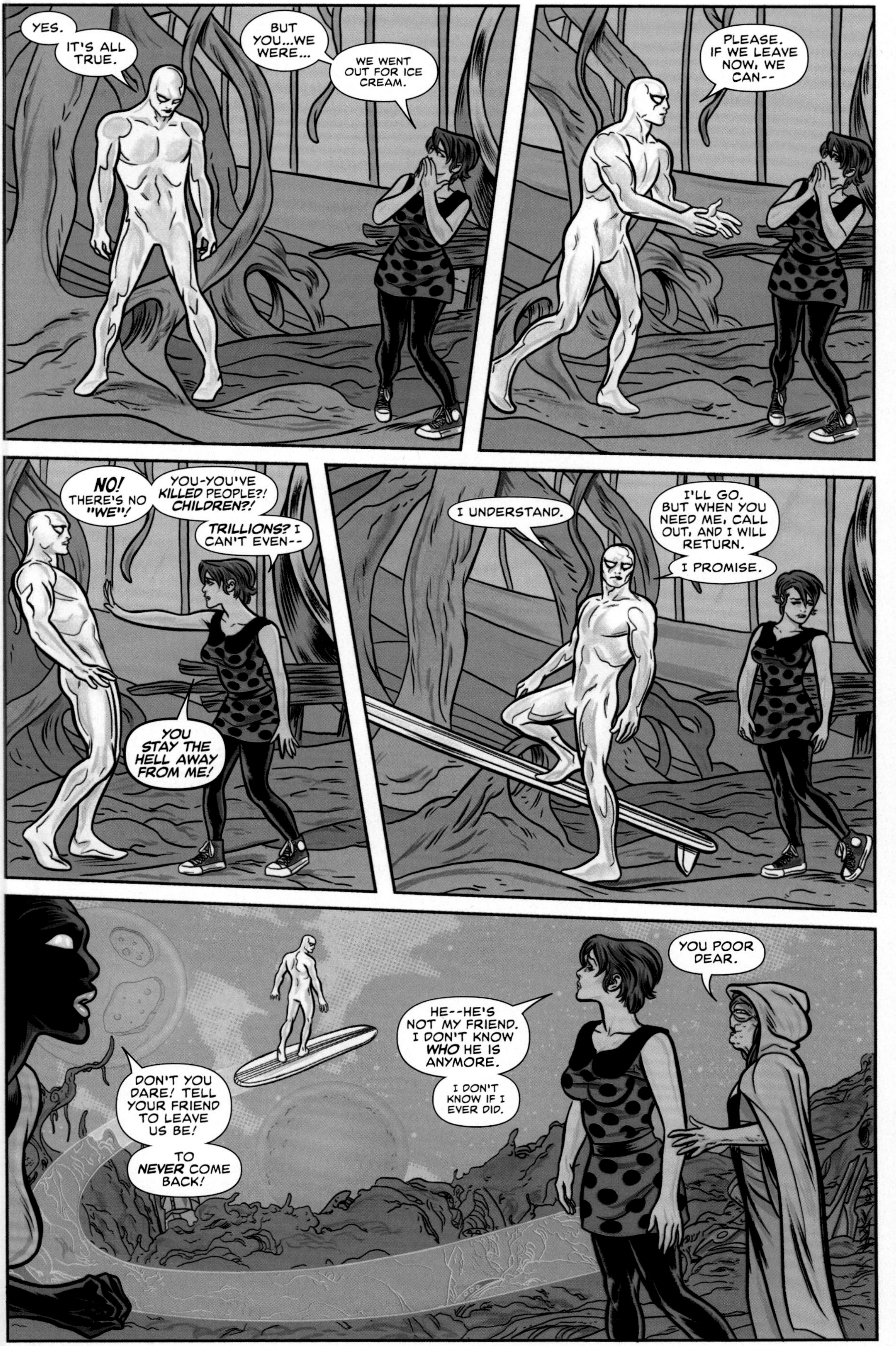

YES.
IT'S ALL TRUE.
BUT YOU...WE WERE...
WE WENT OUT FOR ICE CREAM.
PLEASE. IF WE LEAVE NOW, WE CAN--
NO! THERE'S NO "WE"!
YOU-YOU'VE KILLED PEOPLE?! CHILDREN?!
TRILLIONS? I CAN'T EVEN--
YOU STAY THE HELL AWAY FROM ME!
I UNDERSTAND.
I'LL GO. BUT WHEN YOU NEED ME, CALL OUT, AND I WILL RETURN.
I PROMISE.
DON'T YOU DARE! TELL YOUR FRIEND TO LEAVE US BE!
TO NEVER COME BACK!
HE--HE'S NOT MY FRIEND. I DON'T KNOW WHO HE IS ANYMORE.
I DON'T KNOW IF I EVER DID.
YOU POOR DEAR.

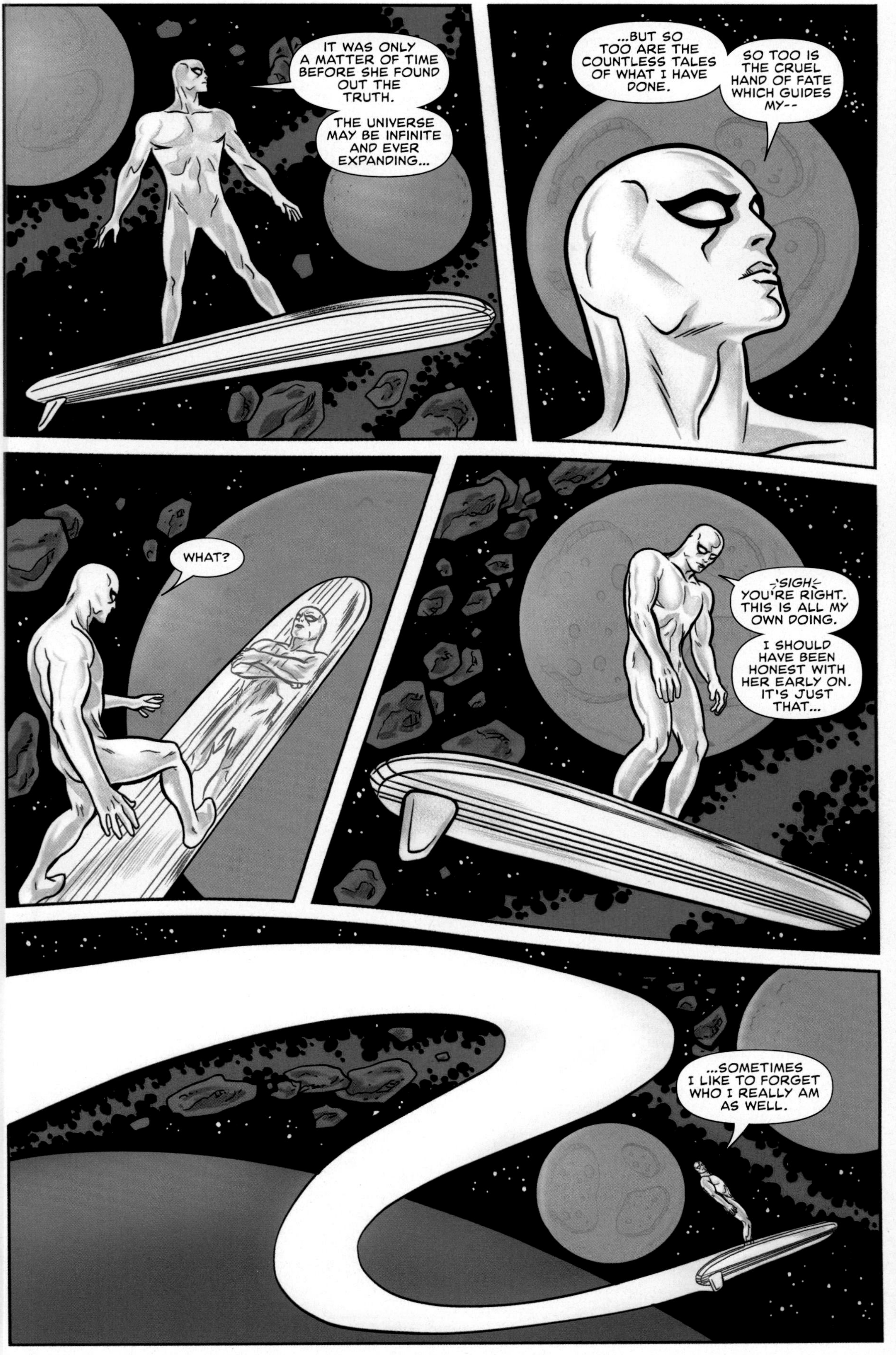
IT WAS ONLY A MATTER OF TIME BEFORE SHE FOUND OUT THE TRUTH.
THE UNIVERSE MAY BE INFINITE AND EVER EXPANDING...
...BUT SO TOO ARE THE COUNTLESS TALES OF WHAT I HAVE DONE.
SO TOO IS THE CRUEL HAND OF FATE WHICH GUIDES MY--
WHAT?
SIGH YOU'RE RIGHT. THIS IS ALL MY OWN DOING.
I SHOULD HAVE BEEN HONEST WITH HER EARLY ON. IT'S JUST THAT...
...SOMETIMES I LIKE TO FORGET WHO I REALLY AM AS WELL.

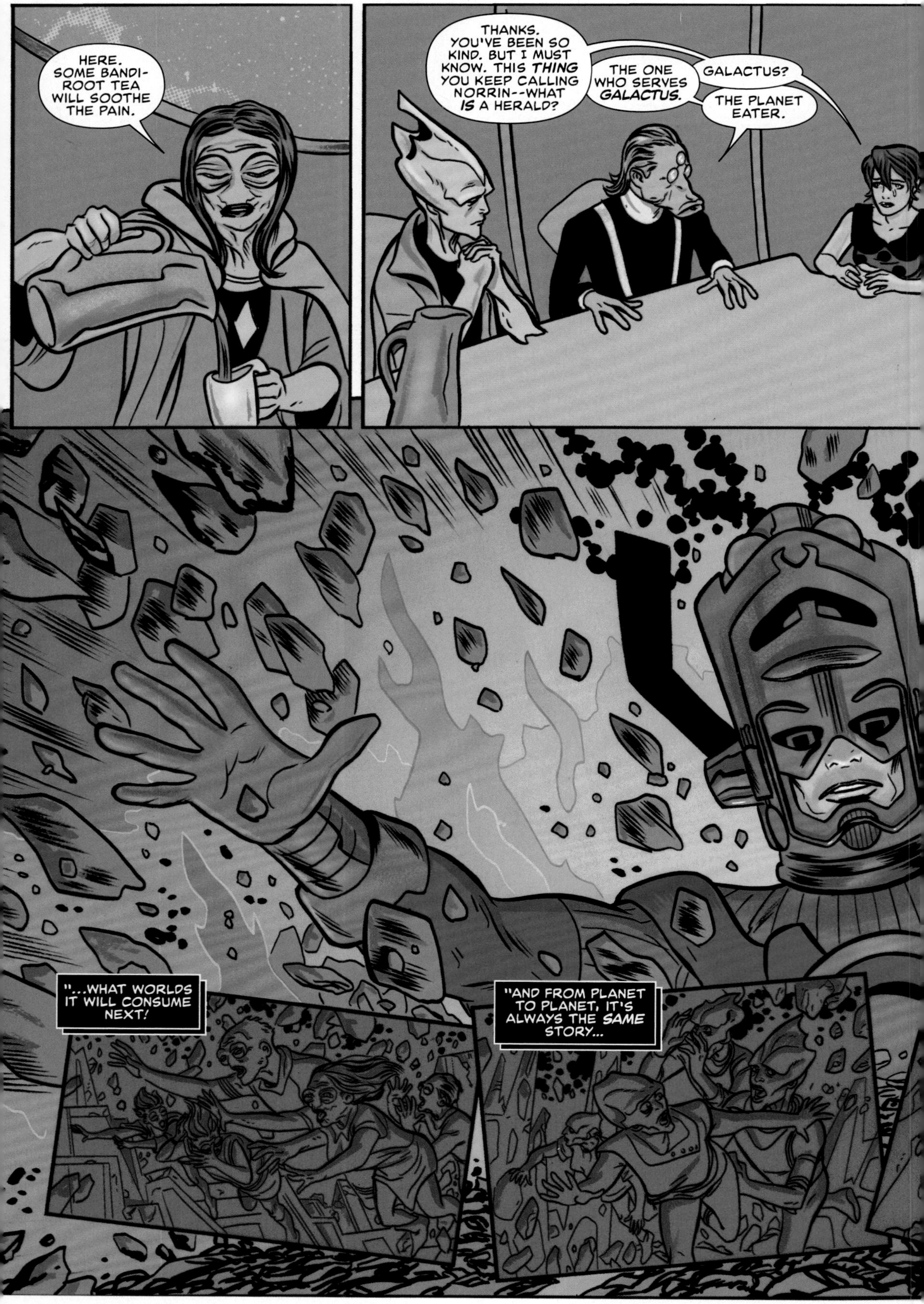
HERE. SOME BANDI-ROOT TEA WILL SOOTHE THE PAIN.
THANKS. YOU'VE BEEN SO KIND. BUT I MUST KNOW. THIS *THING* YOU KEEP CALLING NORRIN--WHAT *IS* A HERALD?
THE ONE WHO SERVES *GALACTUS.*
GALACTUS?
THE PLANET EATER.
"...WHAT WORLDS IT WILL CONSUME NEXT!
"AND FROM PLANET TO PLANET, IT'S ALWAYS THE *SAME* STORY...

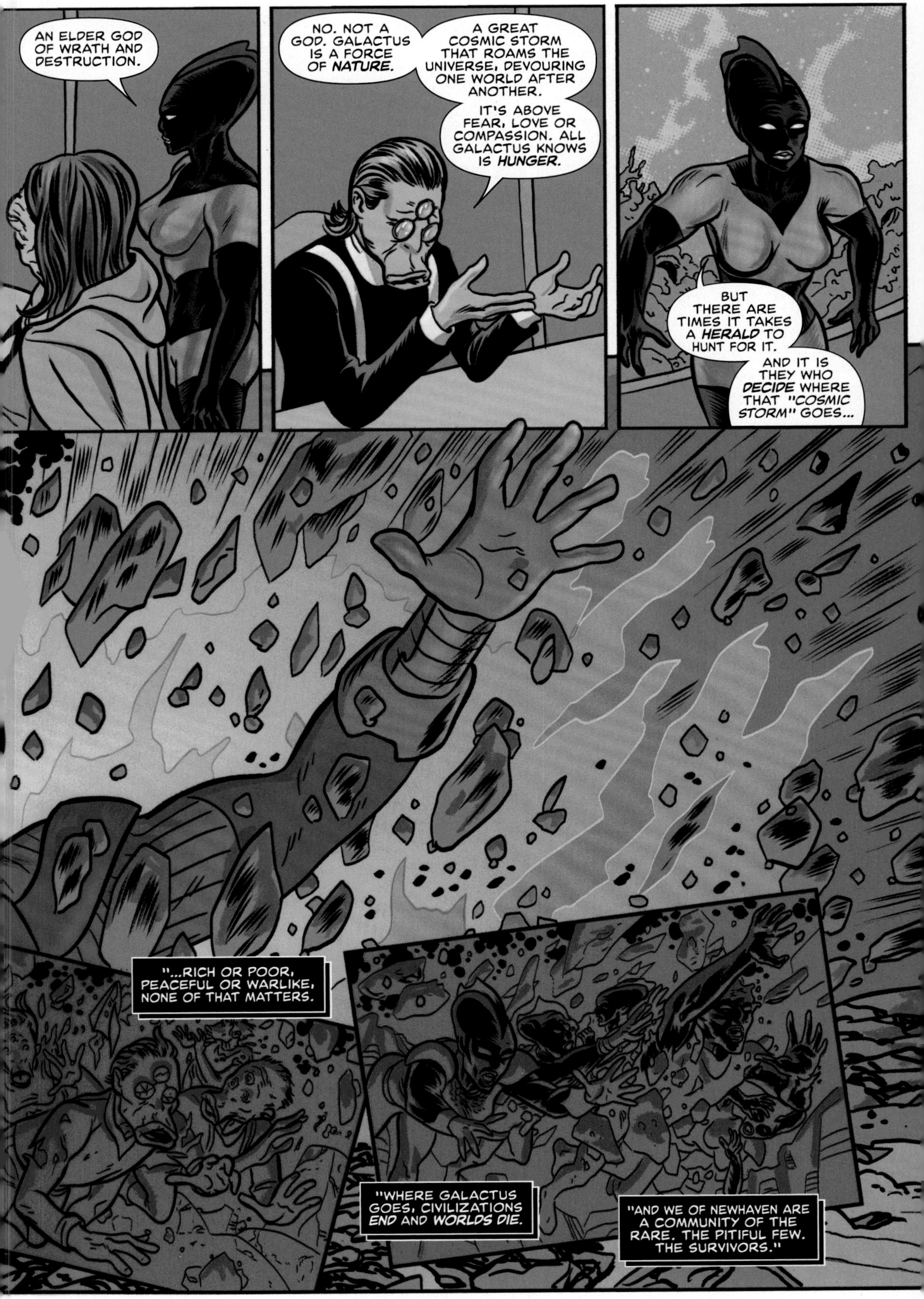
AN ELDER GOD OF WRATH AND DESTRUCTION.
NO. NOT A GOD. GALACTUS IS A FORCE OF NATURE.
A GREAT COSMIC STORM THAT ROAMS THE UNIVERSE, DEVOURING ONE WORLD AFTER ANOTHER.
IT'S ABOVE FEAR, LOVE OR COMPASSION. ALL GALACTUS KNOWS IS HUNGER.
BUT THERE ARE TIMES IT TAKES A HERALD TO HUNT FOR IT.
AND IT IS THEY WHO DECIDE WHERE THAT "COSMIC STORM" GOES...
"...RICH OR POOR, PEACEFUL OR WARLIKE, NONE OF THAT MATTERS.
"WHERE GALACTUS GOES, CIVILIZATIONS END AND WORLDS DIE.
"AND WE OF NEWHAVEN ARE A COMMUNITY OF THE RARE. THE PITIFUL FEW. THE SURVIVORS."

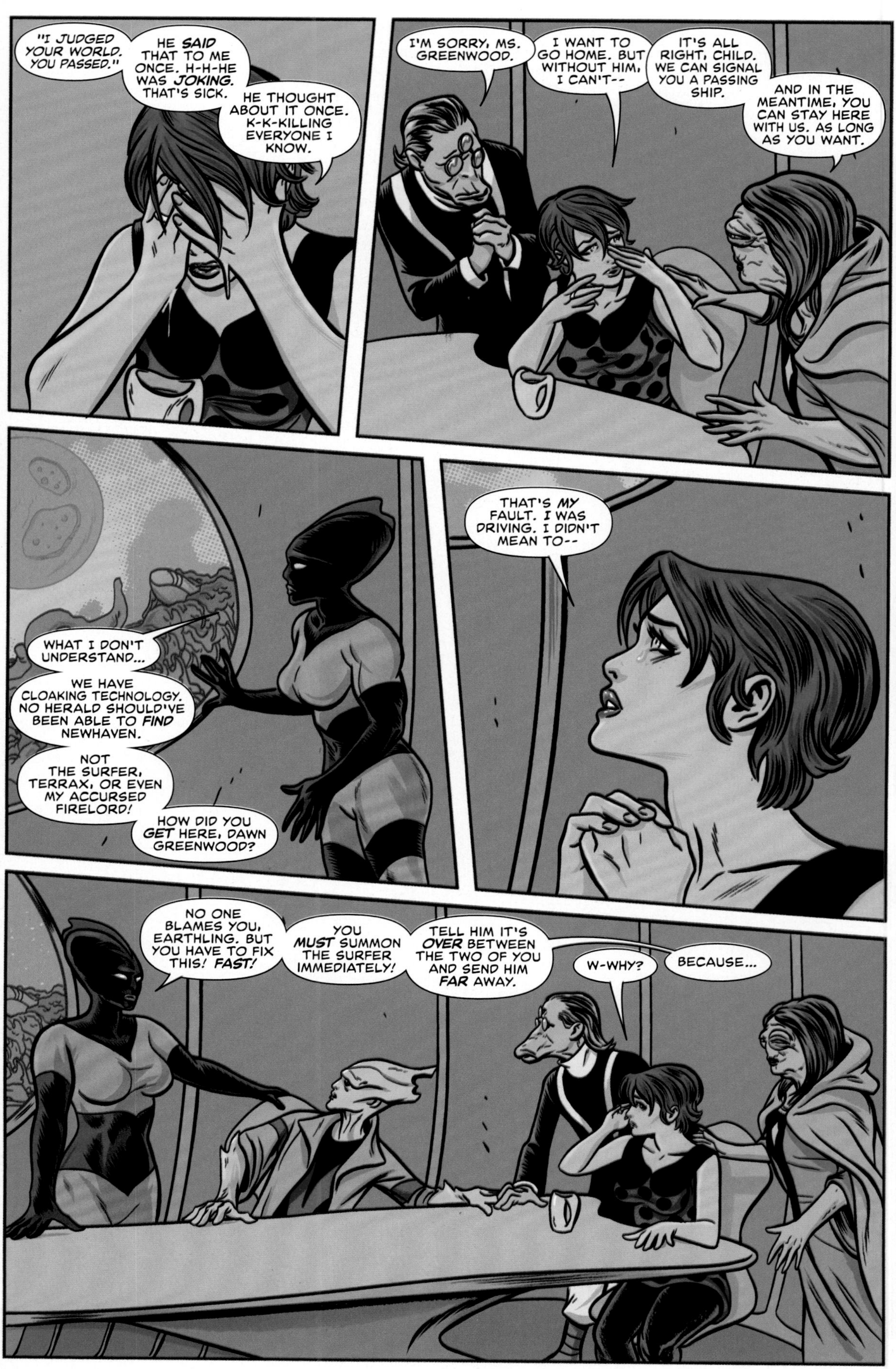
"I JUDGED YOUR WORLD. YOU PASSED."
HE *SAID* THAT TO ME ONCE. H-H-HE WAS *JOKING.* THAT'S SICK.
HE THOUGHT ABOUT IT ONCE. K-K-KILLING EVERYONE I KNOW.
I'M SORRY, MS. GREENWOOD.
I WANT TO GO HOME. BUT WITHOUT HIM, I CAN'T--
IT'S ALL RIGHT, CHILD. WE CAN SIGNAL YOU A PASSING SHIP.
AND IN THE MEANTIME, YOU CAN STAY HERE WITH US. AS LONG AS YOU WANT.
WHAT I DON'T UNDERSTAND...
WE HAVE CLOAKING TECHNOLOGY. NO HERALD SHOULD'VE BEEN ABLE TO *FIND* NEWHAVEN.
NOT THE SURFER, TERRAX, OR EVEN MY ACCURSED FIRELORD!
HOW DID YOU *GET* HERE, DAWN GREENWOOD?
THAT'S *MY* FAULT. *I* WAS DRIVING. I DIDN'T MEAN TO--
NO ONE BLAMES YOU, EARTHLING. BUT YOU HAVE TO FIX THIS! *FAST!*
YOU *MUST* SUMMON THE SURFER IMMEDIATELY!
TELL HIM IT'S *OVER* BETWEEN THE TWO OF YOU AND SEND HIM *FAR* AWAY.
W-WHY?
BECAUSE...

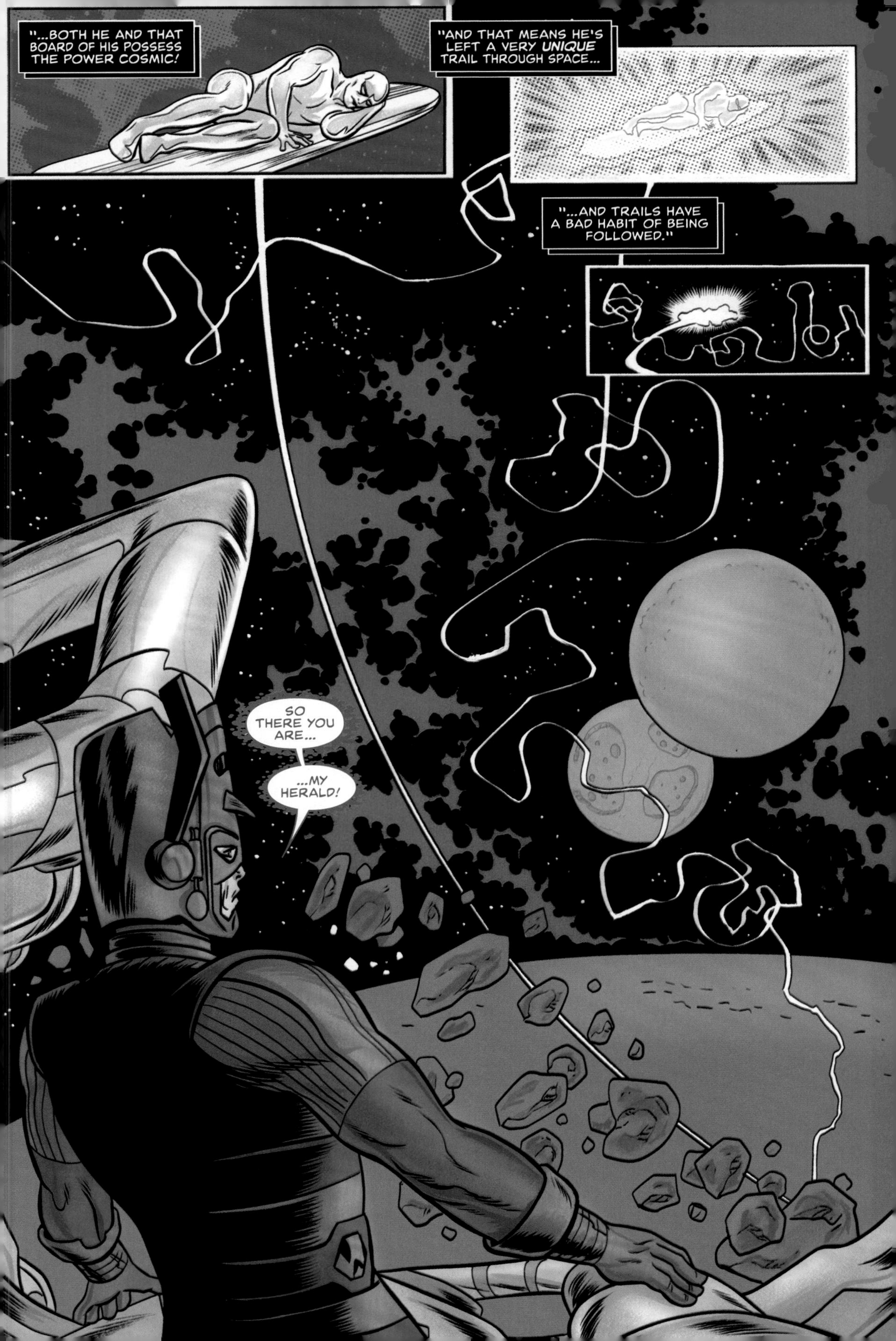
"...BOTH HE AND THAT BOARD OF HIS POSSESS THE POWER COSMIC!
"AND THAT MEANS HE'S LEFT A VERY UNIQUE TRAIL THROUGH SPACE...
"...AND TRAILS HAVE A BAD HABIT OF BEING FOLLOWED."
SO THERE YOU ARE...
...MY HERALD!

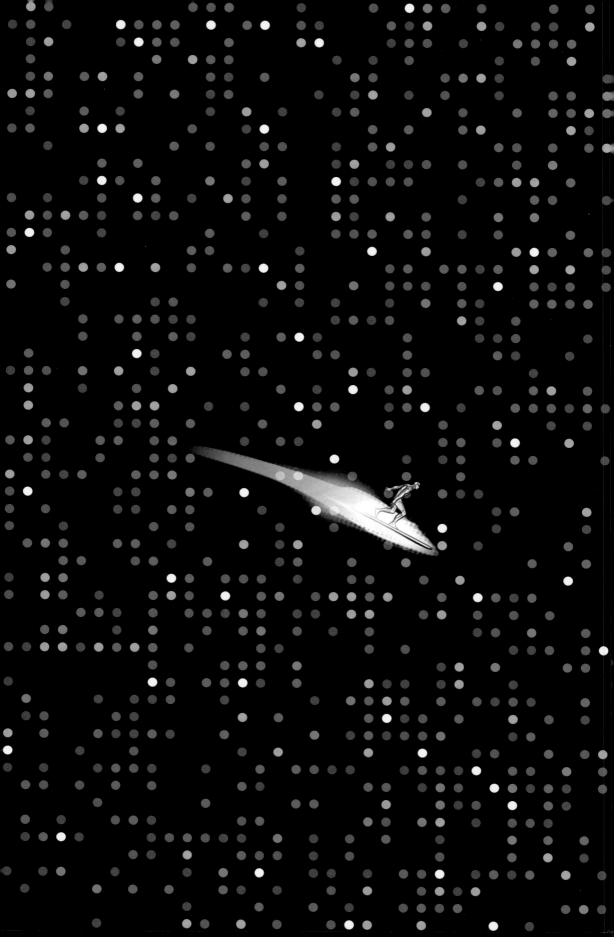

9

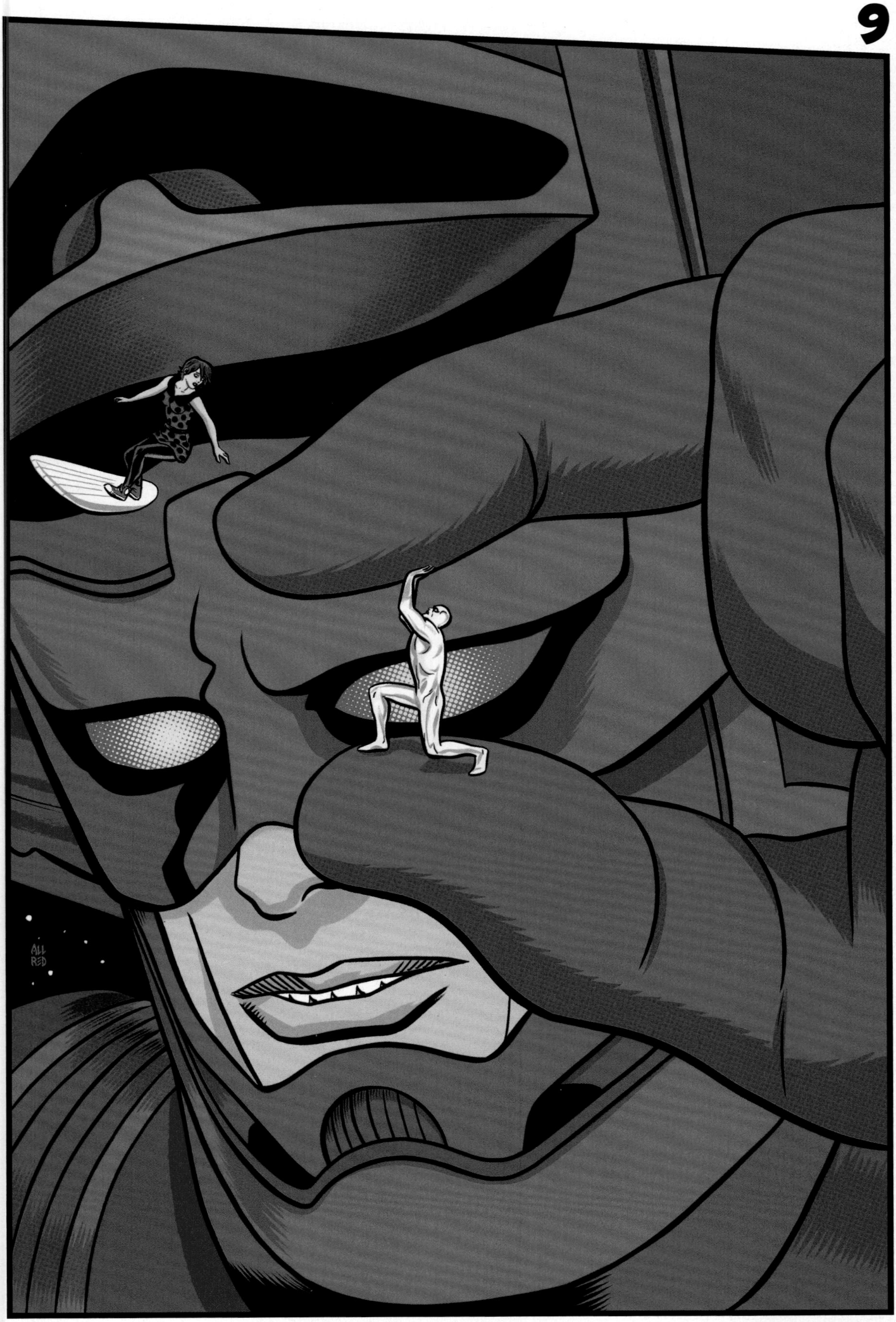
ALL
RED

SLINGSHOT

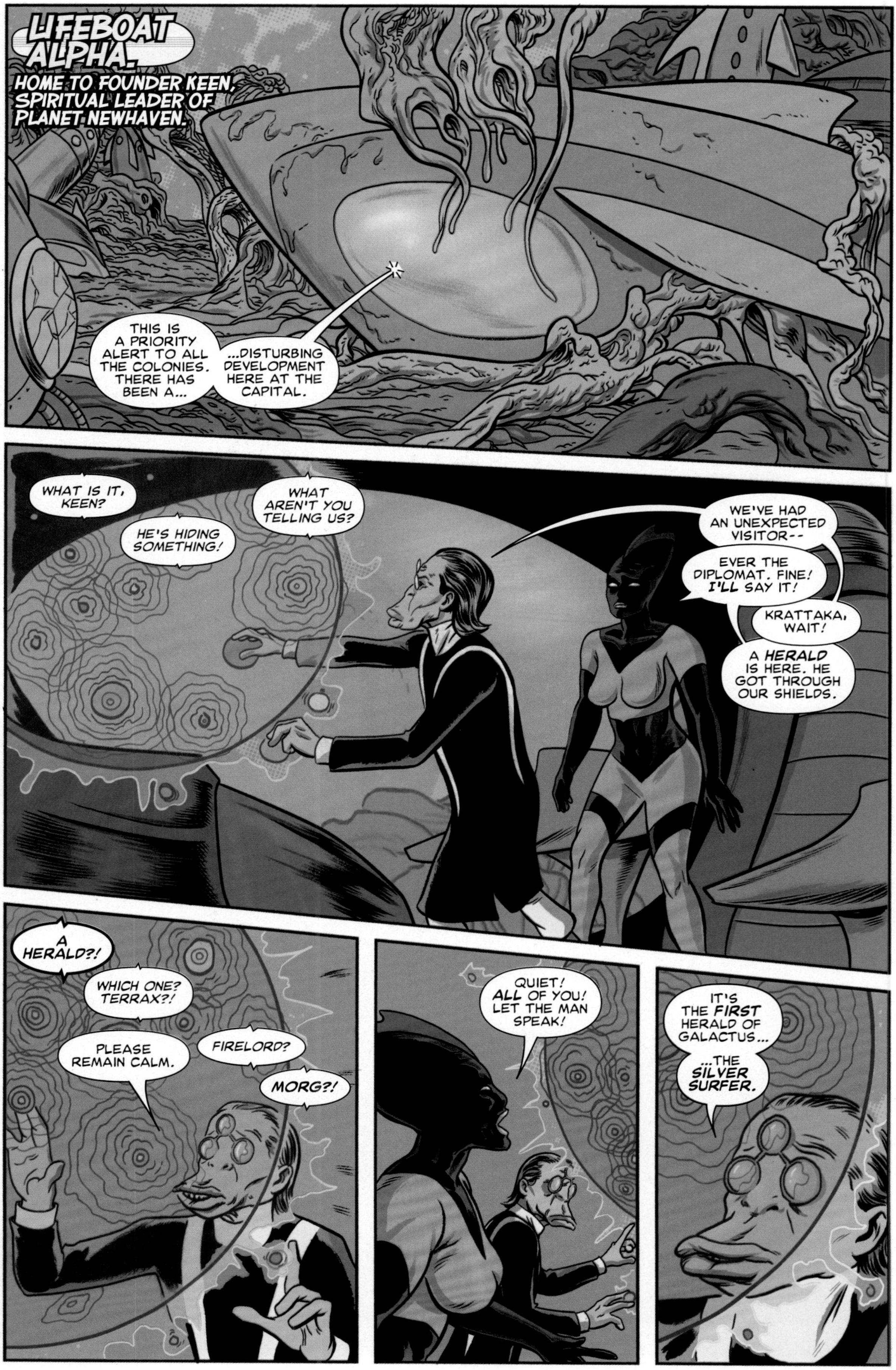
LIFEBOAT ALPHA.
HOME TO FOUNDER KEEN, SPIRITUAL LEADER OF PLANET NEWHAVEN.
THIS IS A PRIORITY ALERT TO ALL THE COLONIES. THERE HAS BEEN A...
...DISTURBING DEVELOPMENT HERE AT THE CAPITAL.
WHAT IS IT, KEEN?
HE'S HIDING SOMETHING!
WHAT AREN'T YOU TELLING US?
WE'VE HAD AN UNEXPECTED VISITOR--
EVER THE DIPLOMAT. FINE! I'LL SAY IT!
KRATTAKA, WAIT!
A HERALD IS HERE. HE GOT THROUGH OUR SHIELDS.
A HERALD?!
WHICH ONE? TERRAX?!
PLEASE REMAIN CALM.
FIRELORD?
MORG?!
QUIET! ALL OF YOU! LET THE MAN SPEAK!
IT'S THE FIRST HERALD OF GALACTUS...
...THE SILVER SURFER.

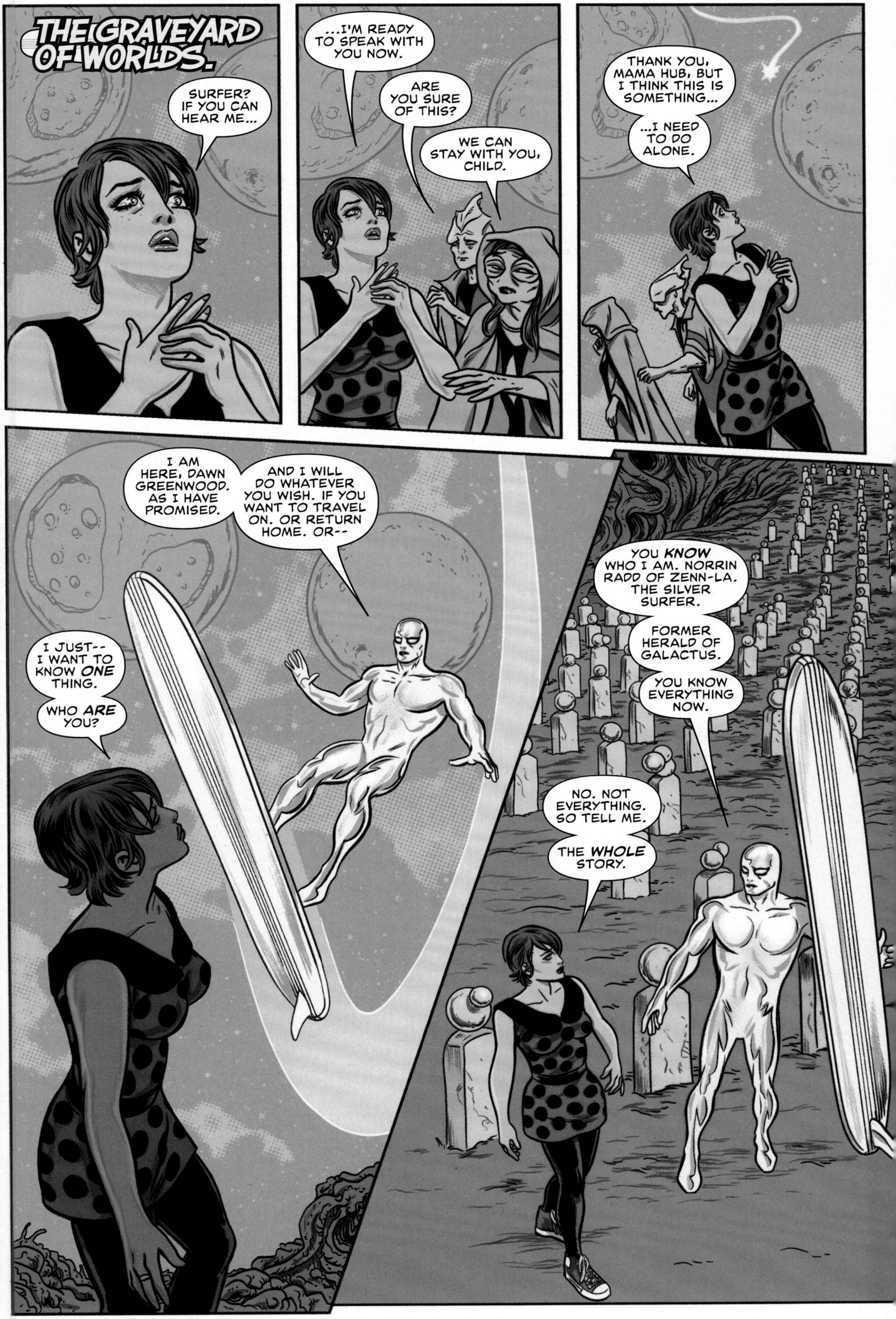
THE GRAVEYARD OF WORLDS.
SURFER? IF YOU CAN HEAR ME...
...I'M READY TO SPEAK WITH YOU NOW.
ARE YOU SURE OF THIS?
WE CAN STAY WITH YOU, CHILD.
THANK YOU, MAMA HUB, BUT I THINK THIS IS SOMETHING...
...I NEED TO DO ALONE.
I AM HERE, DAWN GREENWOOD. AS I HAVE PROMISED.
AND I WILL DO WHATEVER YOU WISH. IF YOU WANT TO TRAVEL ON. OR RETURN HOME. OR--
I JUST-- I WANT TO KNOW ONE THING.
WHO ARE YOU?
YOU KNOW WHO I AM. NORRIN RADD OF ZENN-LA. THE SILVER SURFER.
FORMER HERALD OF GALACTUS.
YOU KNOW EVERYTHING NOW.
NO. NOT EVERYTHING. SO TELL ME.
THE WHOLE STORY.

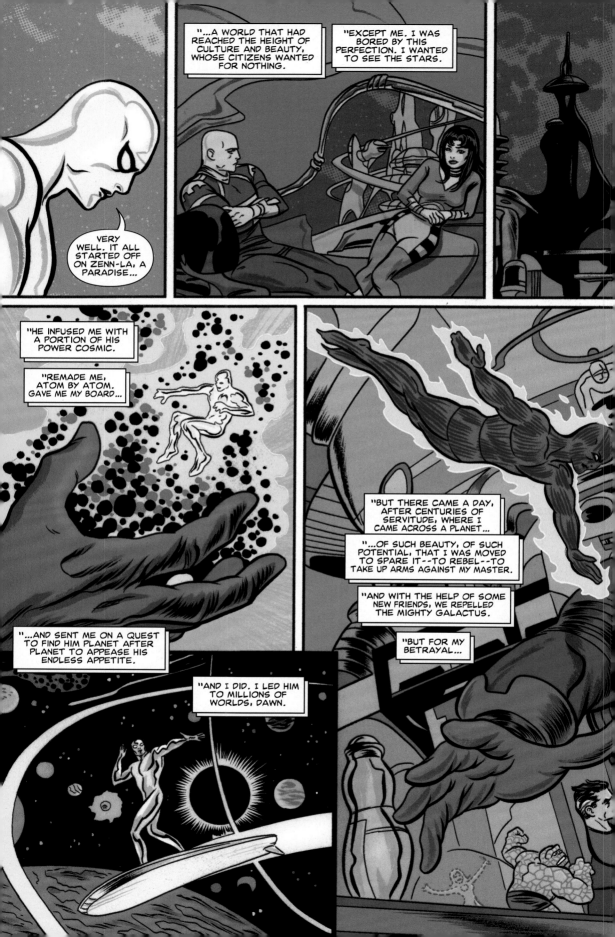

"...A WORLD THAT HAD REACHED THE HEIGHT OF CULTURE AND BEAUTY, WHOSE CITIZENS WANTED FOR NOTHING.

"EXCEPT ME. I WAS BORED BY THIS PERFECTION. I WANTED TO SEE THE STARS.

VERY WELL. IT ALL STARTED OFF ON ZENN-LA, A PARADISE...

"HE INFUSED ME WITH A PORTION OF HIS POWER COSMIC.

"REMADE ME, ATOM BY ATOM. GAVE ME MY BOARD...

"...AND SENT ME ON A QUEST TO FIND HIM PLANET AFTER PLANET TO APPEASE HIS ENDLESS APPETITE.

"AND I DID. I LED HIM TO MILLIONS OF WORLDS, DAWN.

"BUT THERE CAME A DAY, AFTER CENTURIES OF SERVITUDE, WHERE I CAME ACROSS A PLANET...

"...OF SUCH BEAUTY, OF SUCH POTENTIAL, THAT I WAS MOVED TO SPARE IT--TO REBEL--TO TAKE UP ARMS AGAINST MY MASTER.

"AND WITH THE HELP OF SOME NEW FRIENDS, WE REPELLED THE MIGHTY GALACTUS.

"BUT FOR MY BETRAYAL...

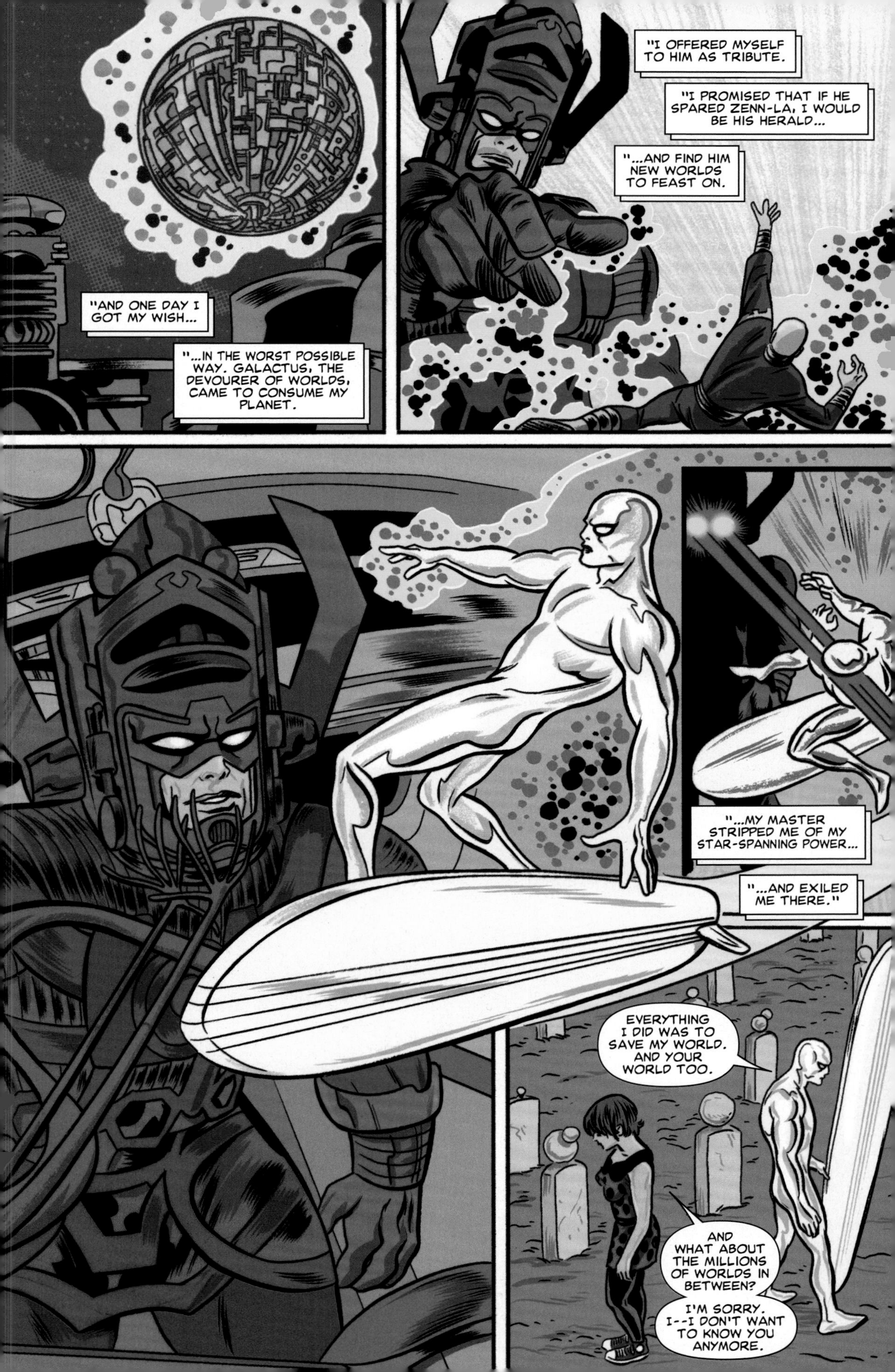
"AND ONE DAY I GOT MY WISH...
"...IN THE WORST POSSIBLE WAY. GALACTUS, THE DEVOURER OF WORLDS, CAME TO CONSUME MY PLANET.
"I OFFERED MYSELF TO HIM AS TRIBUTE.
"I PROMISED THAT IF HE SPARED ZENN-LA, I WOULD BE HIS HERALD...
"...AND FIND HIM NEW WORLDS TO FEAST ON.
"...MY MASTER STRIPPED ME OF MY STAR-SPANNING POWER...
"...AND EXILED ME THERE."
EVERYTHING I DID WAS TO SAVE MY WORLD. AND YOUR WORLD TOO.
AND WHAT ABOUT THE MILLIONS OF WORLDS IN BETWEEN?
I'M SORRY. I--I DON'T WANT TO KNOW YOU ANYMORE.

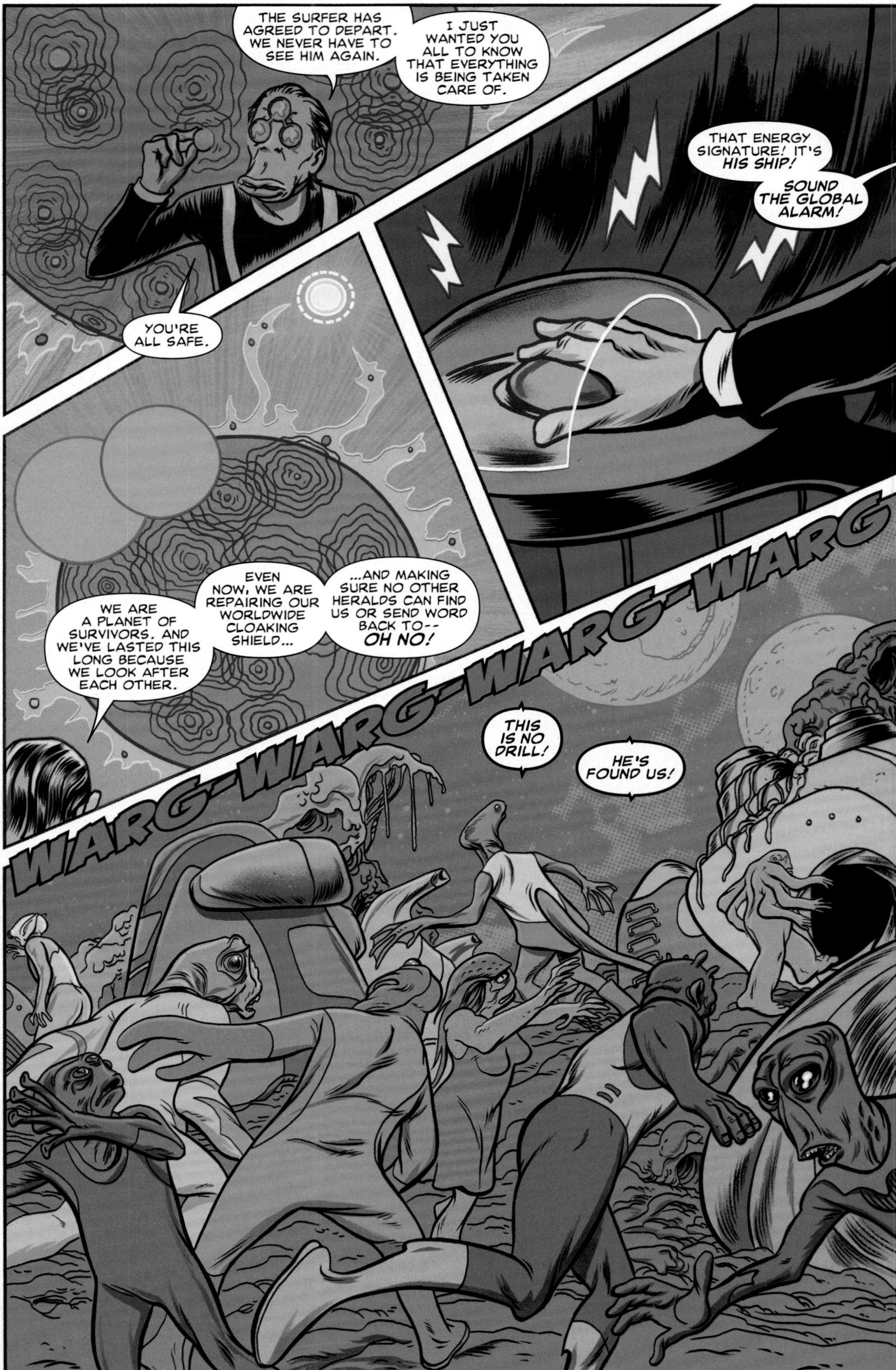
THE SURFER HAS AGREED TO DEPART. WE NEVER HAVE TO SEE HIM AGAIN.
I JUST WANTED YOU ALL TO KNOW THAT EVERYTHING IS BEING TAKEN CARE OF.
YOU'RE ALL SAFE.
WE ARE A PLANET OF SURVIVORS. AND WE'VE LASTED THIS LONG BECAUSE WE LOOK AFTER EACH OTHER.
EVEN NOW, WE ARE REPAIRING OUR WORLDWIDE CLOAKING SHIELD...
...AND MAKING SURE NO OTHER HERALDS CAN FIND US OR SEND WORD BACK TO-- OH NO!
THAT ENERGY SIGNATURE! IT'S HIS SHIP!
SOUND THE GLOBAL ALARM!
WARG-WARG-WARG-WARG-WARG
THIS IS NO DRILL!
HE'S FOUND US!

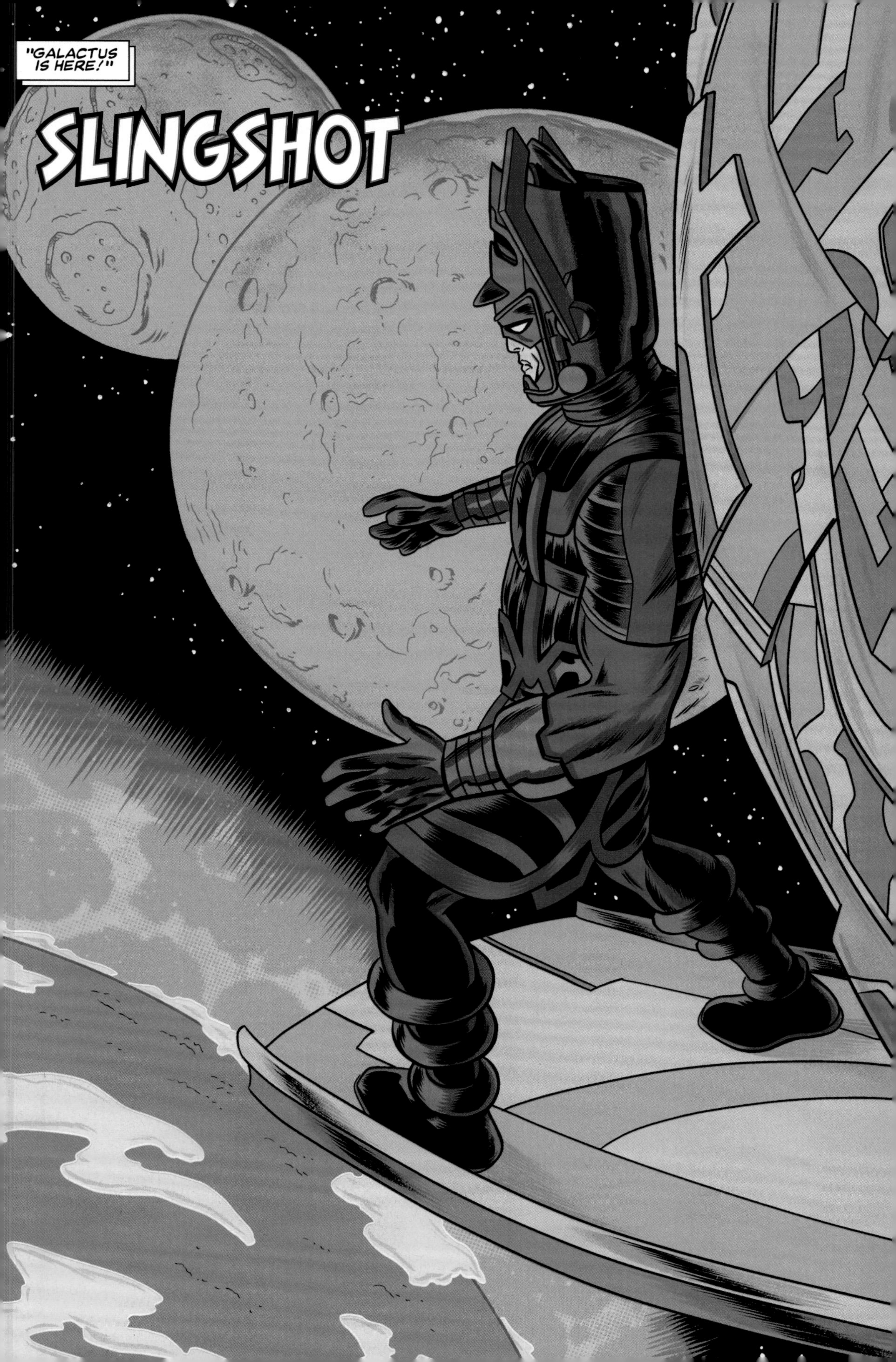
"GALACTUS IS HERE!"
SLINGSHOT

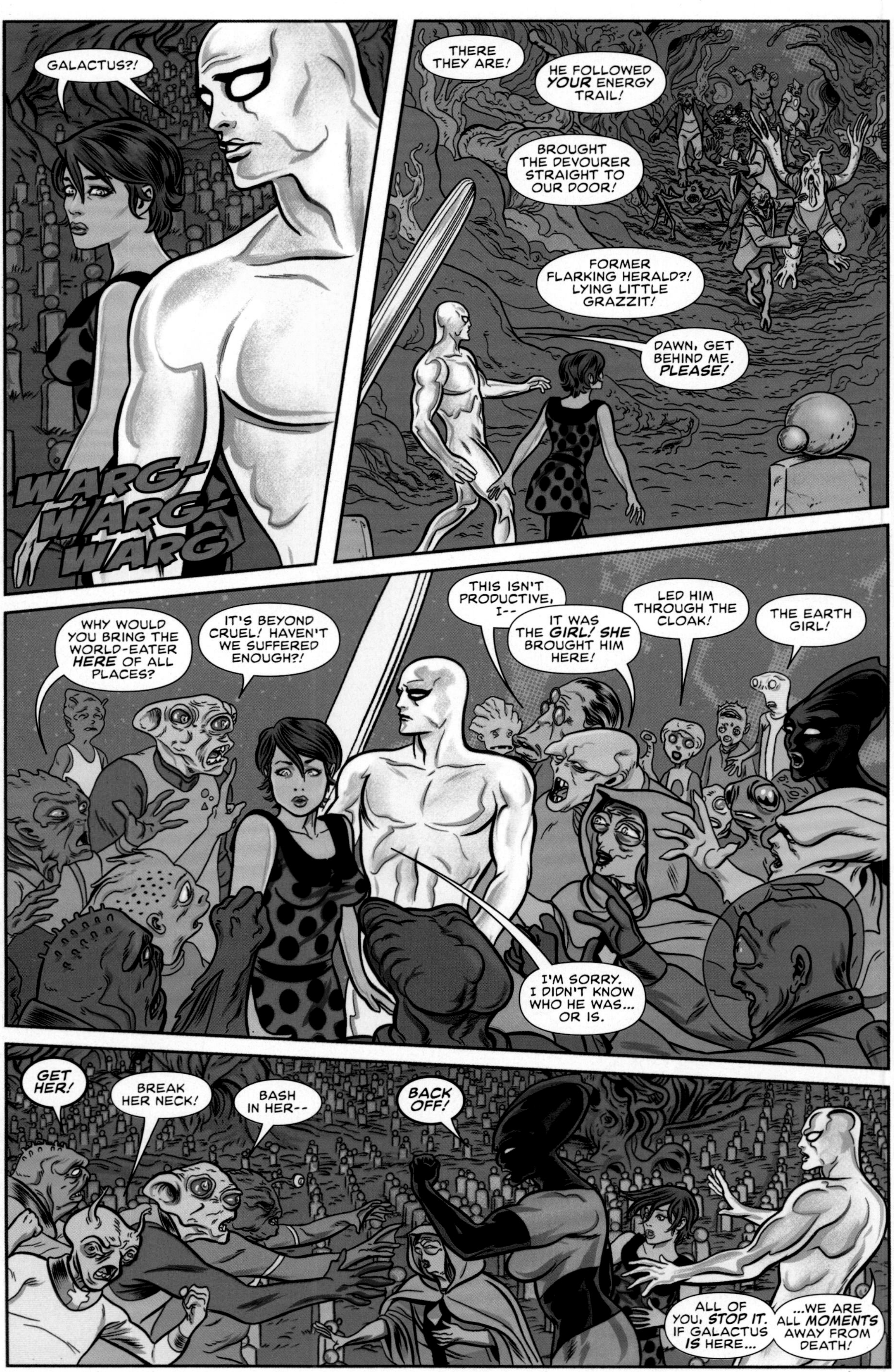
GALACTUS?!
WARG-WARG-WARG
THERE THEY ARE!
HE FOLLOWED YOUR ENERGY TRAIL!
BROUGHT THE DEVOURER STRAIGHT TO OUR DOOR!
FORMER FLARKING HERALD?! LYING LITTLE GRAZZIT!
DAWN, GET BEHIND ME. PLEASE!
WHY WOULD YOU BRING THE WORLD-EATER HERE OF ALL PLACES?
IT'S BEYOND CRUEL! HAVEN'T WE SUFFERED ENOUGH?!
THIS ISN'T PRODUCTIVE, I--
IT WAS THE GIRL! SHE BROUGHT HIM HERE!
LED HIM THROUGH THE CLOAK!
THE EARTH GIRL!
I'M SORRY. I DIDN'T KNOW WHO HE WAS... OR IS.
GET HER!
BREAK HER NECK!
BASH IN HER--
BACK OFF!
ALL OF YOU, STOP IT. IF GALACTUS IS HERE...
...WE ARE ALL MOMENTS AWAY FROM DEATH!

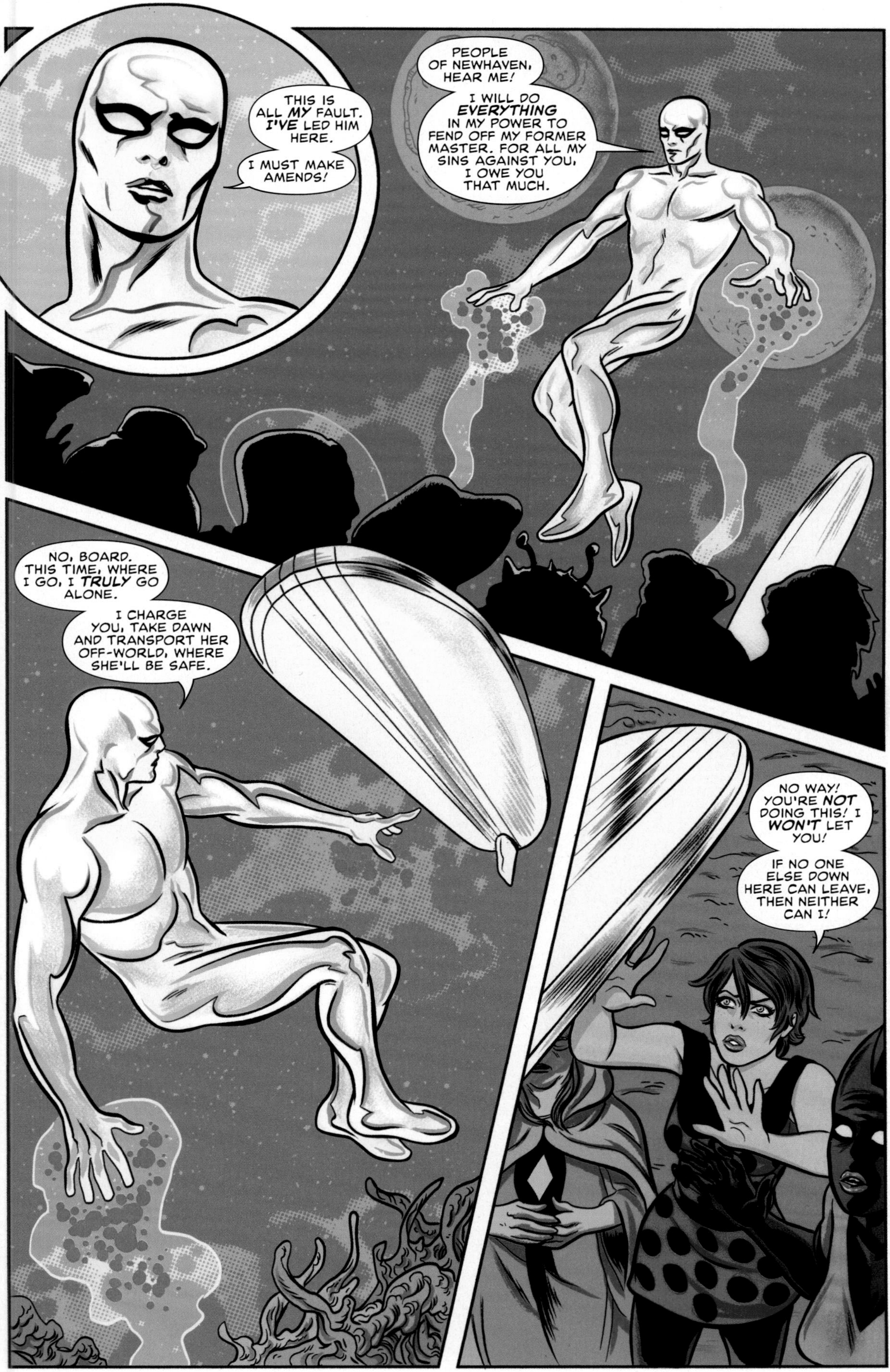
THIS IS ALL *MY* FAULT. *I'VE* LED HIM HERE.
I MUST MAKE AMENDS!
PEOPLE OF NEWHAVEN, HEAR ME!
I WILL DO *EVERYTHING* IN MY POWER TO FEND OFF MY FORMER MASTER. FOR ALL MY SINS AGAINST YOU, I OWE YOU THAT MUCH.
NO, BOARD. THIS TIME, WHERE I GO, I *TRULY* GO ALONE.
I CHARGE YOU, TAKE DAWN AND TRANSPORT HER OFF-WORLD, WHERE SHE'LL BE SAFE.
NO WAY! YOU'RE *NOT* DOING THIS! I *WON'T* LET YOU!
IF NO ONE ELSE DOWN HERE CAN LEAVE, THEN NEITHER CAN I!

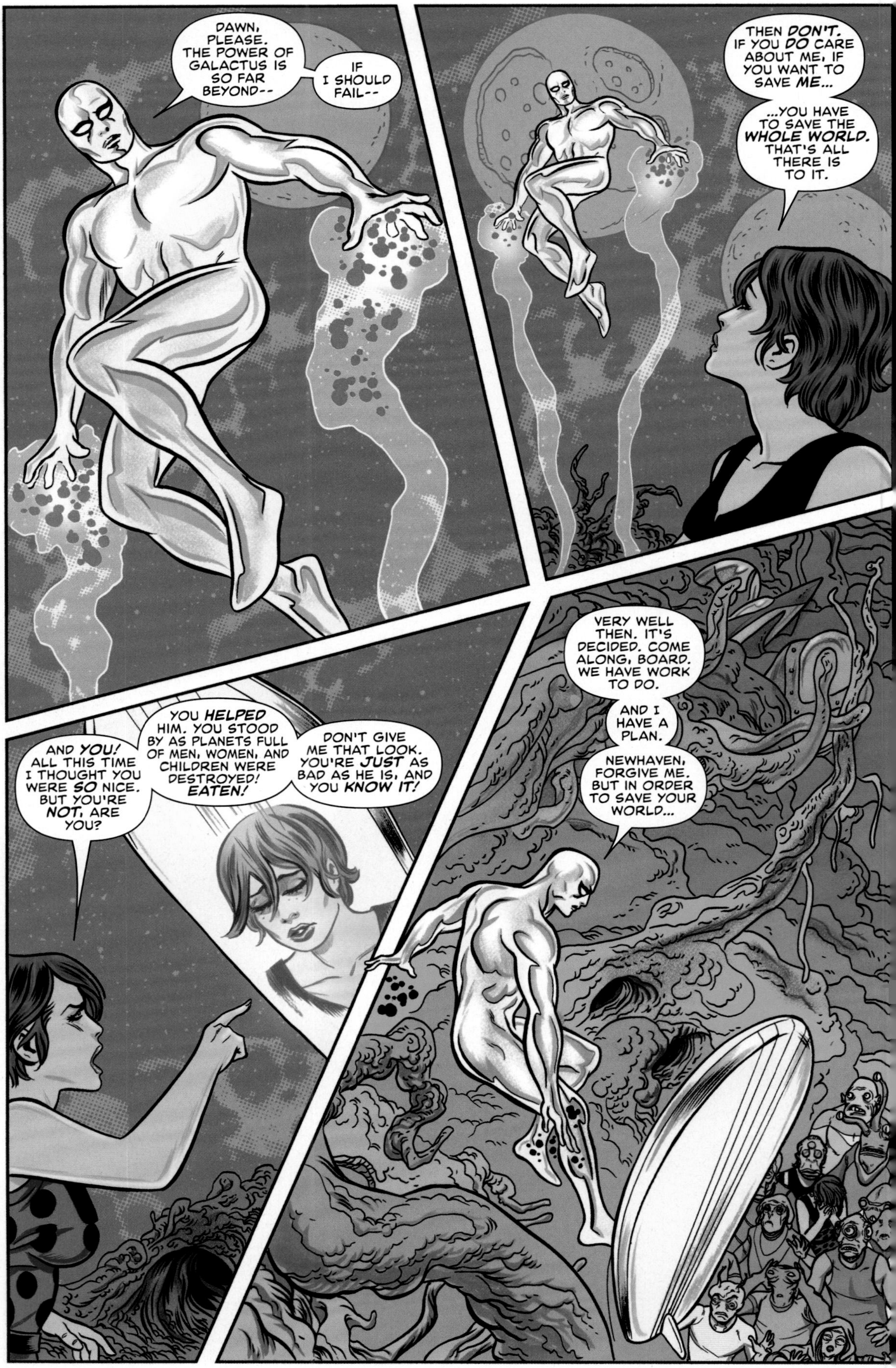

DAWN, PLEASE. THE POWER OF GALACTUS IS SO FAR BEYOND--
IF I SHOULD FAIL--
THEN DON'T. IF YOU DO CARE ABOUT ME, IF YOU WANT TO SAVE ME...
...YOU HAVE TO SAVE THE WHOLE WORLD. THAT'S ALL THERE IS TO IT.
AND YOU! ALL THIS TIME I THOUGHT YOU WERE SO NICE. BUT YOU'RE NOT, ARE YOU?
YOU HELPED HIM. YOU STOOD BY AS PLANETS FULL OF MEN, WOMEN, AND CHILDREN WERE DESTROYED! EATEN!
DON'T GIVE ME THAT LOOK. YOU'RE JUST AS BAD AS HE IS, AND YOU KNOW IT!
VERY WELL THEN. IT'S DECIDED. COME ALONG, BOARD. WE HAVE WORK TO DO.
AND I HAVE A PLAN.
NEWHAVEN, FORGIVE ME. BUT IN ORDER TO SAVE YOUR WORLD...

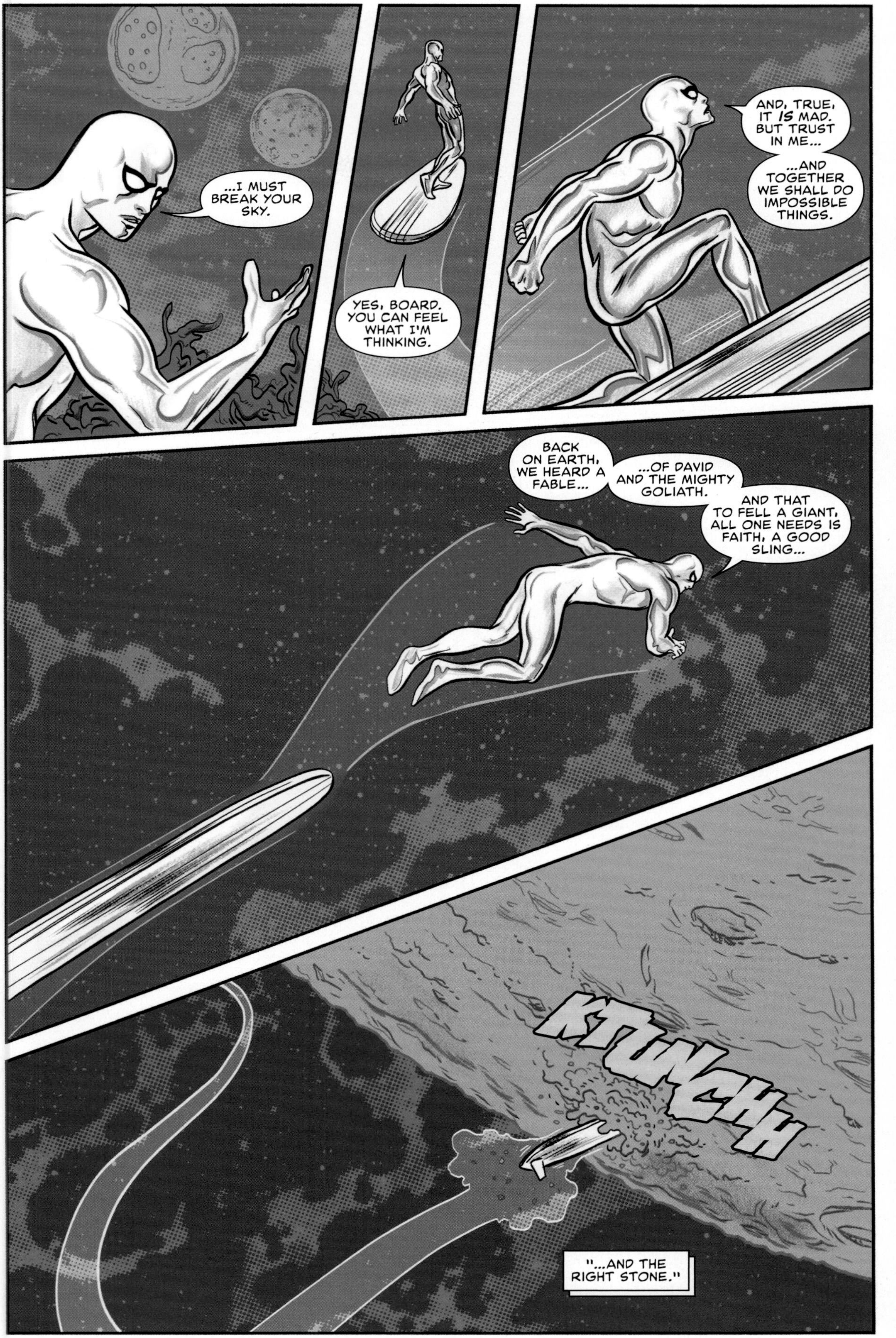
...I MUST BREAK YOUR SKY.
YES, BOARD. YOU CAN FEEL WHAT I'M THINKING.
AND, TRUE, IT IS MAD. BUT TRUST IN ME...
...AND TOGETHER WE SHALL DO IMPOSSIBLE THINGS.
BACK ON EARTH, WE HEARD A FABLE...
...OF DAVID AND THE MIGHTY GOLIATH.
AND THAT TO FELL A GIANT, ALL ONE NEEDS IS FAITH, A GOOD SLING...
KTUNCHH
"...AND THE RIGHT STONE."

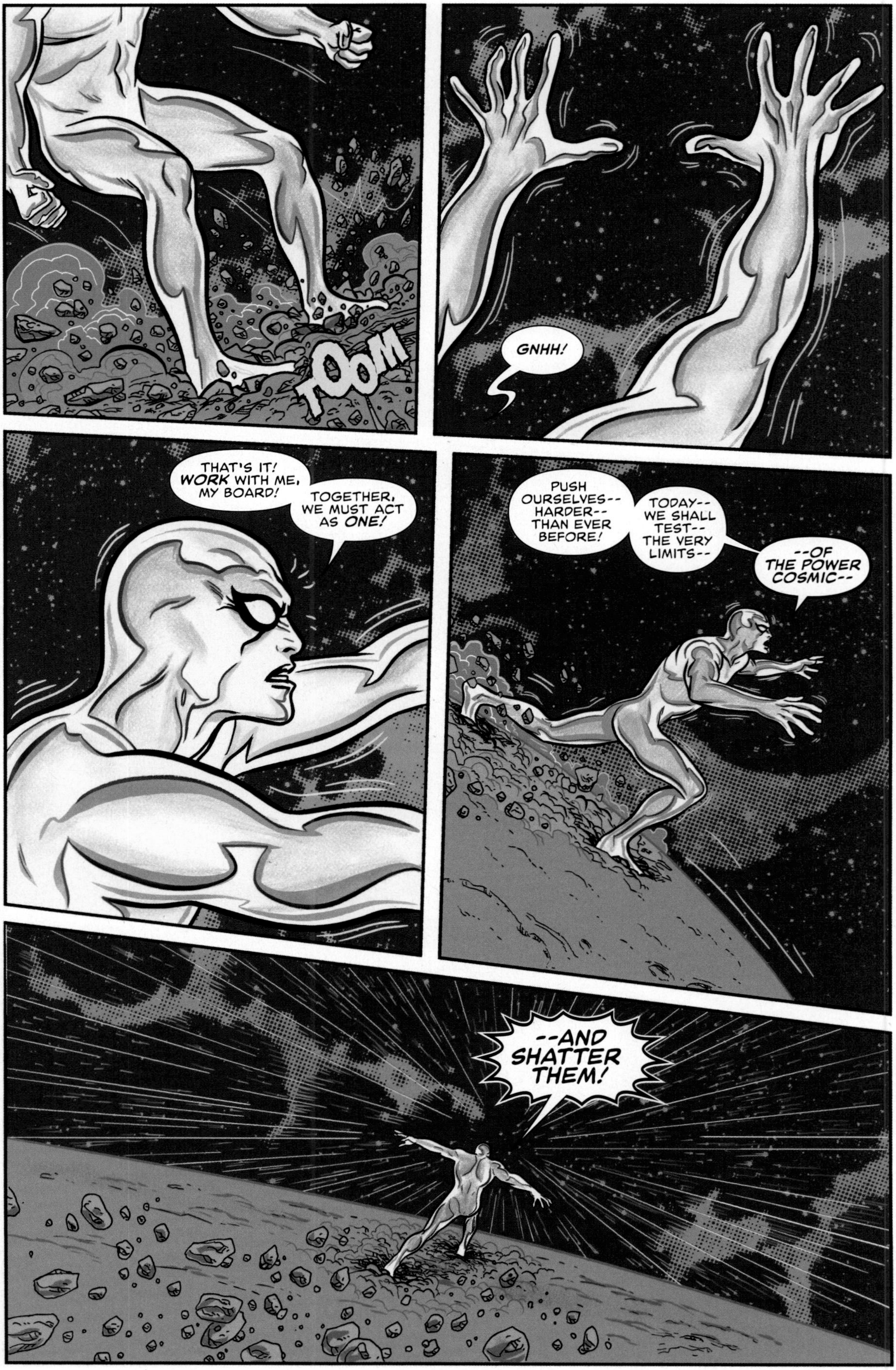
TOOM
GNHH!
THAT'S IT! WORK WITH ME, MY BOARD!
TOGETHER, WE MUST ACT AS ONE!
PUSH OURSELVES--HARDER--THAN EVER BEFORE!
TODAY--WE SHALL TEST--THE VERY LIMITS--
--OF THE POWER COSMIC--
--AND SHATTER THEM!

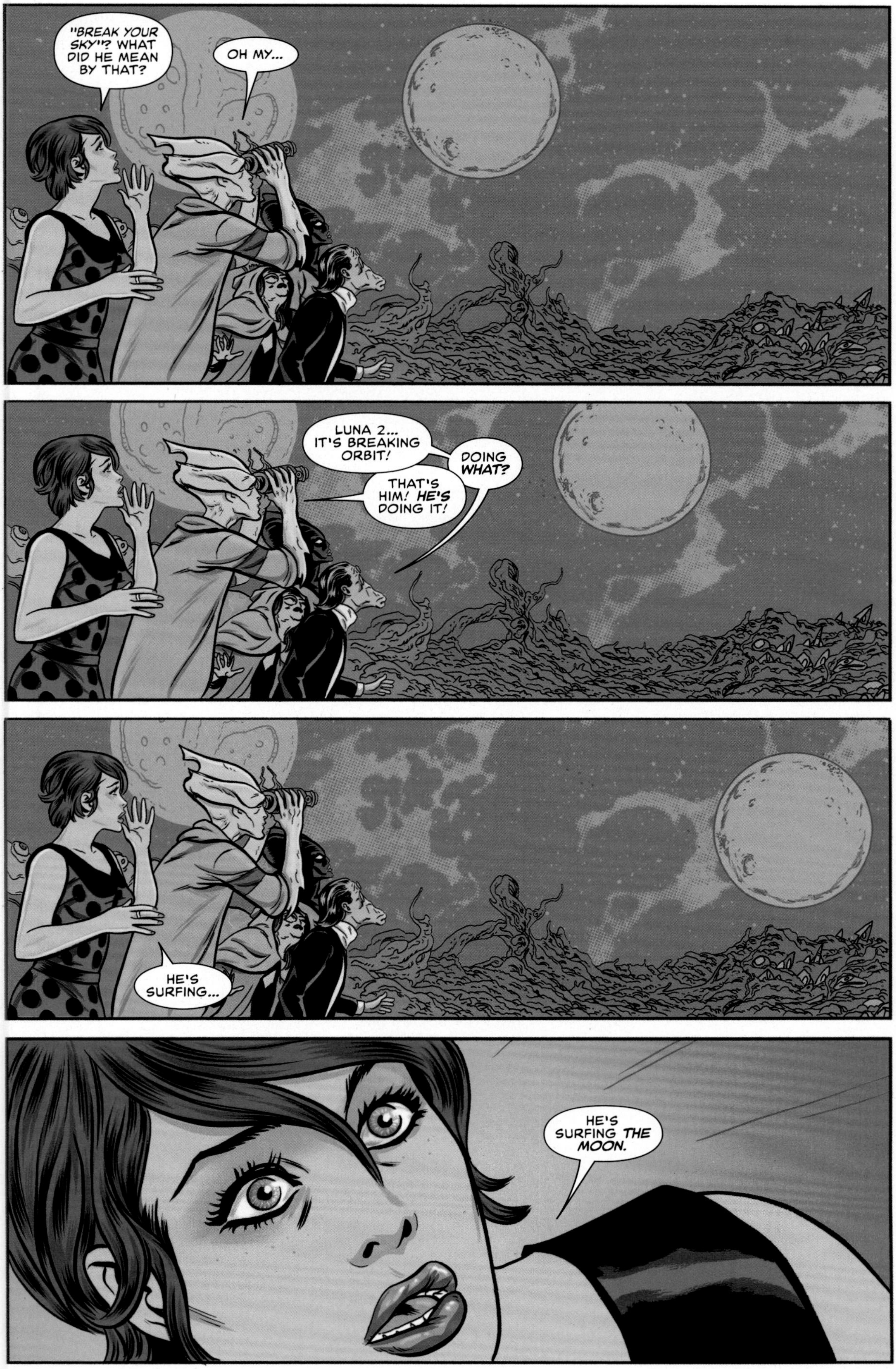
"BREAK YOUR SKY"? WHAT DID HE MEAN BY THAT?
OH MY...
LUNA 2... IT'S BREAKING ORBIT!
DOING *WHAT?*
THAT'S HIM! *HE'S* DOING IT!
HE'S SURFING...
HE'S SURFING *THE MOON.*

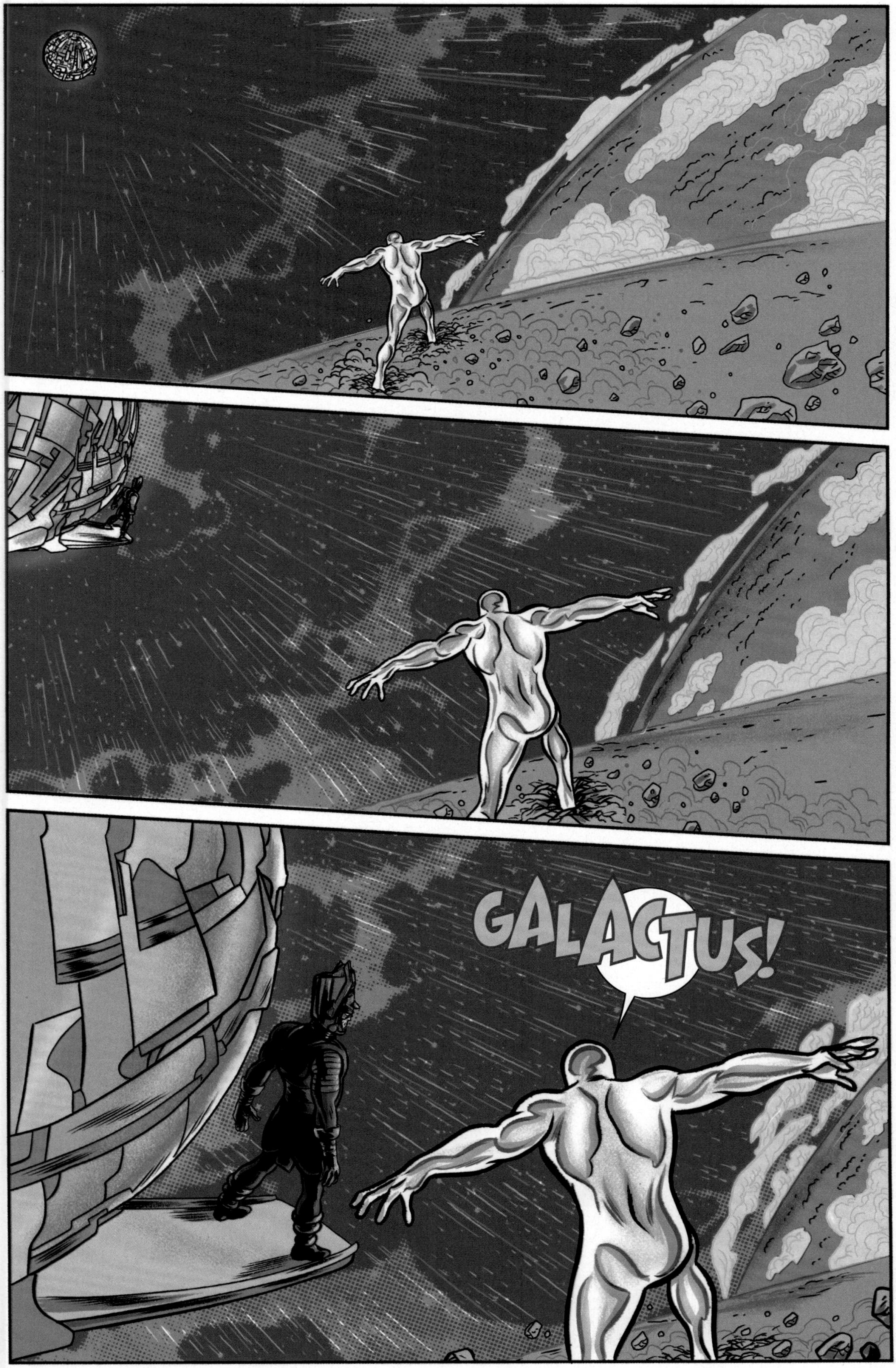
GALACTUS!

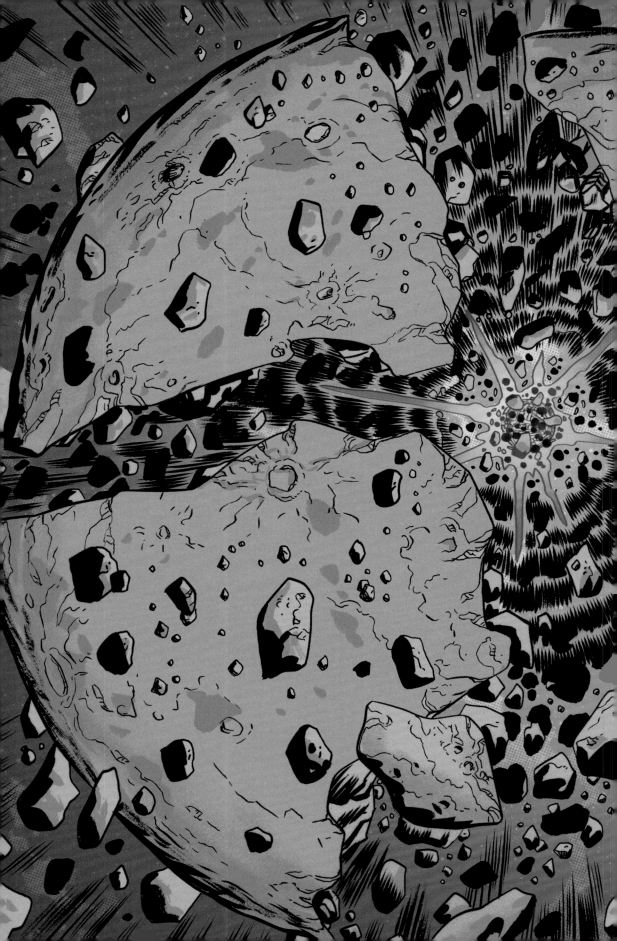

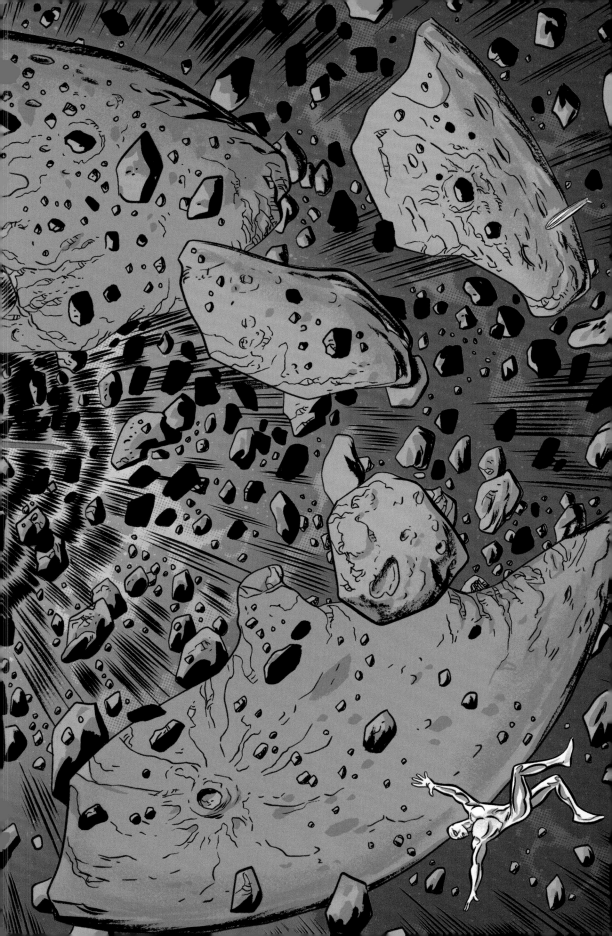

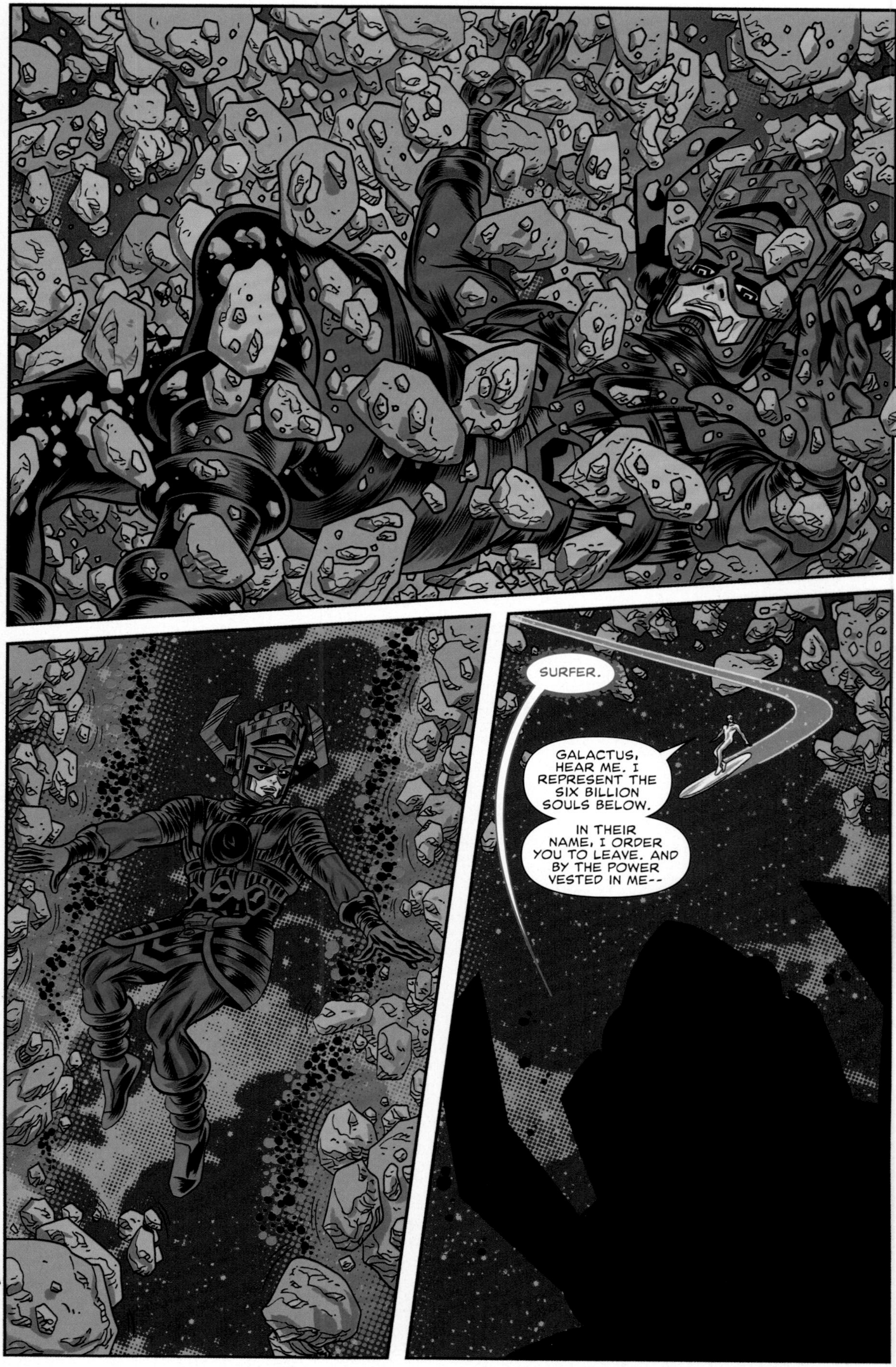

SURFER.
GALACTUS, HEAR ME. I REPRESENT THE SIX BILLION SOULS BELOW.
IN THEIR NAME, I ORDER YOU TO LEAVE. AND BY THE POWER VESTED IN ME--

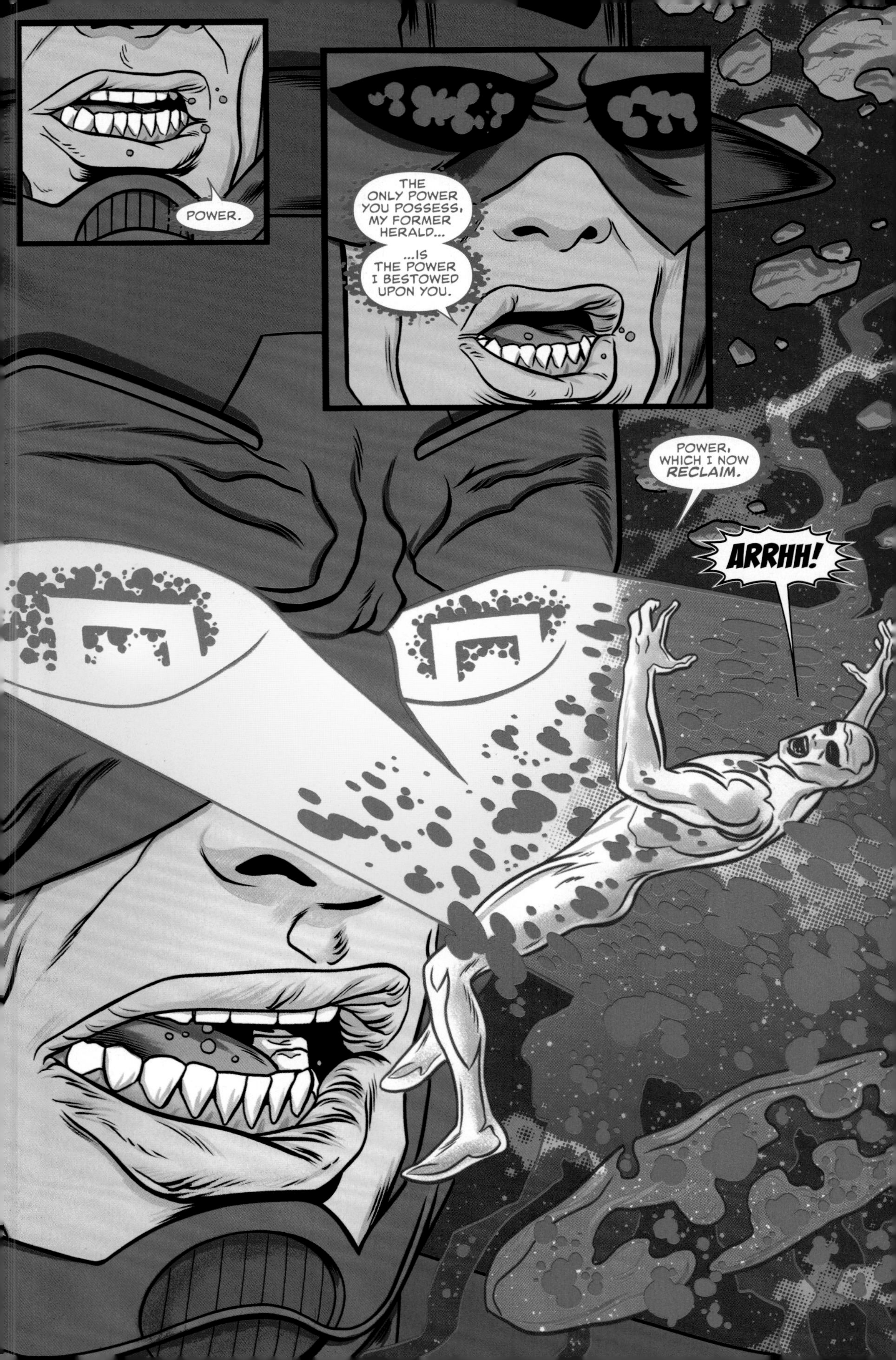
POWER.
THE ONLY POWER YOU POSSESS, MY FORMER HERALD...
...IS THE POWER I BESTOWED UPON YOU.
POWER, WHICH I NOW RECLAIM.
ARRHH!

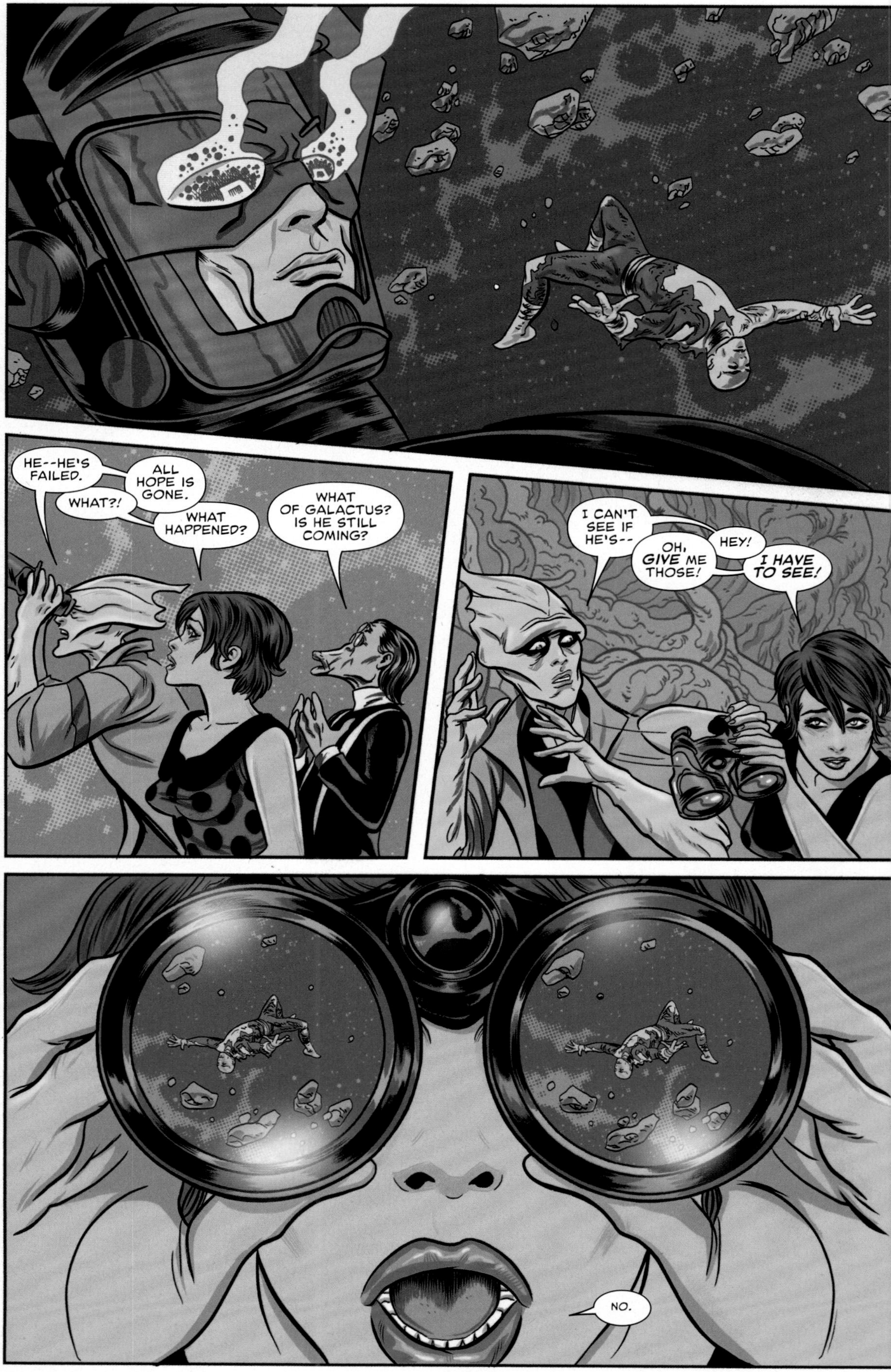

HE--HE'S FAILED.
ALL HOPE IS GONE.
WHAT?!
WHAT HAPPENED?
WHAT OF GALACTUS? IS HE STILL COMING?
I CAN'T SEE IF HE'S--
OH, GIVE ME THOSE!
HEY!
I HAVE TO SEE!
NO.

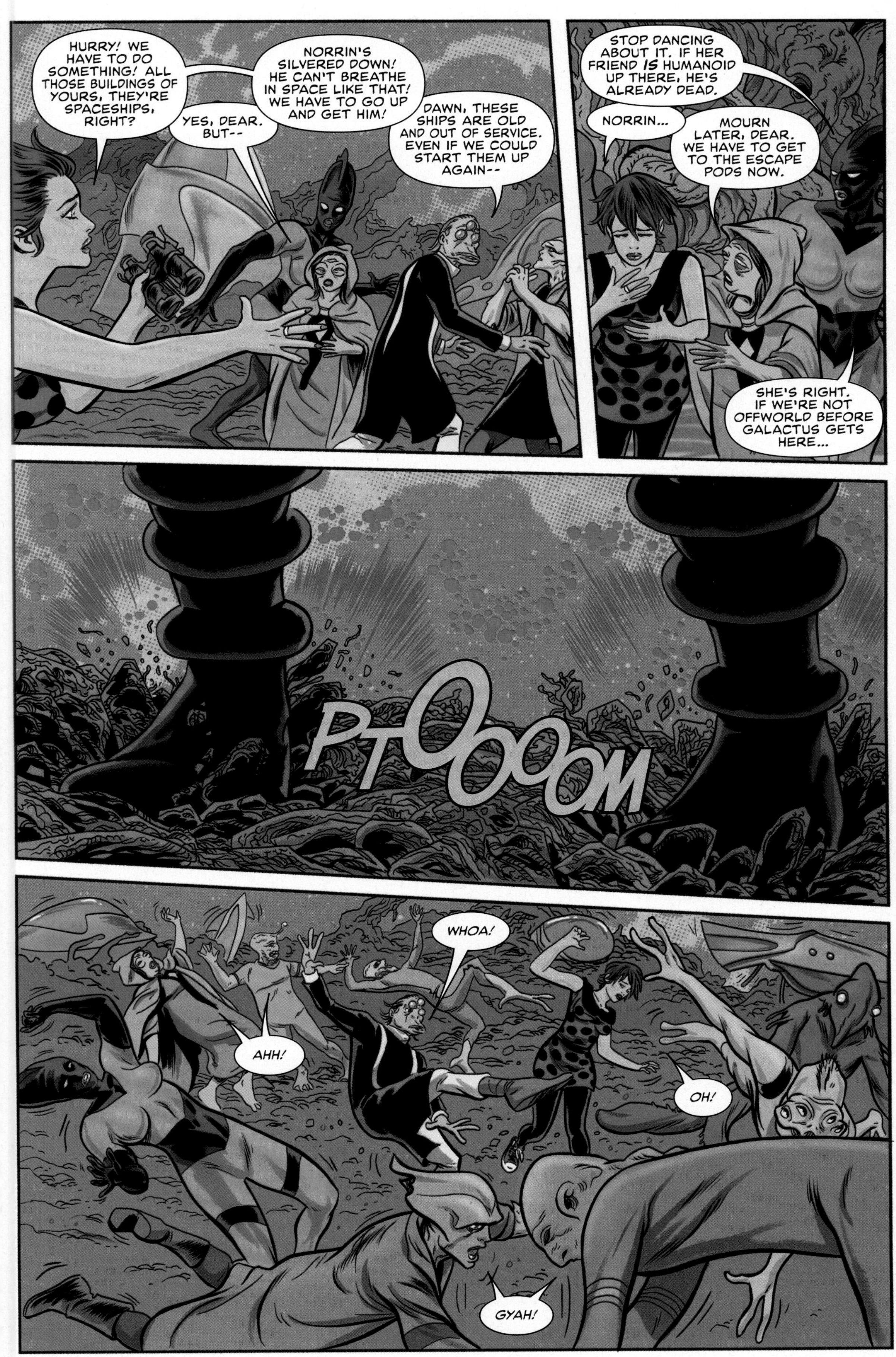

HURRY! WE HAVE TO DO SOMETHING! ALL THOSE BUILDINGS OF YOURS, THEY'RE SPACESHIPS, RIGHT?
YES, DEAR. BUT--
NORRIN'S SILVERED DOWN! HE CAN'T BREATHE IN SPACE LIKE THAT! WE HAVE TO GO UP AND GET HIM!
DAWN, THESE SHIPS ARE OLD AND OUT OF SERVICE. EVEN IF WE COULD START THEM UP AGAIN--
STOP DANCING ABOUT IT. IF HER FRIEND IS HUMANOID UP THERE, HE'S ALREADY DEAD.
NORRIN...
MOURN LATER, DEAR. WE HAVE TO GET TO THE ESCAPE PODS NOW.
SHE'S RIGHT. IF WE'RE NOT OFFWORLD BEFORE GALACTUS GETS HERE...
PTOOOOOM
WHOA!
AHH!
OH!
GYAH!

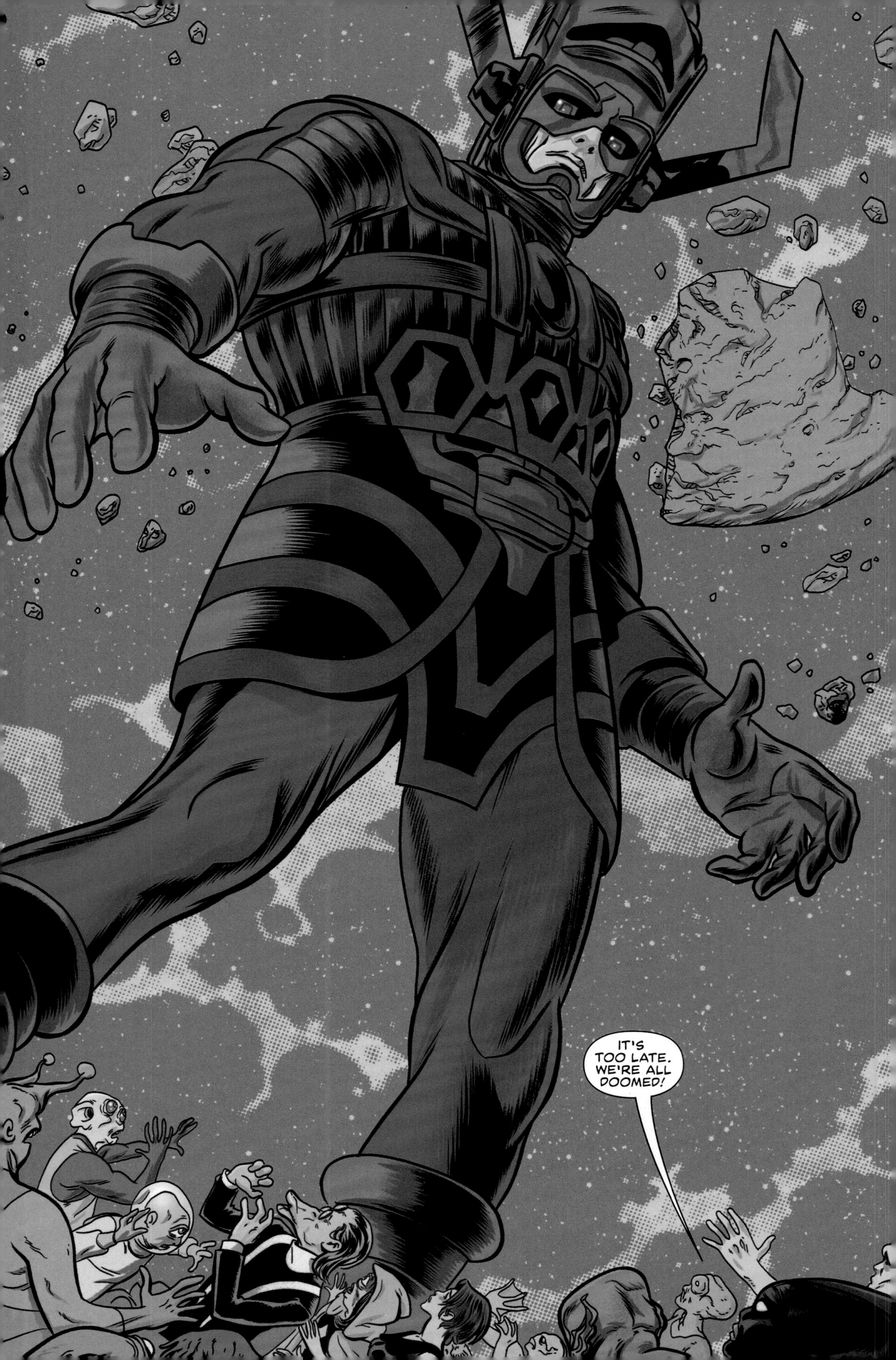
IT'S TOO LATE. WE'RE ALL DOOMED!

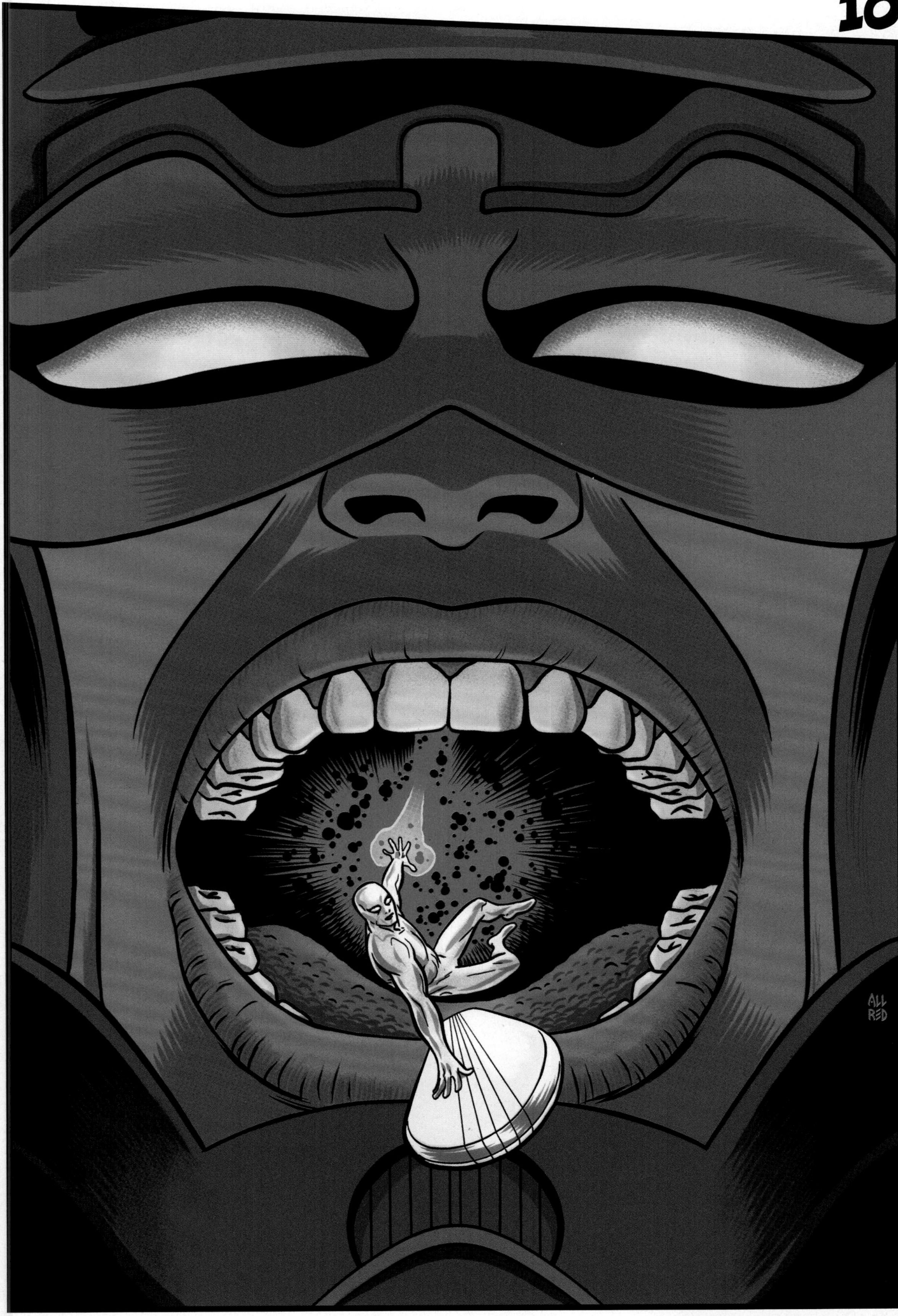
ALL
RED

SMALL SACRIFICE

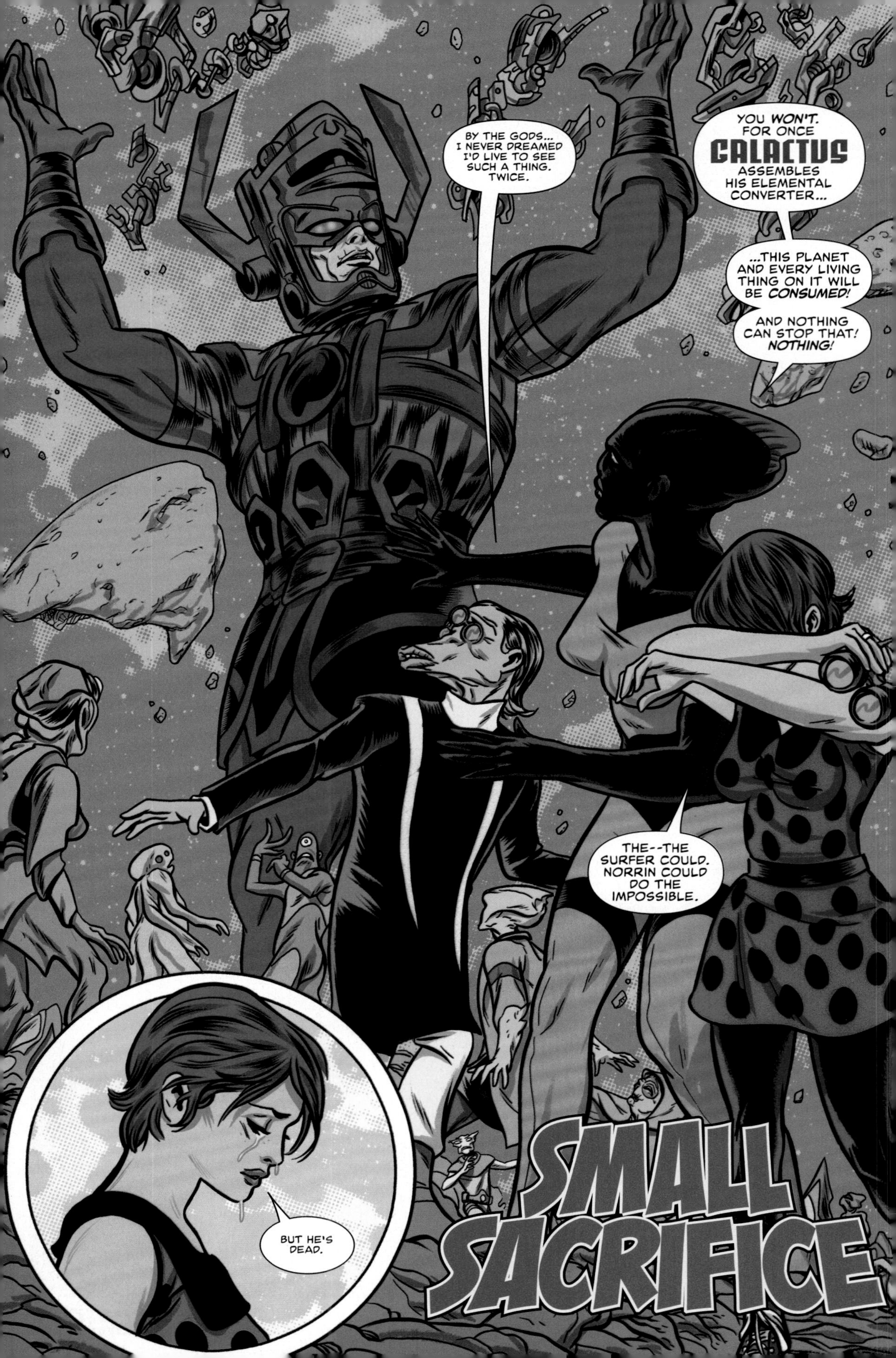
BY THE GODS... I NEVER DREAMED I'D LIVE TO SEE SUCH A THING. TWICE.
YOU WON'T. FOR ONCE GALACTUS ASSEMBLES HIS ELEMENTAL CONVERTER...
...THIS PLANET AND EVERY LIVING THING ON IT WILL BE CONSUMED!
AND NOTHING CAN STOP THAT! NOTHING!
THE--THE SURFER COULD. NORRIN COULD DO THE IMPOSSIBLE.
BUT HE'S DEAD.
SMALL SACRIFICE

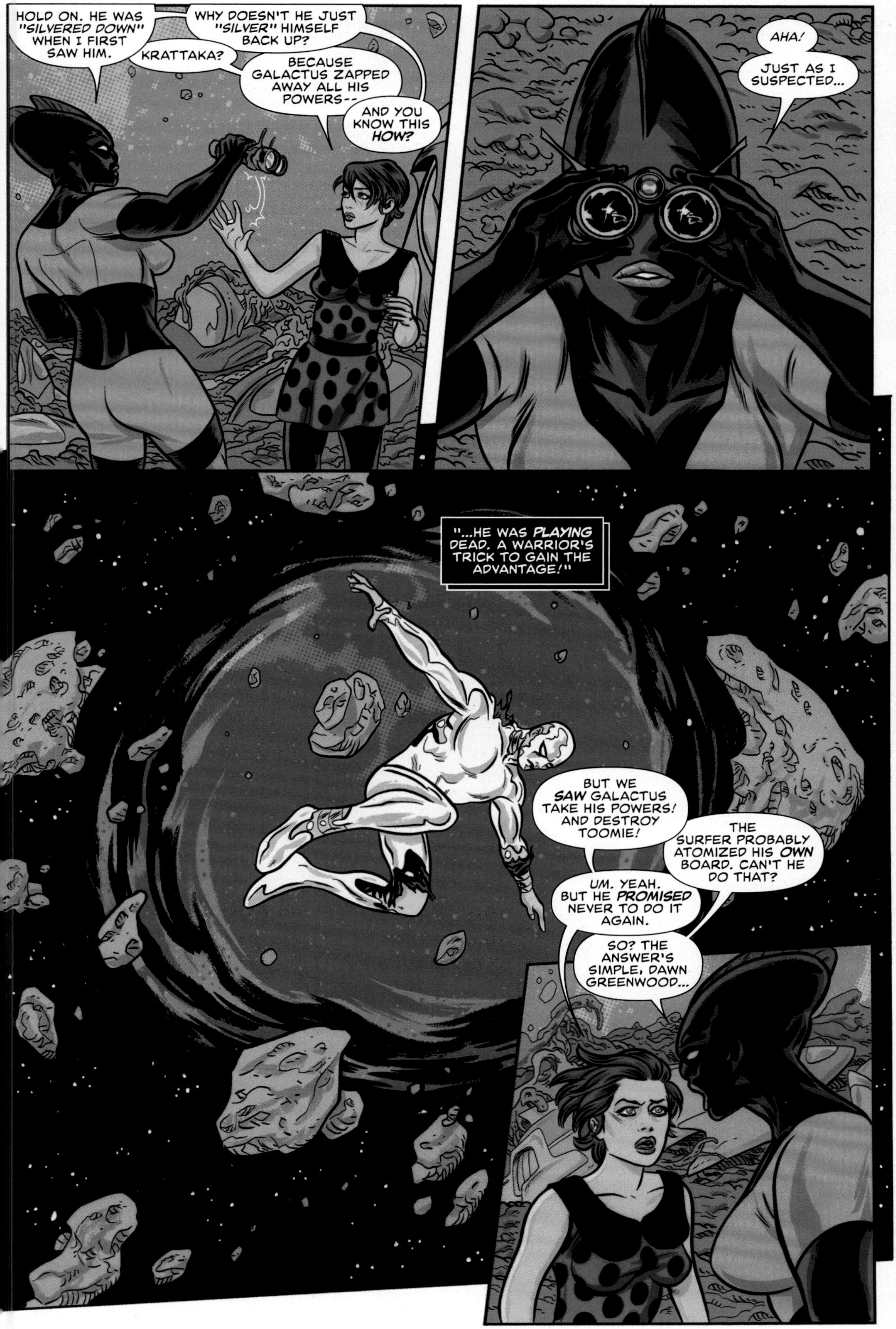
HOLD ON. HE WAS "SILVERED DOWN" WHEN I FIRST SAW HIM.
WHY DOESN'T HE JUST "SILVER" HIMSELF BACK UP?
KRATTAKA?
BECAUSE GALACTUS ZAPPED AWAY ALL HIS POWERS--
AND YOU KNOW THIS HOW?
AHA!
JUST AS I SUSPECTED...
"...HE WAS PLAYING DEAD. A WARRIOR'S TRICK TO GAIN THE ADVANTAGE!"
BUT WE SAW GALACTUS TAKE HIS POWERS! AND DESTROY TOOMIE!
THE SURFER PROBABLY ATOMIZED HIS OWN BOARD. CAN'T HE DO THAT?
UM. YEAH. BUT HE PROMISED NEVER TO DO IT AGAIN.
SO? THE ANSWER'S SIMPLE, DAWN GREENWOOD...

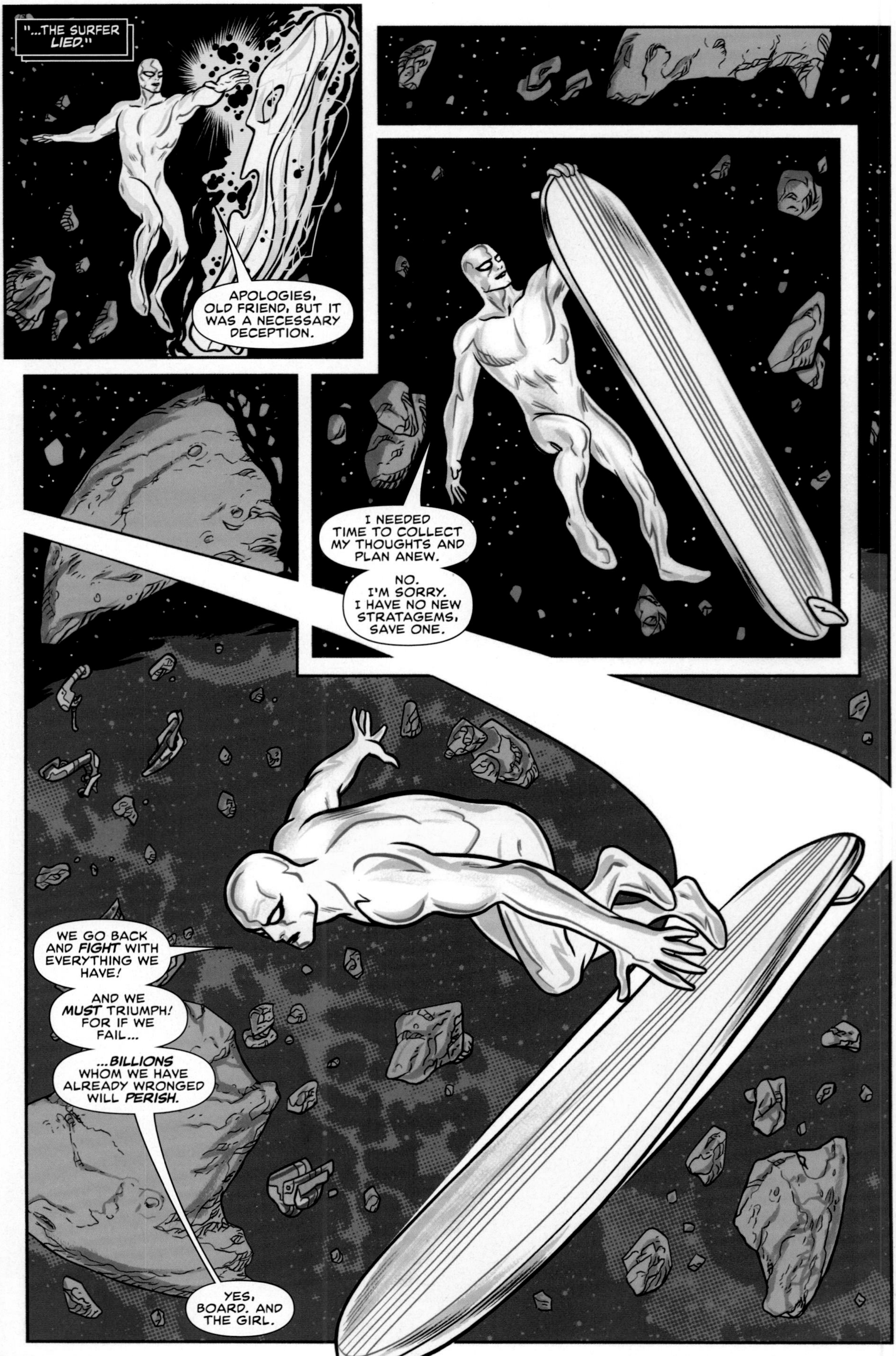
"...THE SURFER *LIED*."
APOLOGIES, OLD FRIEND, BUT IT WAS A NECESSARY DECEPTION.
I NEEDED TIME TO COLLECT MY THOUGHTS AND PLAN ANEW.
NO. I'M SORRY. I HAVE NO NEW STRATAGEMS, SAVE ONE.
WE GO BACK AND *FIGHT* WITH EVERYTHING WE HAVE!
AND WE *MUST* TRIUMPH! FOR IF WE FAIL...
...*BILLIONS* WHOM WE HAVE ALREADY WRONGED WILL *PERISH*.
YES, BOARD. AND THE GIRL.

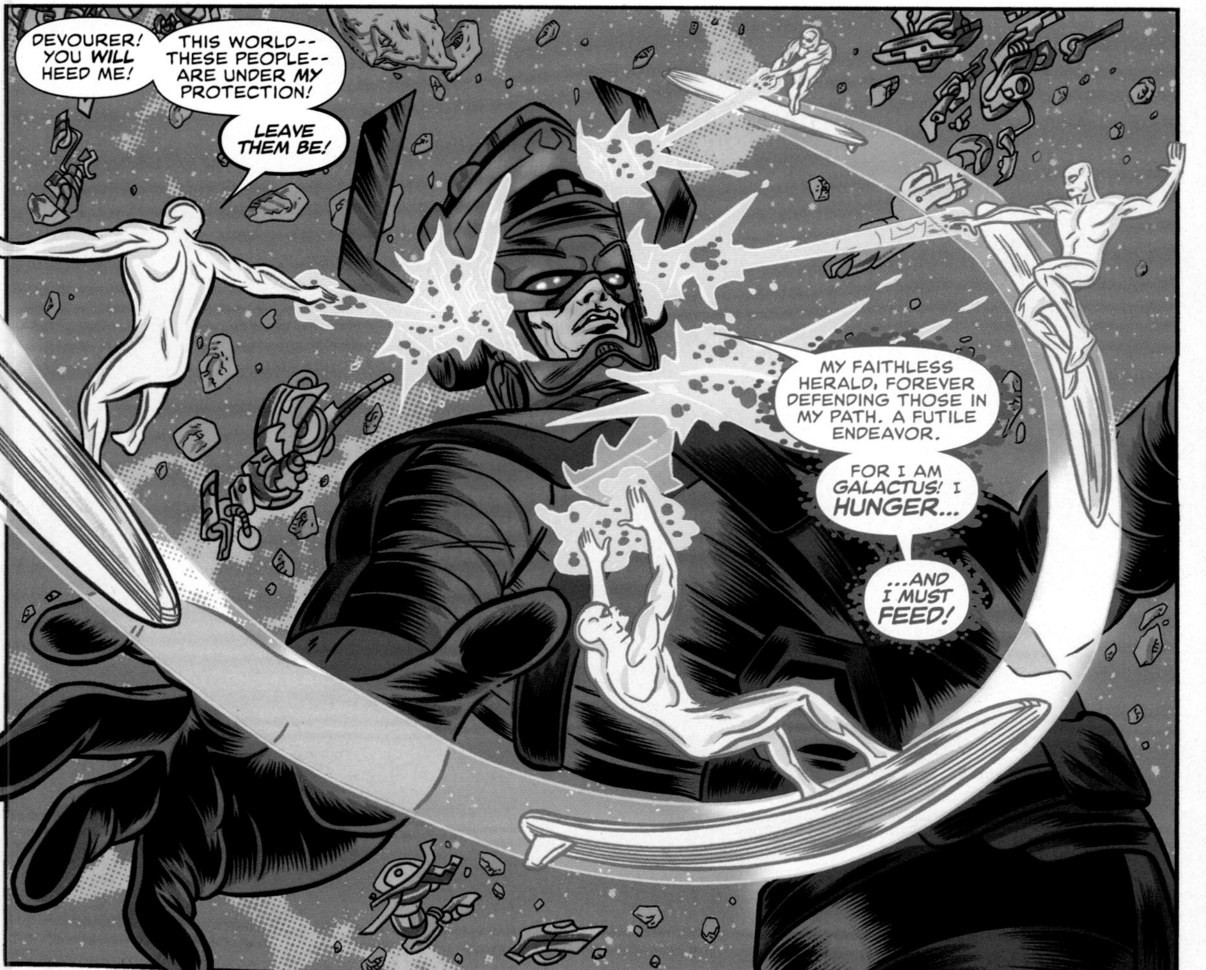
DEVOURER! YOU WILL HEED ME!
THIS WORLD-- THESE PEOPLE-- ARE UNDER MY PROTECTION!
LEAVE THEM BE!
MY FAITHLESS HERALD, FOREVER DEFENDING THOSE IN MY PATH. A FUTILE ENDEAVOR.
FOR I AM GALACTUS! I HUNGER...
...AND I MUST FEED!

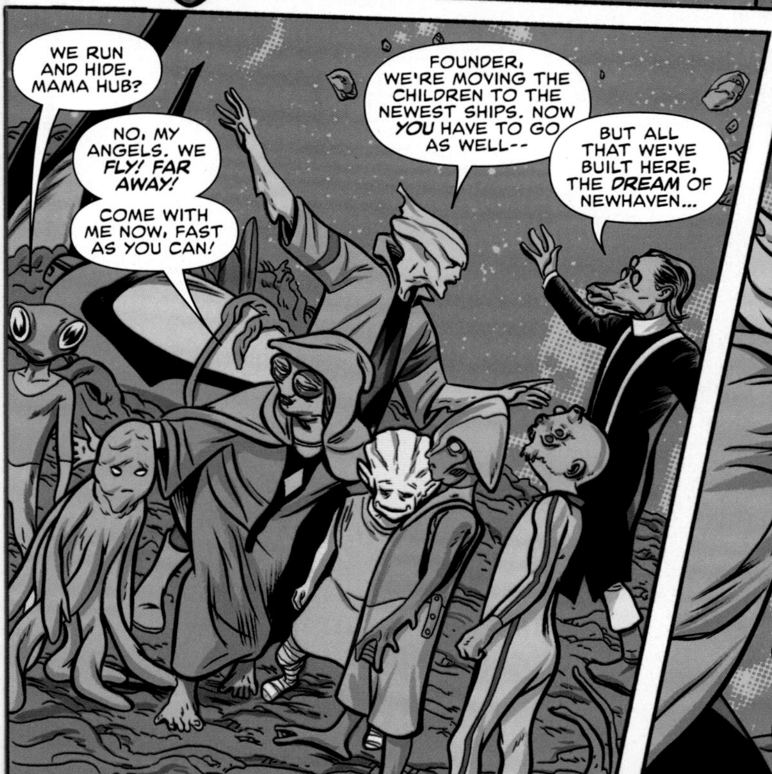
WE RUN AND HIDE, MAMA HUB?
NO, MY ANGELS. WE FLY! FAR AWAY!
COME WITH ME NOW, FAST AS YOU CAN!
FOUNDER, WE'RE MOVING THE CHILDREN TO THE NEWEST SHIPS. NOW YOU HAVE TO GO AS WELL--
BUT ALL THAT WE'VE BUILT HERE, THE DREAM OF NEWHAVEN...

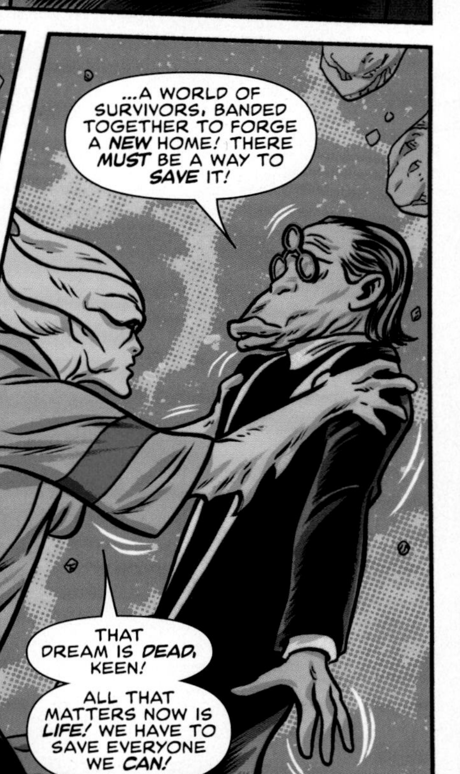
...A WORLD OF SURVIVORS, BANDED TOGETHER TO FORGE A NEW HOME! THERE MUST BE A WAY TO SAVE IT!
THAT DREAM IS DEAD, KEEN!
ALL THAT MATTERS NOW IS LIFE! WE HAVE TO SAVE EVERYONE WE CAN!

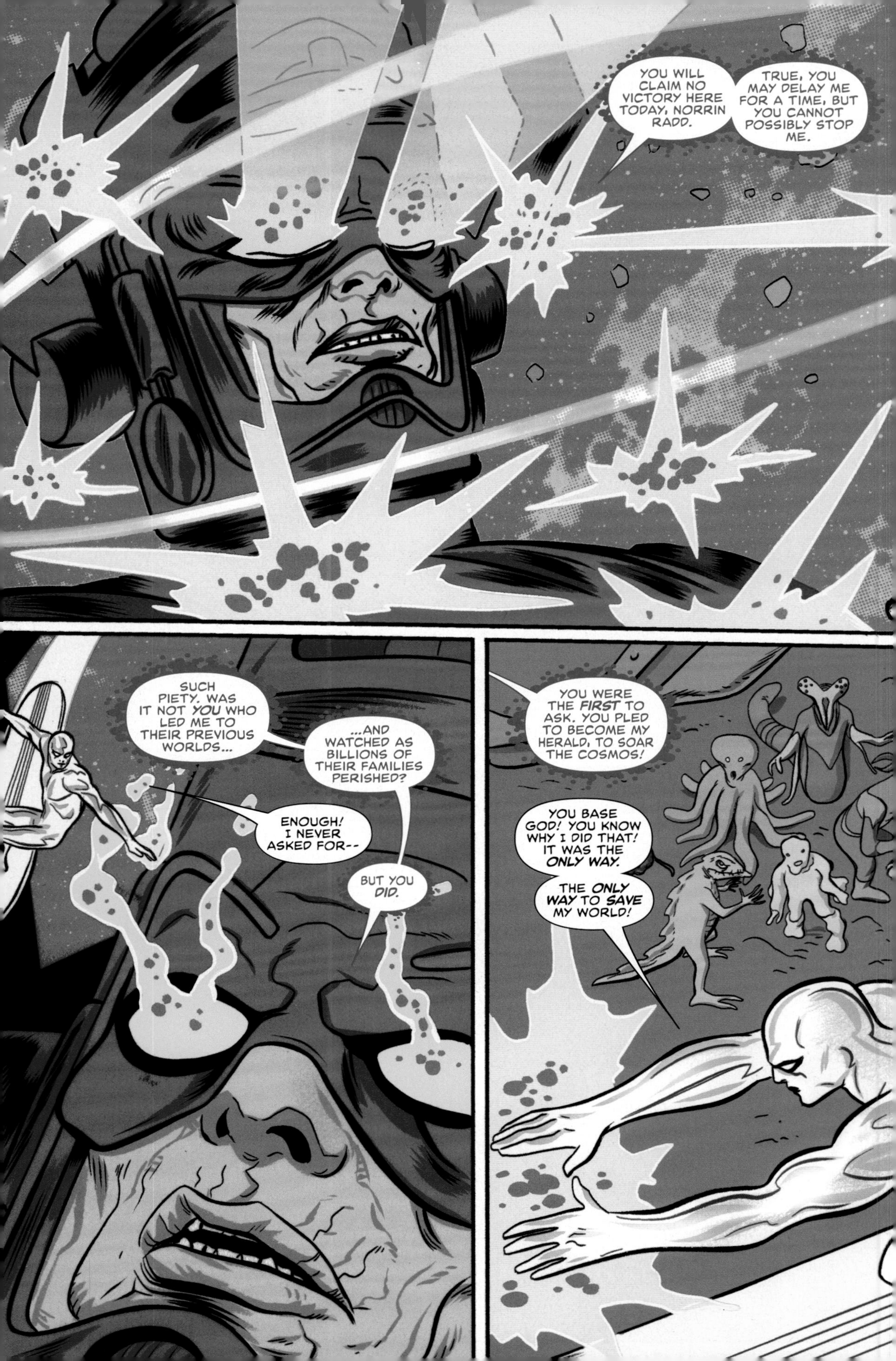
YOU WILL CLAIM NO VICTORY HERE TODAY, NORRIN RADD.
TRUE, YOU MAY DELAY ME FOR A TIME, BUT YOU CANNOT POSSIBLY STOP ME.
SUCH PIETY. WAS IT NOT YOU WHO LED ME TO THEIR PREVIOUS WORLDS...
...AND WATCHED AS BILLIONS OF THEIR FAMILIES PERISHED?
ENOUGH! I NEVER ASKED FOR--
BUT YOU DID.
YOU WERE THE FIRST TO ASK. YOU PLED TO BECOME MY HERALD, TO SOAR THE COSMOS!
YOU BASE GOD! YOU KNOW WHY I DID THAT! IT WAS THE ONLY WAY.
THE ONLY WAY TO SAVE MY WORLD!

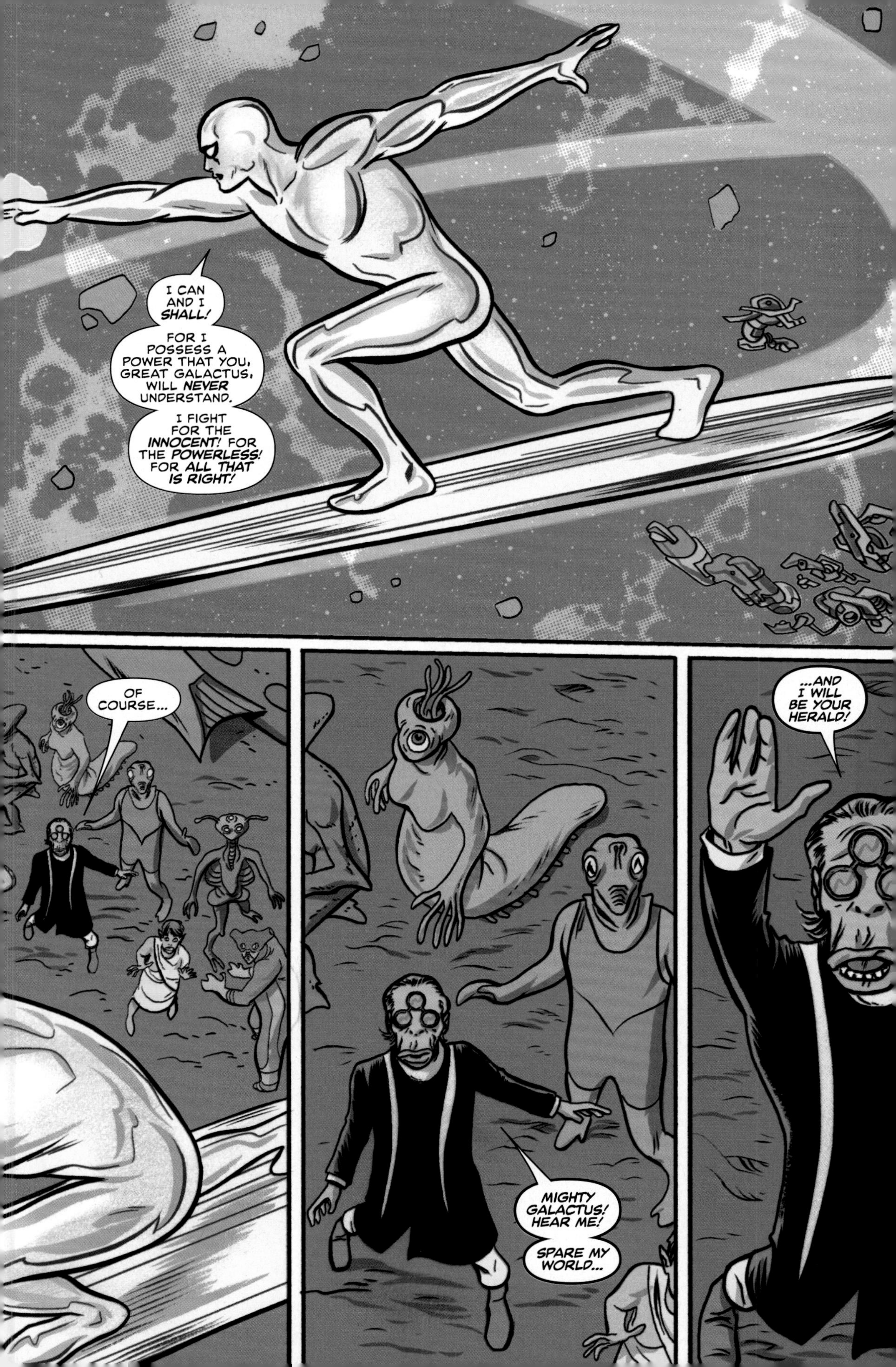
I CAN AND I SHALL!
FOR I POSSESS A POWER THAT YOU, GREAT GALACTUS, WILL NEVER UNDERSTAND.
I FIGHT FOR THE INNOCENT! FOR THE POWERLESS! FOR ALL THAT IS RIGHT!
OF COURSE...
MIGHTY GALACTUS! HEAR ME!
SPARE MY WORLD...
...AND I WILL BE YOUR HERALD!

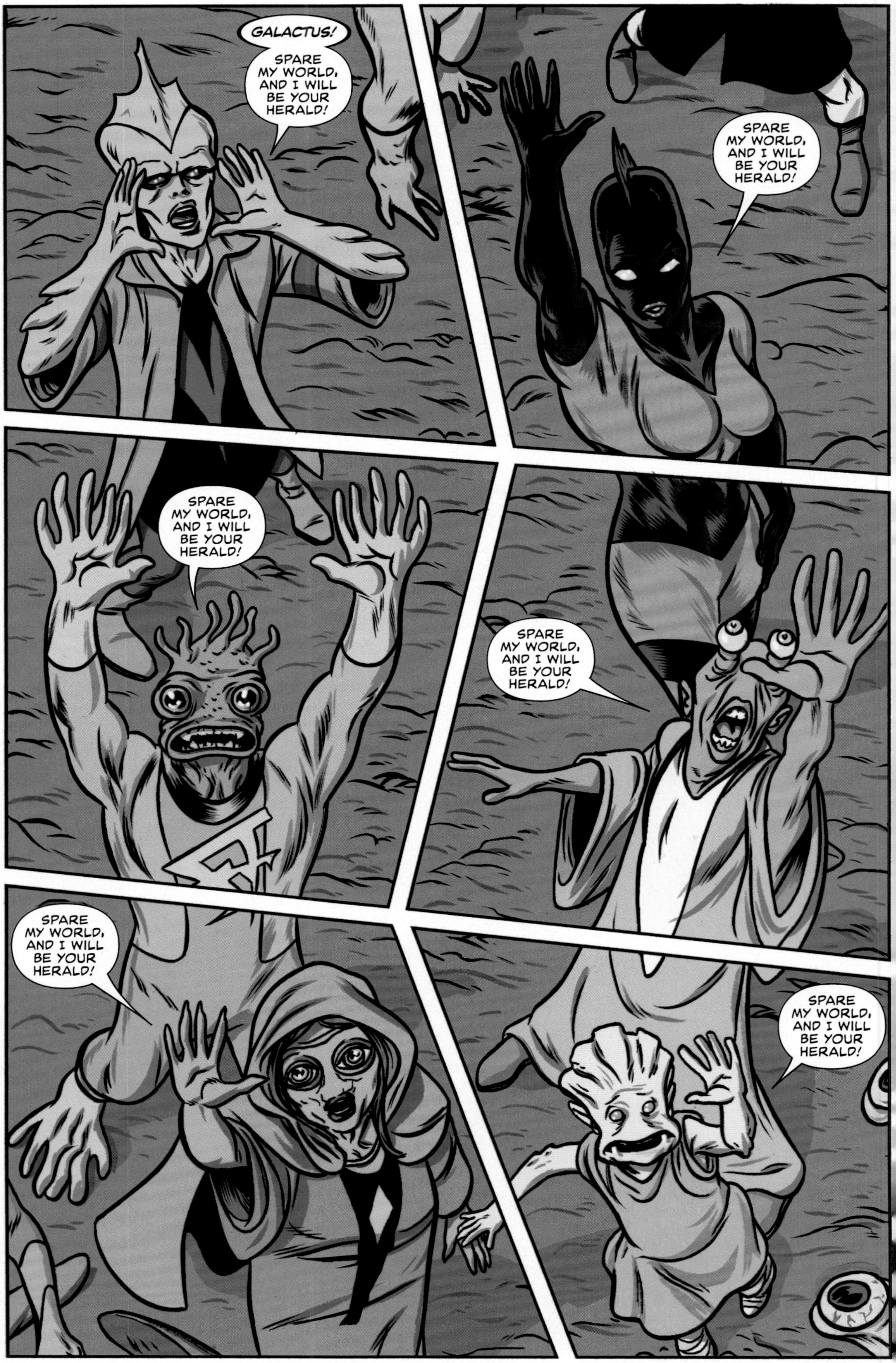
GALACTUS!
SPARE MY WORLD, AND I WILL BE YOUR HERALD!
SPARE MY WORLD, AND I WILL BE YOUR HERALD!
SPARE MY WORLD, AND I WILL BE YOUR HERALD!
SPARE MY WORLD, AND I WILL BE YOUR HERALD!
SPARE MY WORLD, AND I WILL BE YOUR HERALD!
SPARE MY WORLD, AND I WILL BE YOUR HERALD!

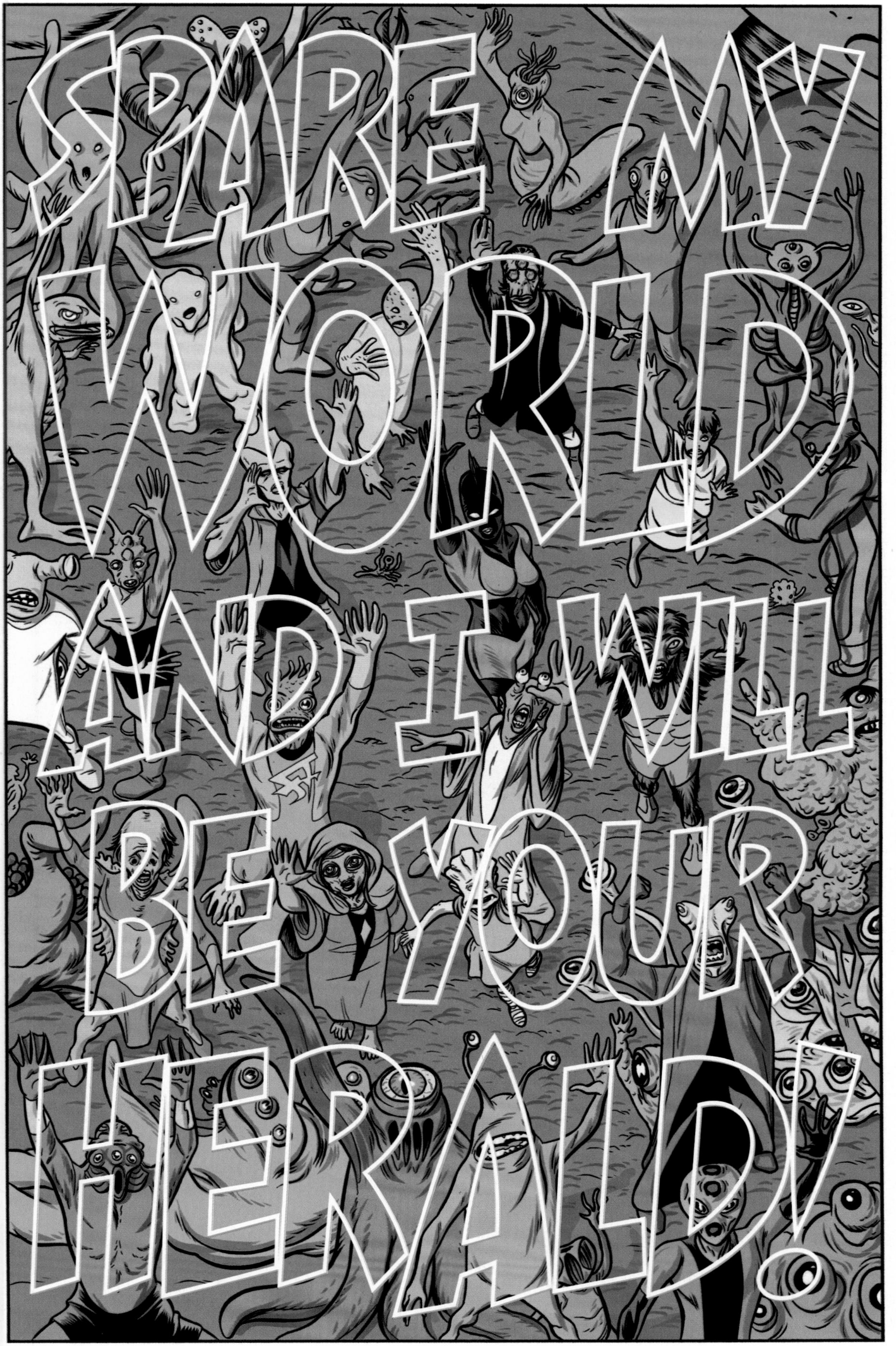
SPARE MY WORLD AND I WILL BE YOUR HERALD!

ACROSS THE PLANET, THE WORD SPREADS--

"SPARE MY WORLD, AND I WILL BE YOUR HERALD!"

ON RADIO WAVES, TELEPATHIC FIELDS, TRIBAL DRUMS--

"SPARE MY WORLD, AND I WILL BE YOUR HERALD!"

CITIES, NATIONS, WHOLE CONTINENTS CRY OUT IN *ONE* VOICE--

"SPARE MY WORLD, AND I WILL BE YOUR HERALD!"

WHAT NOBLE SOULS.

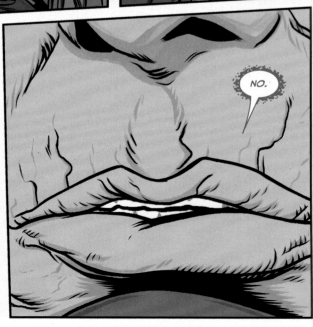

NO.

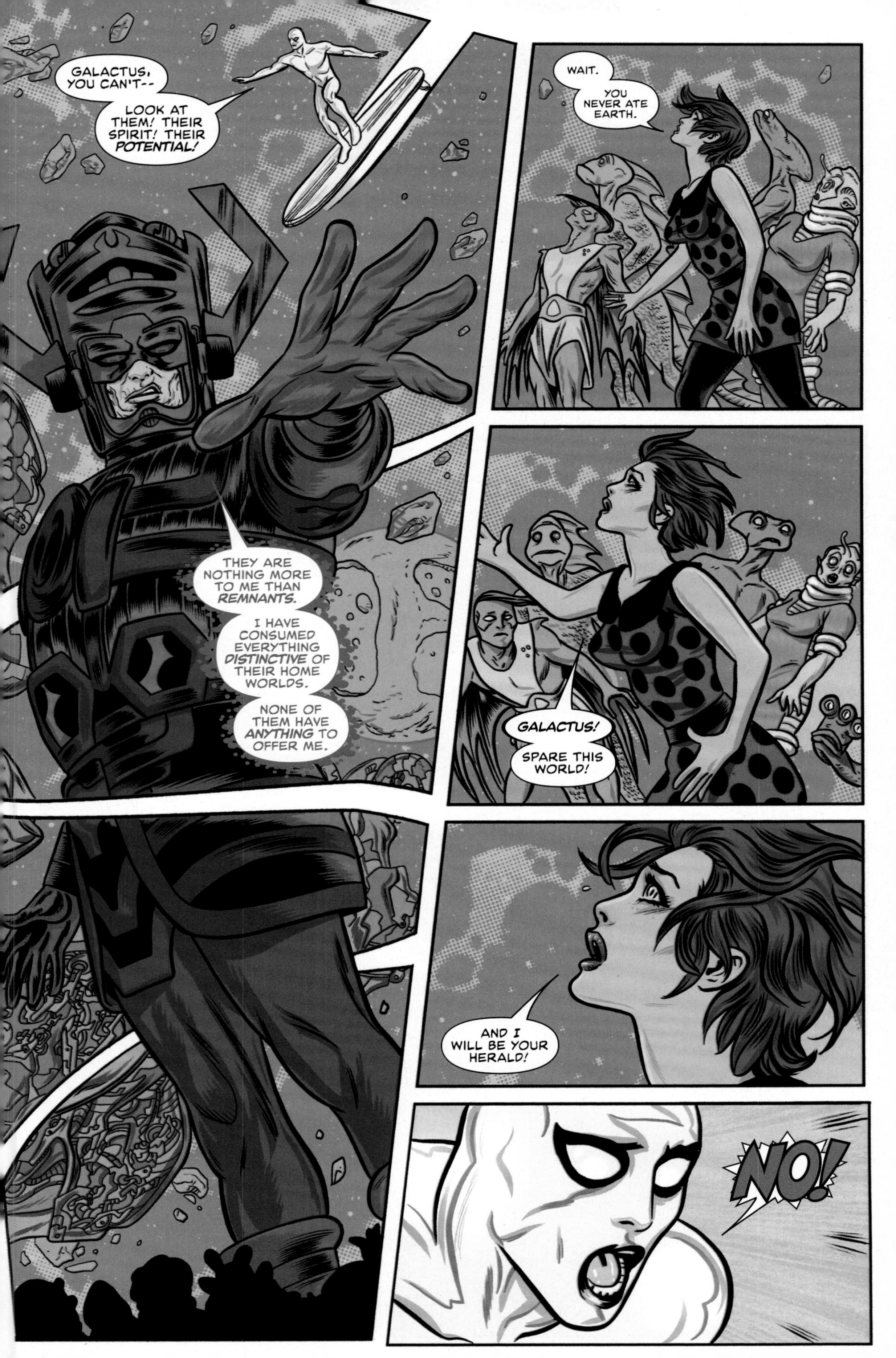
GALACTUS, YOU CAN'T--
LOOK AT THEM! THEIR SPIRIT! THEIR POTENTIAL!
THEY ARE NOTHING MORE TO ME THAN REMNANTS.
I HAVE CONSUMED EVERYTHING DISTINCTIVE OF THEIR HOME WORLDS.
NONE OF THEM HAVE ANYTHING TO OFFER ME.
WAIT.
YOU NEVER ATE EARTH.
GALACTUS!
SPARE THIS WORLD!
AND I WILL BE YOUR HERALD!
NO!

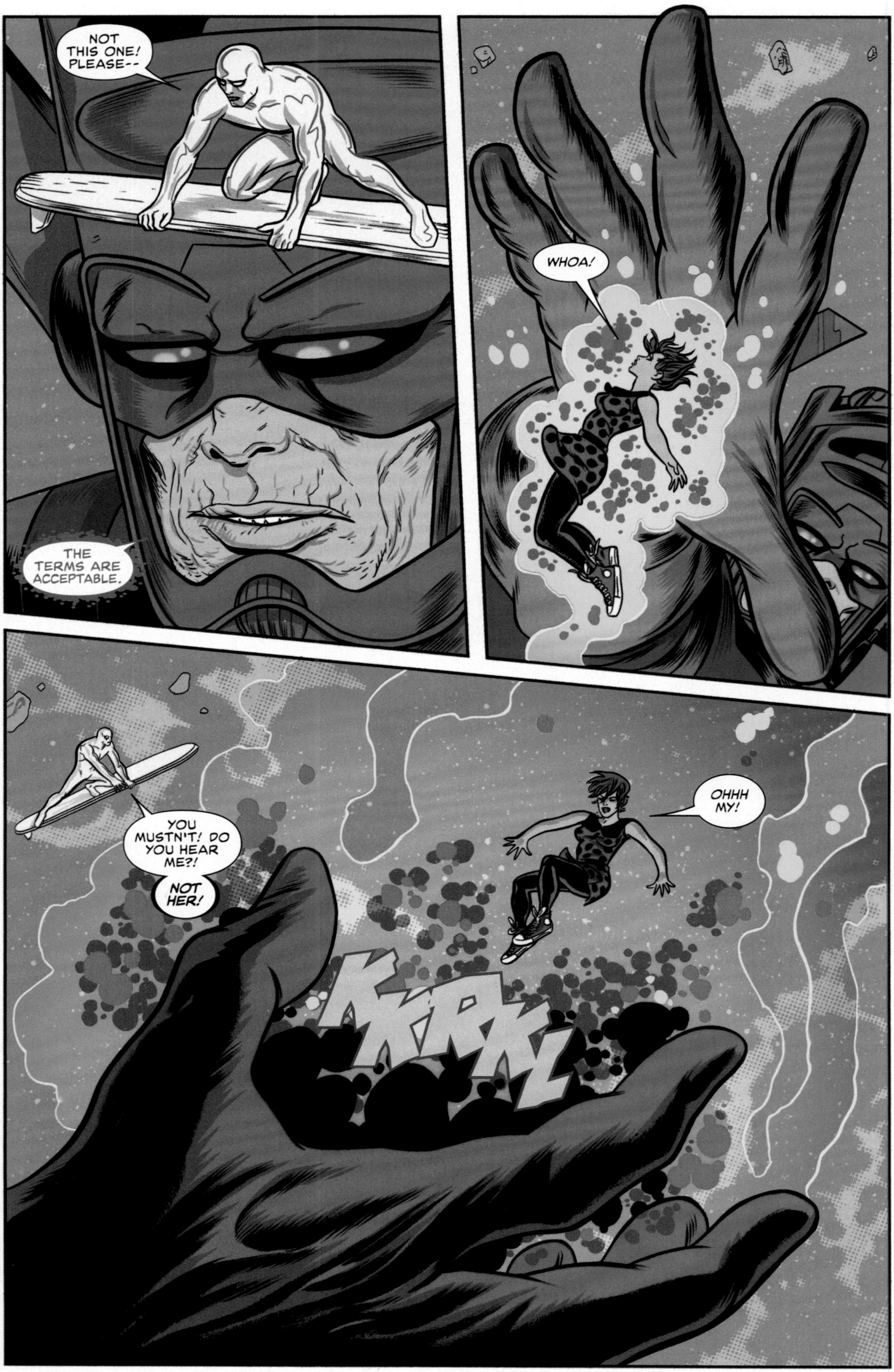
NOT THIS ONE! PLEASE--
THE TERMS ARE ACCEPTABLE.
WHOA!
YOU MUSTN'T! DO YOU HEAR ME?!
NOT HER!
OHHH MY!

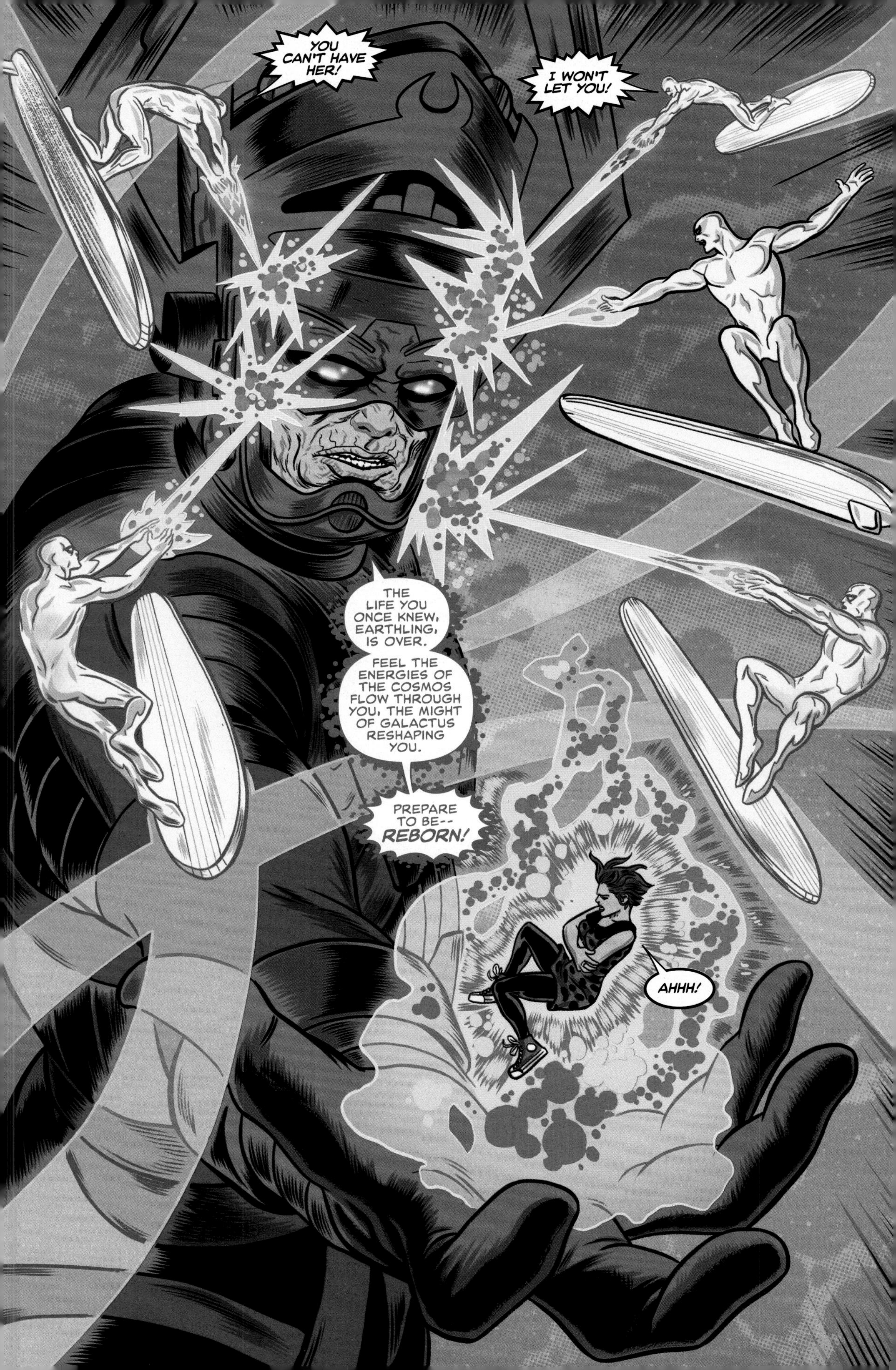
YOU CAN'T HAVE HER!
I WON'T LET YOU!
THE LIFE YOU ONCE KNEW, EARTHLING, IS OVER.
FEEL THE ENERGIES OF THE COSMOS FLOW THROUGH YOU, THE MIGHT OF GALACTUS RESHAPING YOU.
PREPARE TO BE-- REBORN!
AHHH!

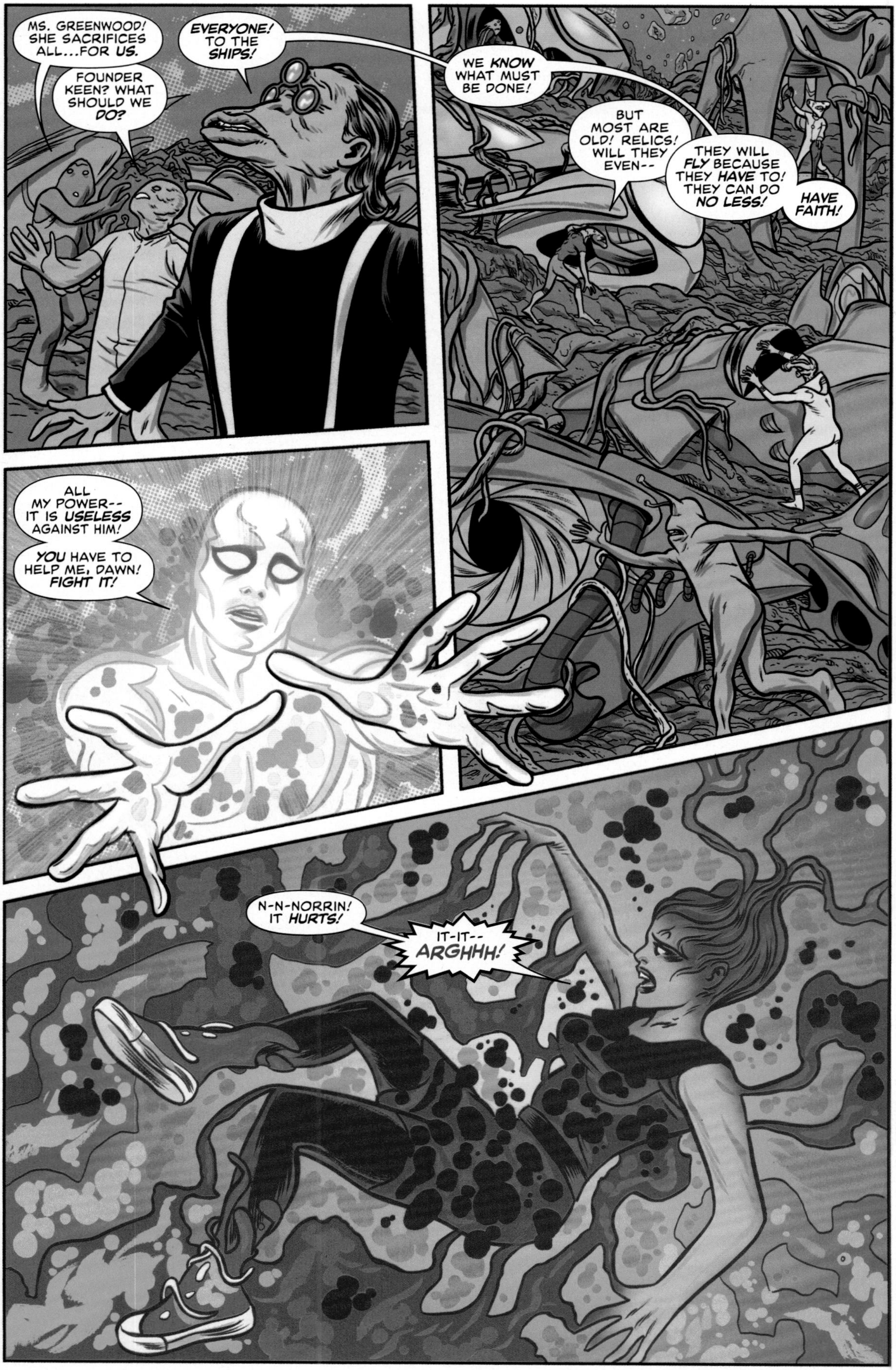
MS. GREENWOOD! SHE SACRIFICES ALL...FOR US.
FOUNDER KEEN? WHAT SHOULD WE DO?
EVERYONE! TO THE SHIPS!
WE KNOW WHAT MUST BE DONE!
BUT MOST ARE OLD! RELICS! WILL THEY EVEN--
THEY WILL FLY BECAUSE THEY HAVE TO! THEY CAN DO NO LESS!
HAVE FAITH!
ALL MY POWER--IT IS USELESS AGAINST HIM!
YOU HAVE TO HELP ME, DAWN! FIGHT IT!
N-N-NORRIN! IT HURTS!
IT-IT--ARGHHH!

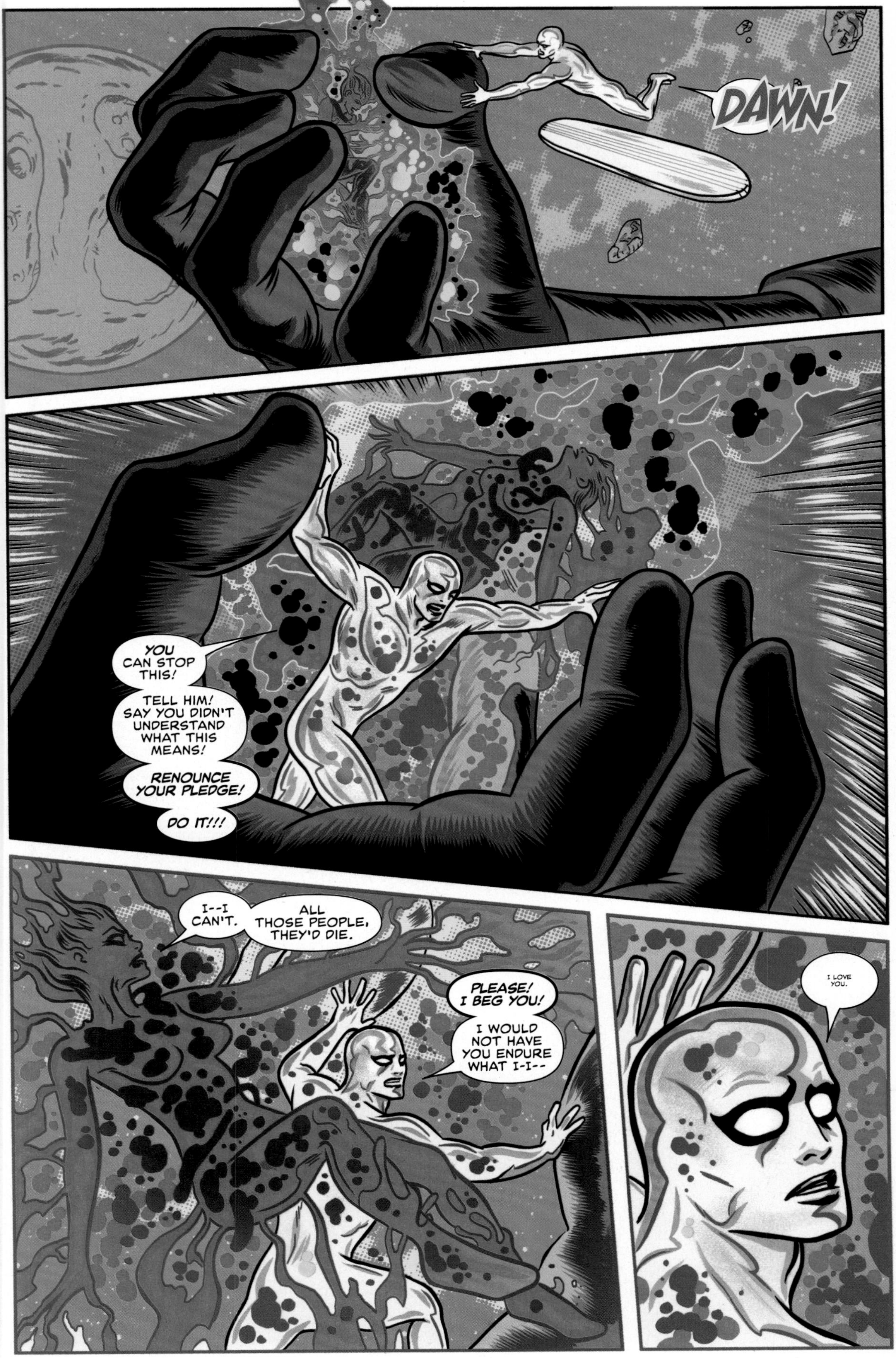
DAWN!
YOU CAN STOP THIS!
TELL HIM! SAY YOU DIDN'T UNDERSTAND WHAT THIS MEANS!
RENOUNCE YOUR PLEDGE!
DO IT!!!
I--I CAN'T.
ALL THOSE PEOPLE, THEY'D DIE.
PLEASE! I BEG YOU!
I WOULD NOT HAVE YOU ENDURE WHAT I-I--
I LOVE YOU.

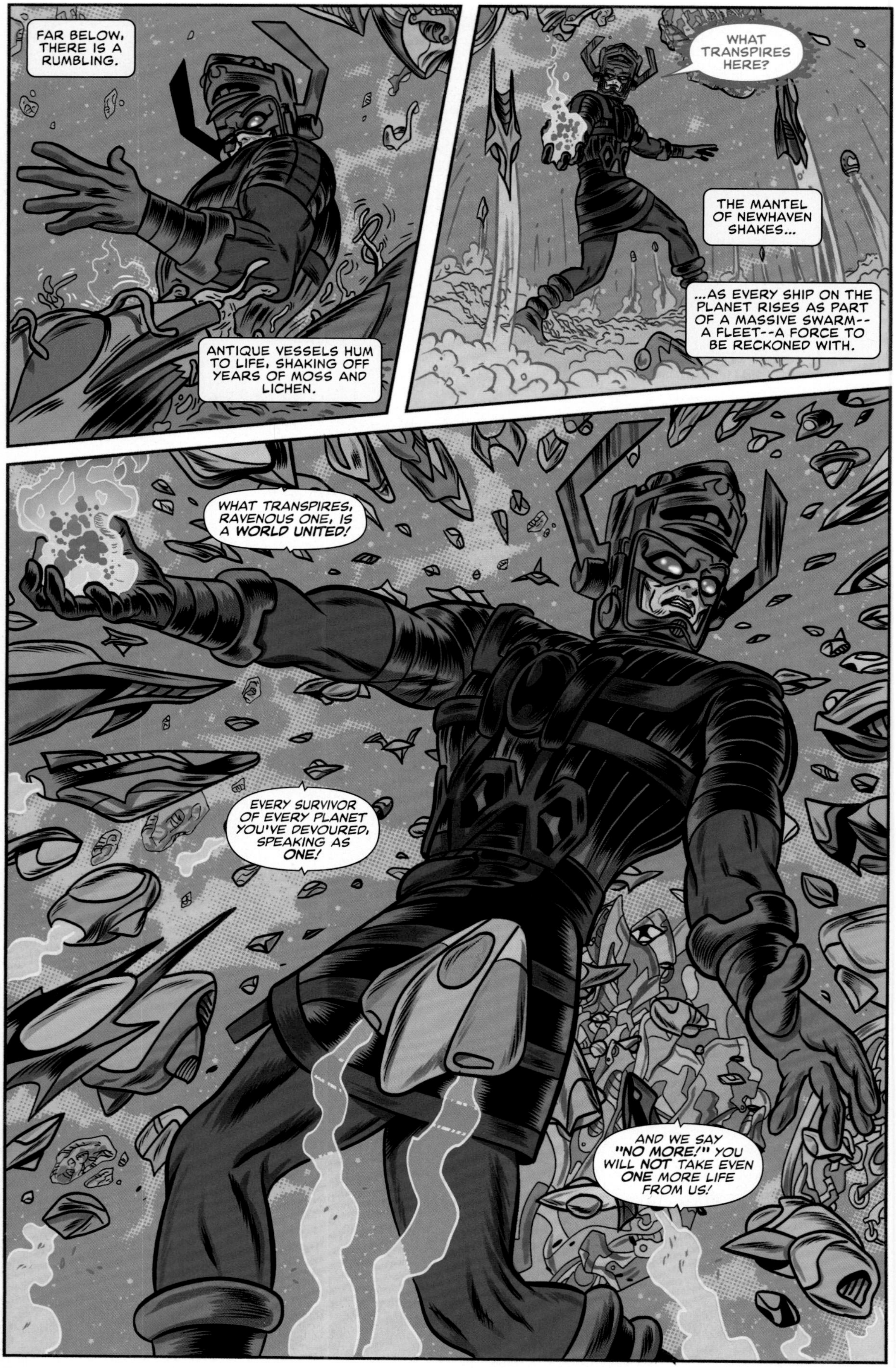
FAR BELOW, THERE IS A RUMBLING.
ANTIQUE VESSELS HUM TO LIFE, SHAKING OFF YEARS OF MOSS AND LICHEN.
WHAT TRANSPIRES HERE?
THE MANTEL OF NEWHAVEN SHAKES...
...AS EVERY SHIP ON THE PLANET RISES AS PART OF A MASSIVE SWARM--A FLEET--A FORCE TO BE RECKONED WITH.
WHAT TRANSPIRES, RAVENOUS ONE, IS A WORLD UNITED!
EVERY SURVIVOR OF EVERY PLANET YOU'VE DEVOURED, SPEAKING AS ONE!
AND WE SAY "NO MORE!" YOU WILL NOT TAKE EVEN ONE MORE LIFE FROM US!

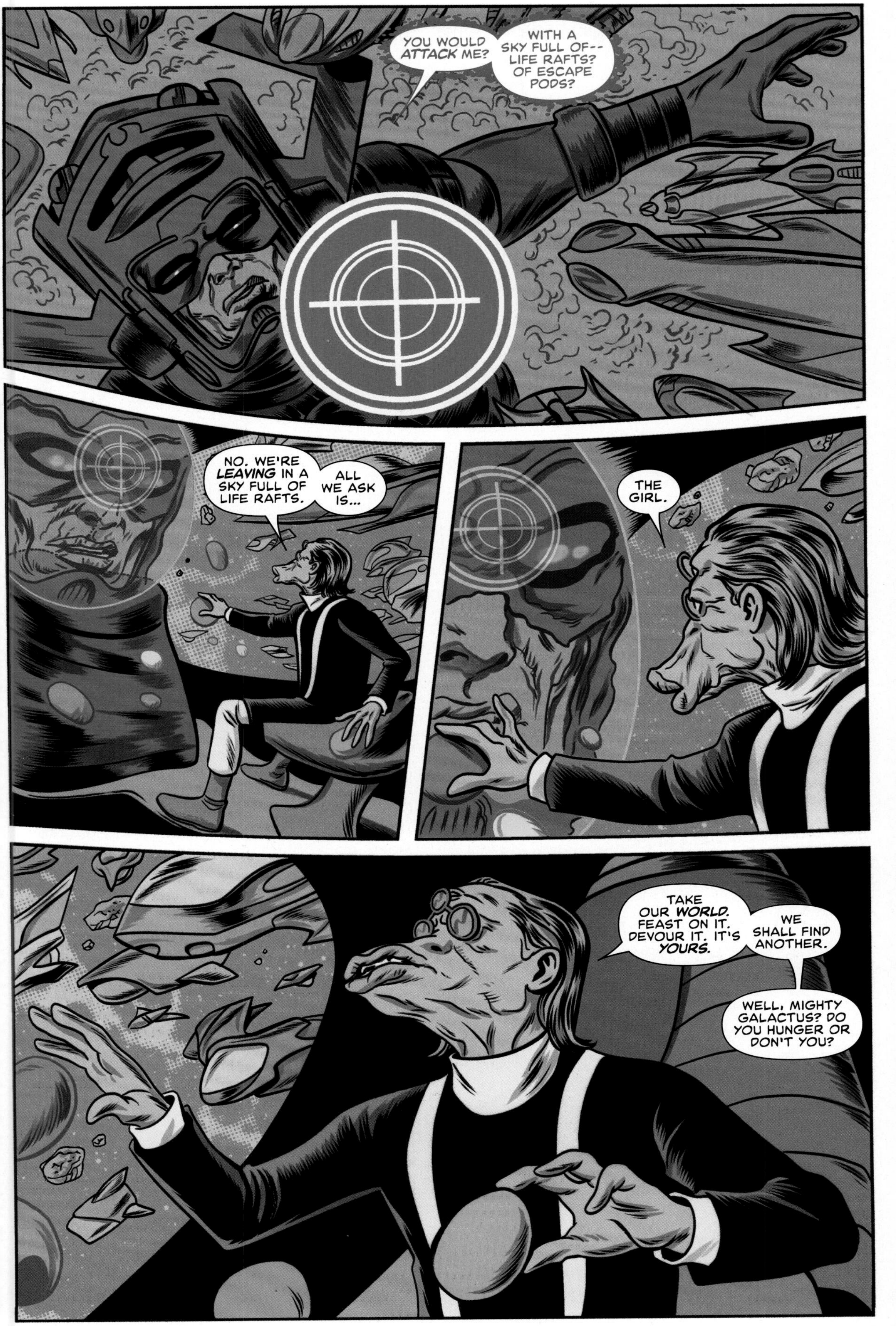
YOU WOULD ATTACK ME?
WITH A SKY FULL OF-- LIFE RAFTS? OF ESCAPE PODS?
NO. WE'RE LEAVING IN A SKY FULL OF LIFE RAFTS.
ALL WE ASK IS...
THE GIRL.
TAKE OUR WORLD. FEAST ON IT. DEVOUR IT. IT'S YOURS.
WE SHALL FIND ANOTHER.
WELL, MIGHTY GALACTUS? DO YOU HUNGER OR DON'T YOU?

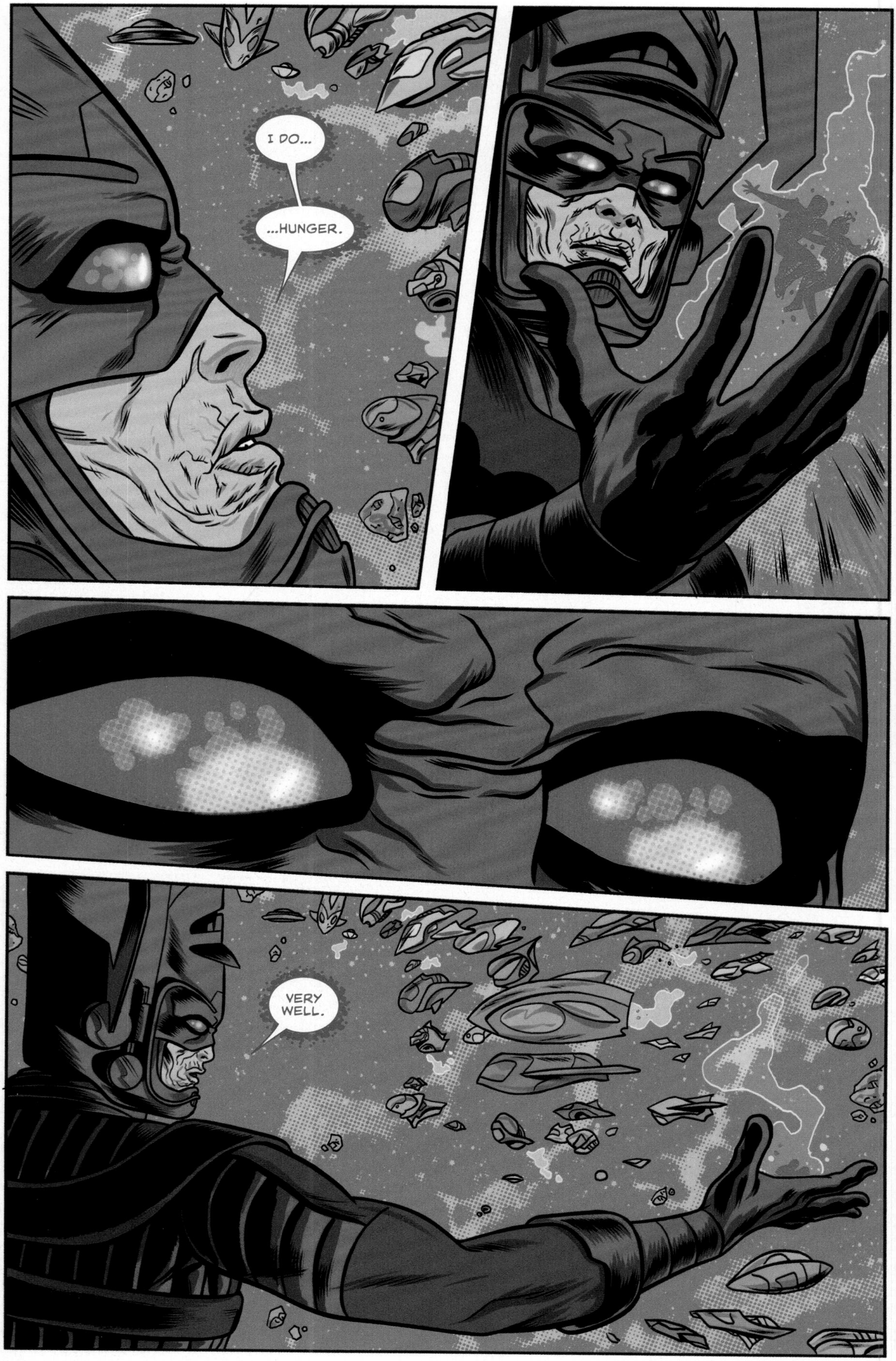
I DO...
...HUNGER.
VERY WELL.

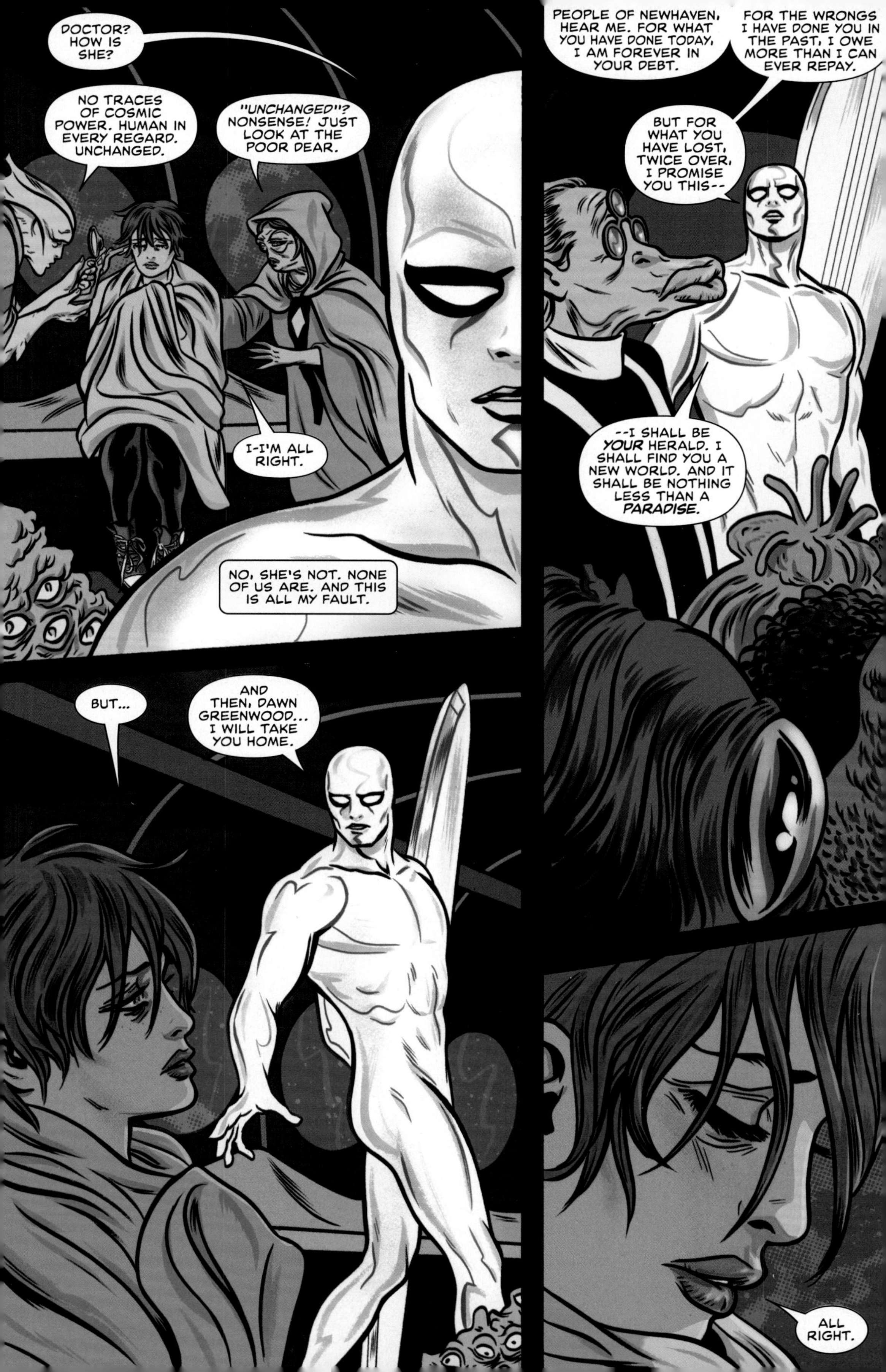
DOCTOR? HOW IS SHE?
NO TRACES OF COSMIC POWER. HUMAN IN EVERY REGARD. UNCHANGED.
"UNCHANGED"? NONSENSE! JUST LOOK AT THE POOR DEAR.
I-I'M ALL RIGHT.
NO, SHE'S NOT. NONE OF US ARE. AND THIS IS ALL MY FAULT.
PEOPLE OF NEWHAVEN, HEAR ME. FOR WHAT YOU HAVE DONE TODAY, I AM FOREVER IN YOUR DEBT.
FOR THE WRONGS I HAVE DONE YOU IN THE PAST, I OWE MORE THAN I CAN EVER REPAY.
BUT FOR WHAT YOU HAVE LOST, TWICE OVER, I PROMISE YOU THIS--
--I SHALL BE *YOUR* HERALD. I SHALL FIND YOU A NEW WORLD. AND IT SHALL BE NOTHING LESS THAN A *PARADISE*.
BUT...
AND THEN, DAWN GREENWOOD... I WILL TAKE YOU HOME.
ALL RIGHT.

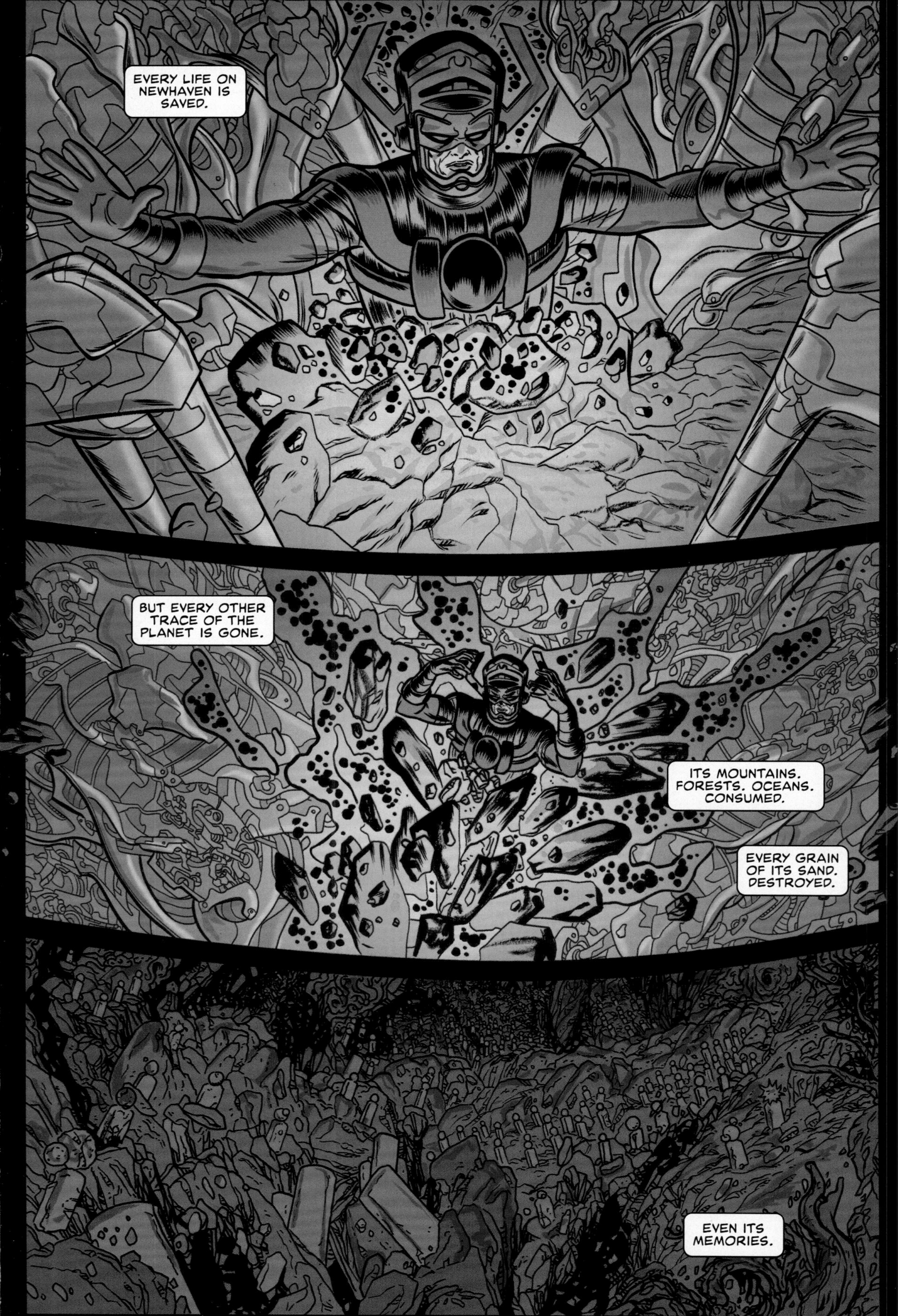
EVERY LIFE ON NEWHAVEN IS SAVED.
BUT EVERY OTHER TRACE OF THE PLANET IS GONE.
ITS MOUNTAINS. FORESTS. OCEANS. CONSUMED.
EVERY GRAIN OF ITS SAND. DESTROYED.
EVEN ITS MEMORIES.

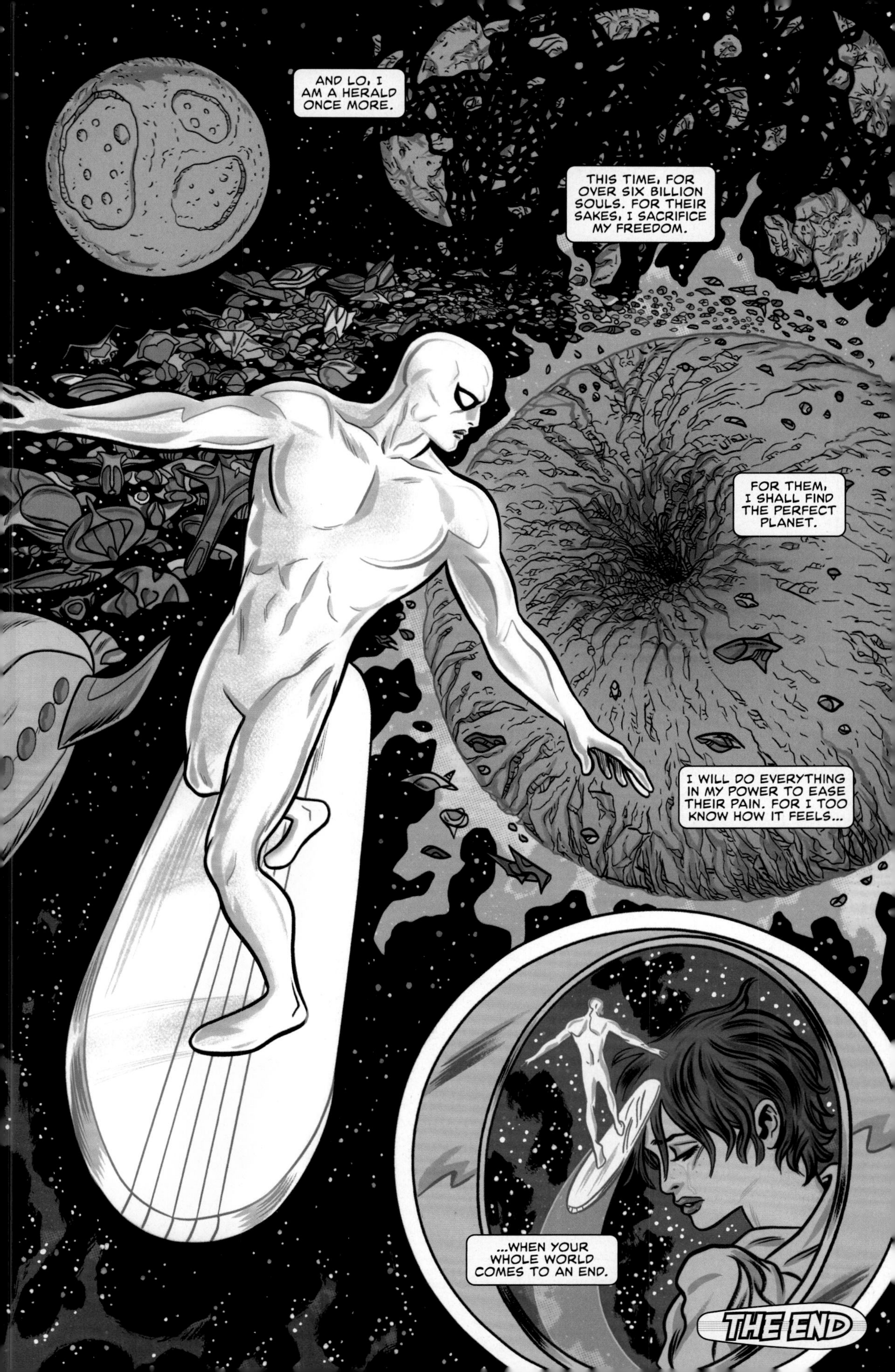
AND LO, I AM A HERALD ONCE MORE.
THIS TIME, FOR OVER SIX BILLION SOULS. FOR THEIR SAKES, I SACRIFICE MY FREEDOM.
FOR THEM, I SHALL FIND THE PERFECT PLANET.
I WILL DO EVERYTHING IN MY POWER TO EASE THEIR PAIN. FOR I TOO KNOW HOW IT FEELS...
...WHEN YOUR WHOLE WORLD COMES TO AN END.
THE END

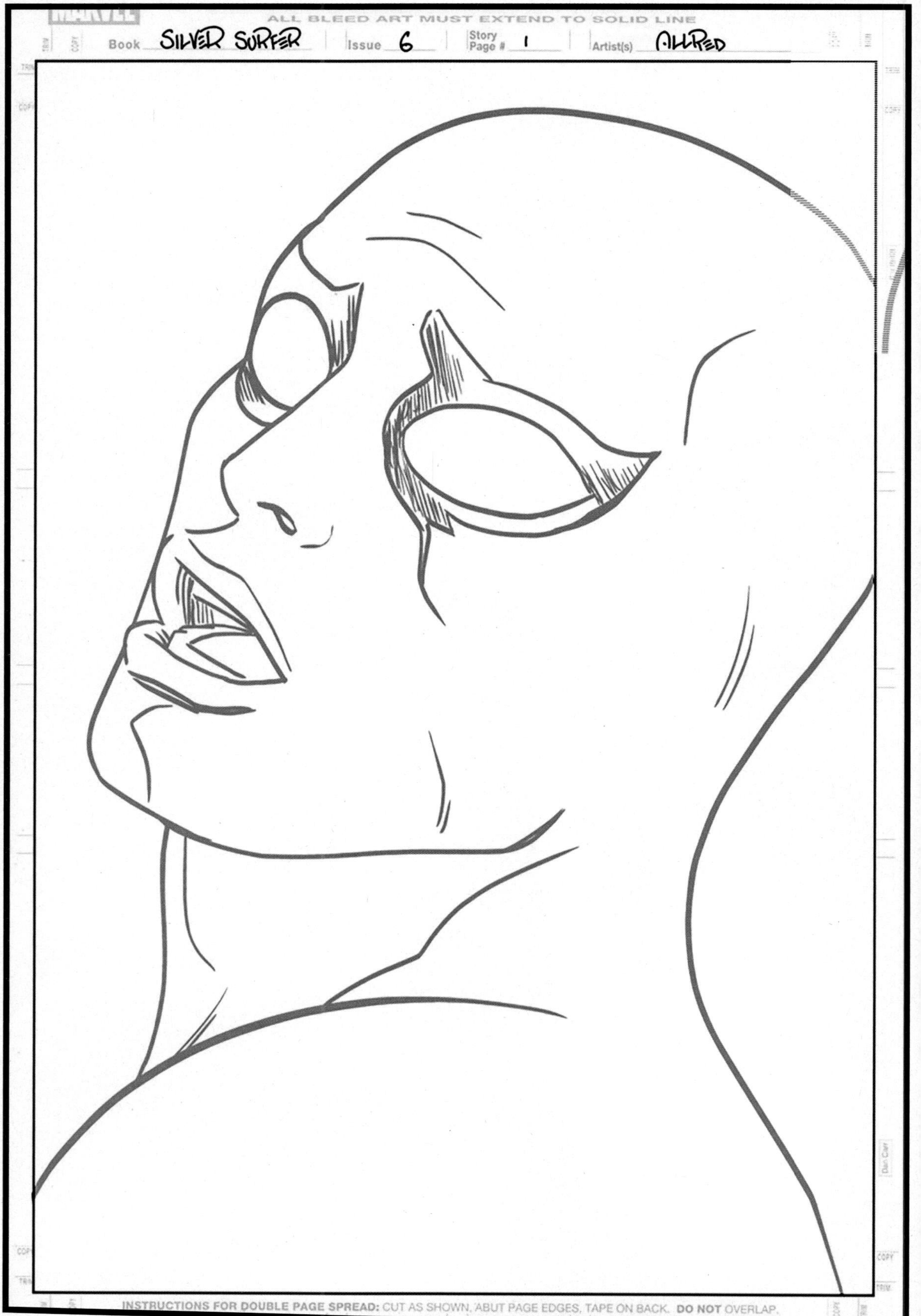
ALL BLEED ART MUST EXTEND TO SOLID LINE
Book SILVER SURFER
Issue 6
Story Page # 1
Artist(s) ALLRED
INSTRUCTIONS FOR DOUBLE PAGE SPREAD: CUT AS SHOWN, ABUT PAGE EDGES, TAPE ON BACK. DO NOT OVERLAP.

#6, PAGE 1 ART BY MICHAEL ALLRED

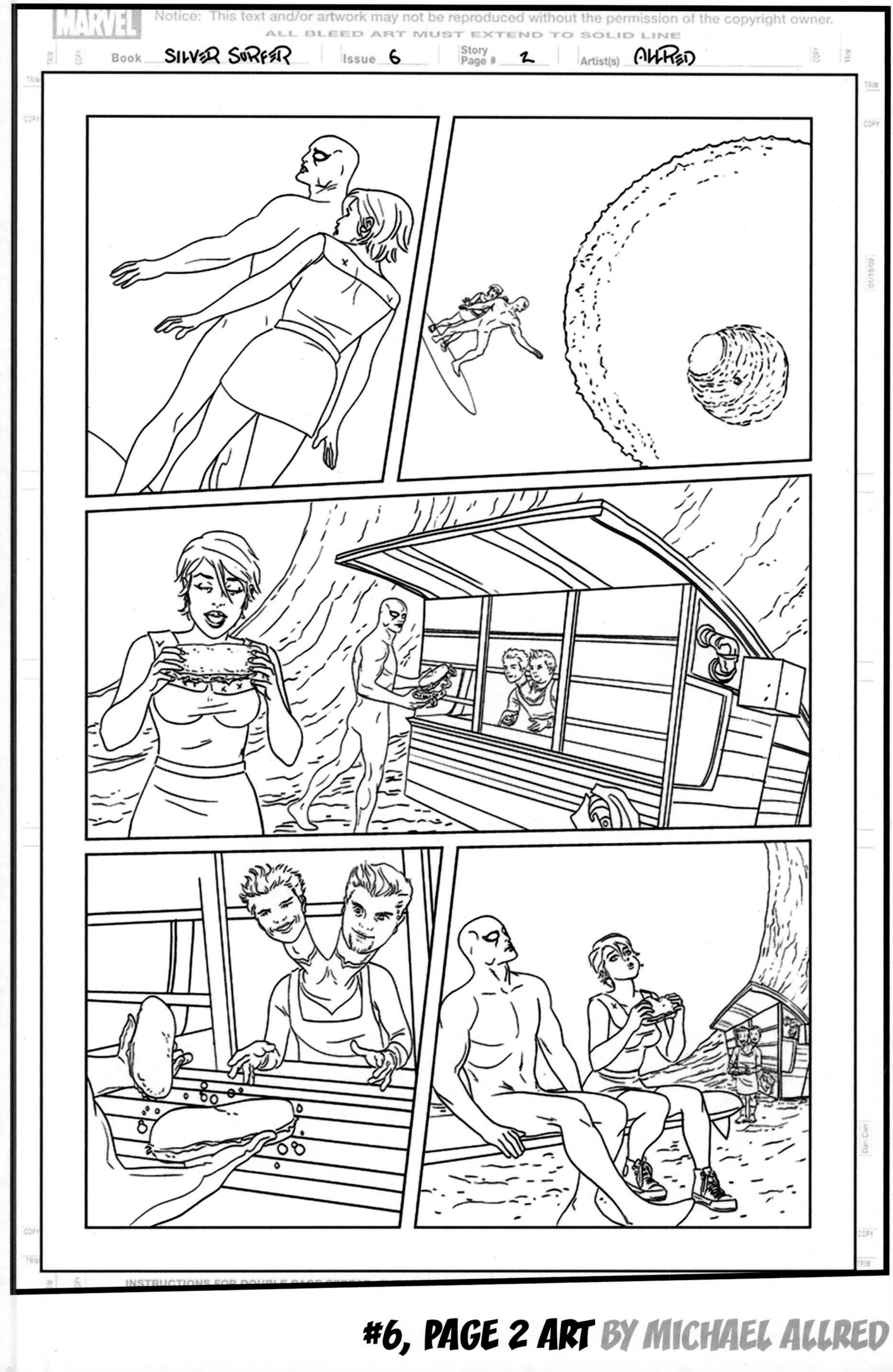
MARVEL
Notice: This text and/or artwork may not be reproduced without the permission of the copyright owner.
ALL BLEED ART MUST EXTEND TO SOLID LINE
Book SILVER SURFER
Issue 6
Story Page # 2
Artist(s) ALLRED

#6, PAGE 2 ART BY MICHAEL ALLRED

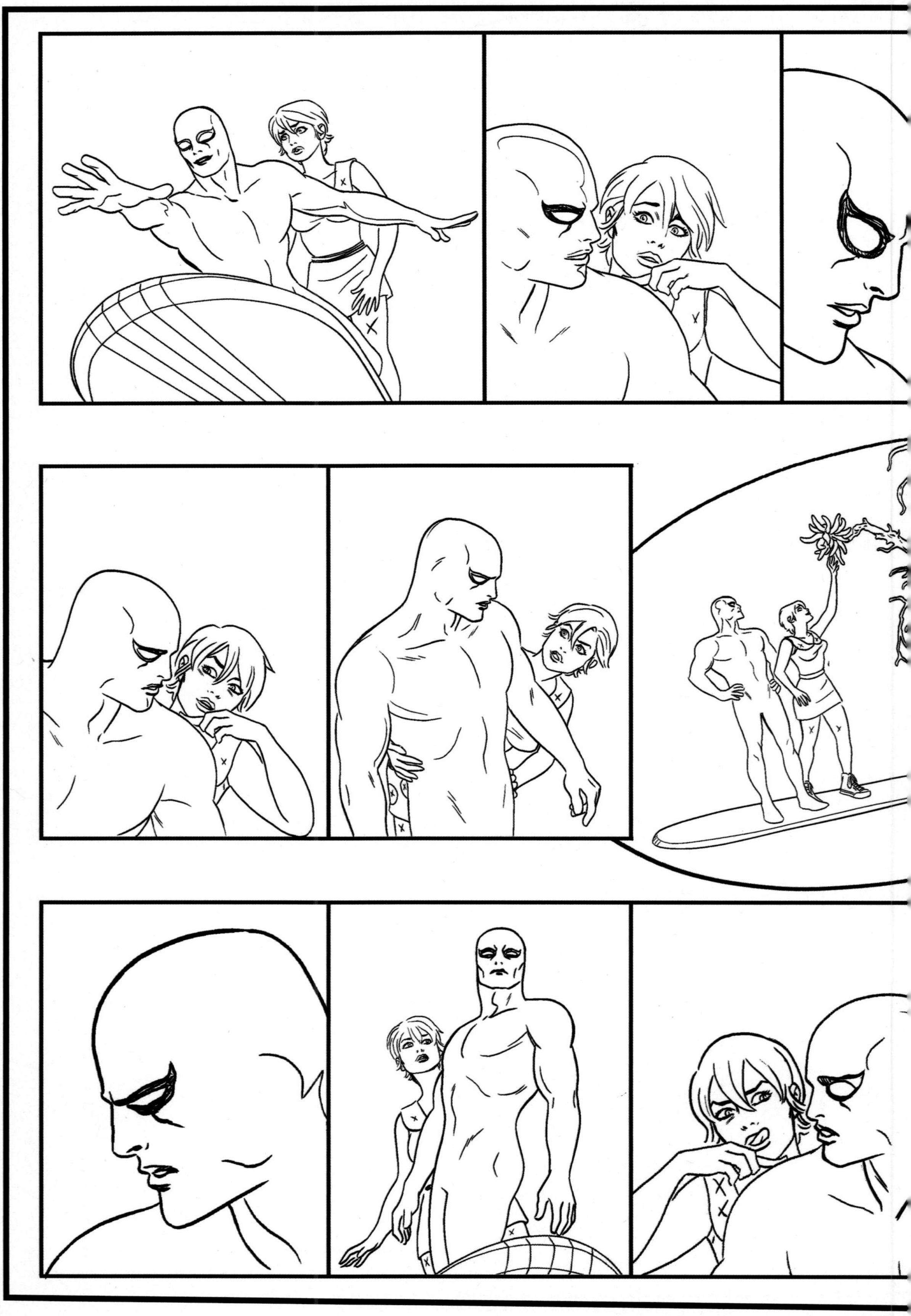

#6, PAGES 3-4 ART BY MICHAEL ALLRED

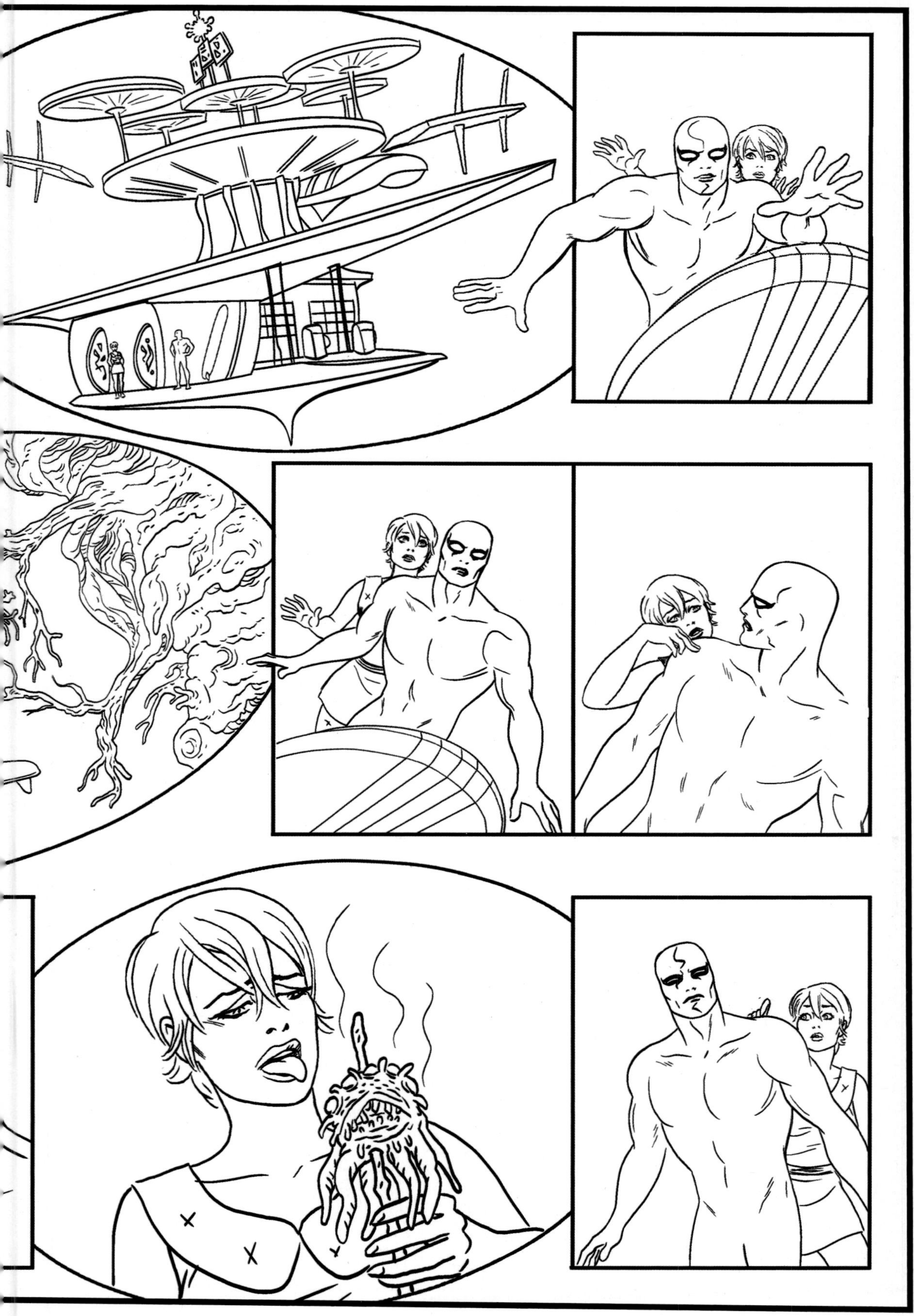

#6, PAGE 5 ART *BY MICHAEL ALLRED*